Bunker Diplomacy:
An Arab-American in the U.S. Foreign Service

BUNKER DIPLOMACY

AN ARAB-AMERICAN IN THE U.S. FOREIGN SERVICE

---

*Personal Reflections on 25 Years of
U.S. Policy in the Middle East*

NABEEL KHOURY

Westphalia Press
An Imprint of the Policy Studies Organization
Washington, DC
2019

BUNKER DIPLOMACY:
AN ARAB-AMERICAN IN THE U.S. FOREIGN SERVICE
All Rights Reserved © 2019 by Policy Studies Organization

Westphalia Press
An imprint of Policy Studies Organization
1527 New Hampshire Ave., NW
Washington, D.C. 20036
info@ipsonet.org

ISBN: 978-1-63391-911-2

Cover and interior design by Jeffrey Barnes
jbarnesbook.design

Daniel Gutierrez-Sandoval, Executive Director
PSO and Westphalia Press

Updated material and comments on this edition
can be found at the Westphalia Press website:
www.westphaliapress.org

For MargaretAnne
Who has always been there

And

To the memory of my father
Abdo As'ad Khoury

Contents

PROLOGUE

On Sept. 11, 2012, militants, likely affiliated with al-Qaʾeda, attacked the U.S. Consulate in Benghazi, Libya, killing Ambassador J. Christopher Stevens and Sean Smith, another Foreign Service Officer serving with Chris. The two followed procedure and hid out in the safe haven inside the building when the attack started and consulate walls were breached. Both died of smoke inhalation when the attackers set fire to the building. Neither a CIA rescue team in Benghazi nor a naval force stationed offshore, both awaiting instructions from Washington, could arrive in time to save the American diplomats. Chris Stevens, a gentle soul who believed in reaching out in friendship to all nations, had gone to Libya with the intention of doing just that in order to gain hearts and minds, and to assist the Libyan people in building a stable democracy. By 2012, however, U.S. diplomacy from behind high walls and under fire had unfortunately become all too common in the Middle East—a far cry from the open-door cultural centers we staffed when I first joined the service in 1987.

ACKNOWLEDGMENTS

My father taught me the love of the word and its ability to inspire and influence early on in life. I recall being inspired in my teens by the words of Gibran Kahlil Gibran as by the poetry of al-Mutanabi and Nizar Qabbani. From then on, if it wasn't written down, it didn't exist for me. Every significant experience in my life was penned in essays either to myself, in letters to my father and friends or sent to a newspaper and, in those early years, it tended to be my favorite newspaper in Lebanon, the late Ghassan Tueini's An-Nahar.

Inspired and emotionally moved by events I witnessed and people I met over 25 fascinating years of working for the U.S. Department of State—almost all in the Middle East or working on the region's issues from Washington, I very much wanted to put it all down on paper but couldn't do so while still in the service. It was mostly a question of time—the pace of foreign service work leaving very little for contemplating, let alone writing—but also because the sensitivity of some of the issues necessitated some detachment before committing pen to paper.

Upon retirement, in 2013, I went to work for the Chicago Council on Global Affairs and discussed two ideas with my colleagues there: A book to reflect on my years in the foreign service and a special project to promote a peaceful transition to democracy in Yemen. There were no council resources to dedicate to either. Elizabeth Marquardt, who was my colleague and dear friend during my 2 years in Chicago, was very encouraging and put me in touch with Carol Mann in New York. I eventually submitted a book proposal to the Carol Mann agency in 2014 and sample chapters in 2015. With advice from Carol's readers/reviewers, I developed the idea further and the book project was finally launched upon my return to Washington.

Of all the Arab countries where I lived and worked, Yemen has stayed with me the most—if for nothing else, as I told a dear friend recently, because Yemenis (thankfully) never leave one alone. I have fond memories from my 7 years in Morocco and am still in touch with dear friends there, but I have rarely written any commentaries on events there—both friends and events in Morocco are however very much present in this book. I left Yemen in 2007 but have never stopped working on Yemen issues to this day. The two chapters on Yemen in this book do not do justice to my experience there nor to my continued involvement. My dearest Yemeni friends, Afrah Nasser, Amat al-Alim al-Soswa and Sama'a al-Hamadani, have kept me in touch via constant discussions and sharing of contacts with people on the ground inside Yemen throughout this terrible war that continues to consume the country. To them, I owe a debt of gratitude for their continued friendship, for letting me share their concerns and for considering me one of their own. I'm grateful to Afrah Nasser, in particular, for her advice and for constantly reminding me to stick to my own imposed deadlines for finishing the book.

In a similar vein, conversations with Mohamad Abu Lahoum, Mohamad al-Tayeb, Abdelwahab al-Hajry, Faisal Abu Ras, Abdelwahab Hajar, and Mustapha Noman kept me engaged and updated on important events and perspectives on Yemen and the broader region. April Longley-Alley, a longtime friend and top notch researcher through her work with the Crisis Group, has constantly offered helpful insights and rigorous analysis of Yemen events.

My many lunch conversations with Tom Krajeski, my boss in Yemen and my friend thereafter, were reminders of the many anecdotes of the more pleasant moments in Yemen.

The short bibliography at the end of this book is not meant as an exhaustive list of books relevant to the topics I touch on in the text—that would be an impossible task. They are rather, books that have influenced my thinking on some of the topics I discuss or authors with whom I have had interesting conversations, particularly on Yemen, Morocco, and Egypt.

My comrade-in-arms (often literally) Alaa al-Sadr gets special mention for keeping me updated on Iraq events and for his continued comradeship well after my brief stint in Baghdad ended in 2003.

MargaretAnne Francella Khoury, ever my personal editor and advisor over the years, was the first to read the finished manuscript and offer critical comments and advice.

Finally, ambassador Mark Hambley, my first boss in the foreign service, and always my friend and supporter, read the entire manuscript in a matter of days, loved it, and connected me with Daniel Gutierrez who replied with a cheerful, "We'd be delighted to publish you," on behalf of Westphalia Press.

Preface

Coming Full Circle

I stepped out of the plane from Amman and was escorted to a special section of Baghdad's International Airport where a helicopter was waiting to fly me and another visitor directly to the American Embassy compound in the Green Zone (now dubbed the International Zone). We were handed bullet-proof vests and helmets and urged to put them on. It was deja-vu for me, 10 years after my stint as State Department spokesperson in Baghdad in 2003, when security conditions were horrendous and taking a helicopter flight over the city was like playing Russian roulette. But this was February 16, 2014; I had recently retired from the Department of State and was back in Baghdad as a guest speaker not as a member of the Coalition Provisional Authority (AKA occupation authority). Memories of chaos and violence floated through my mind, but my anxiety levels went down when the helos proved to be civilian, marines with guns sticking out of the windows were missing from the picture and the city seemed calm, peaceful, and downright pretty as we flew over it.

Another source of comfort was the presence of my longtime friend, Egyptian-American Alaa eddine al-Sadr (Al), who had worked closely with me in 2003 and was back at the Embassy as a special advisor on cultural affairs and Arab media. Al was in charge of my program this time with Iraqi ministries, media, and think tank scholars. He and I had dodged bullets together in downtown Baghdad, been bombed at the Rashid hotel, and otherwise put ourselves in harm's way as we carried out our mission back then to seek out and establish contact with the postwar Iraqi media, to explain U.S. policy in Iraq to the pan-Arab media represented in various parts of the city and listen to their ideas, criticisms, and needs. The perils of public diplomacy in war zones are not often highlighted, or indeed much known by the

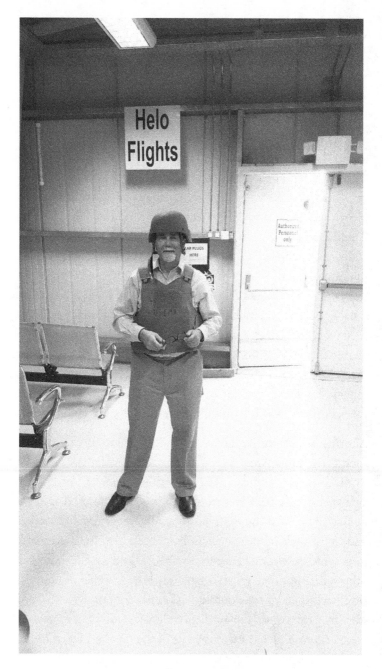

Preparing for Helo ride at BIA.

average American. In war zones, soldiers, diplomats, and journalists mingle and often face the same dangers, with those briefing journalists, not to mention the journalists themselves, being the least protected.

I had heard that the new U.S. Embassy, Baghdad (opened in 2008), was the largest embassy in the world, but I assumed that meant a huge building with state-of-the-art security measures around it. I was unprepared for the first view of the outside—a wall that stretched for several city blocks surrounded the compound (a wall that would make even Donald Trump proud!). The embassy was in fact a city within a city, including roads, several residential buildings, huge cafeterias, fully equipped gymnasiums, an Olympic size swimming pool, and even a soccer field. The chancery was indeed large and built along Inman standards+, i.e. features had been added to the outdated specs recommended in the 1985 Inman report as safety measures to be built into all U.S. embassy buildings in light of the terrorist attacks against U.S. facilities in the Middle East, starting with the attack on Embassy Beirut in 1983. The embassy was built for the last war. If we had had such a magnificent edifice back in 2003, it would have been a much safer facility than the buildings we used back then (The Republican Palace, the al-Rashid hotel, and sundry other facilities within the Green Zone). This embassy would also have been a more appropriate facility for the large diplomatic mission we had back in 2003. Suffice it to say, the size of the compound was incongruous with the small diplomatic mission in 2014 and the modest political goals set once U.S. troops were withdrawn in 2011.

My return visit to Baghdad was also cause to reflect on the course my life had taken since I left my ancestral home in Lebanon in 1971 to pursue a Ph.D. at the State University of New York at Albany. I had started out on my professional career as an academic, teaching international relations and reflecting on U.S. policy in the Middle East, then joined the U.S. foreign service and spent the next 25 years as an American diplomat working in the Middle East or on Middle East issues. Having just retired from that career, I was back in an Arab country as an analyst working for a think tank and teaching again. I had come full circle. It was time to take stock of a lifetime of involvement in and reflection on U.S. policy in this ever-turbulent region. What had I gained and what had I lost on a personal level, and what had actually changed for the United States in the region? The wall around U.S. Embassy Baghdad tells part of the story: We moved from open and inviting diplomatic and cultural facilities when I joined in 1987 to walled-in, fortified and forbidding establishments that reflected a rising hatred of, and ever-increasing dangers for Americans overseas. It was more than a question of image; it was a reflection of failed policies, certainly in the Middle East and perhaps in the rest of the world as well.

Baghdad by air, 2014.

CHAPTER 1

FORMATIVE YEARS

"You have your Lebanon and I have mine"

I was born into a Greek Catholic family which acquired the name Khoury, meaning priest, because our paternal ancestor, a priest, was one of the three Greek brothers who immigrated to Lebanon escaping Greek-Turkish wars in the early nineteenth century and settled in the village of Hammana in the Matn mountains above Beirut.

Three influences early in my life helped shape me: Gibran Kahlil Gibran, Lebanese-American philosopher, poet, and artist; Fairuz, Lebanon's first lady of song, often referred to as Lebanon's ambassador to the stars; and friendship. Fairuz, through her pure heavenly voice, gave me a deeper appreciation of the beauty of Lebanon and helped put my love for it into words. It is the Lebanon in its purest form, idealistic, loving, and proud. Fairuz not only enshrined the simplicity of village life, first loves, and nostalgia for both but also soared well beyond Lebanon and sang about Jerusalem, Damascus, and Mecca (Islam's holiest shrine). As a Christian, she inspired me to think beyond the parochial Lebanese-Christian identity to a broader sense of belonging to everything that is beautiful in Arab history and culture. One of the miracles this soulful singer accomplished was uniting all Lebanese even at the height of their fractiousness in the middle of the country's civil war. I recall in 1981, in mid-civil war, Fairuz and her group performed the musical Petra—the story of a Sparta-like city-state facing off with the Roman empire—first performed in Jordan in 1978. In Lebanon, it took on the meaning of resilience of a small country in the face of great regional dangers. The performance started with the song "Rij'it el-asfoura" meaning, birds have returned to sing again, symbolizing a peri-

1

od of hope in Lebanon's long civil war (premature optimism as it turned out), and ended with the song "Bhibbak Ya Libnan," I love you Oh Lebanon. The mixed audience of Lebanese Christians and Muslims of all political shades responded wildly to her. There wasn't a dry eye in the house that night.

On a literary level, Gibran inspired a similar sentiment, one of an enduring country of boundless love and beauty, in stark contrast to the realities of war and conflict at the time (early twentieth century), Gibran wrote lamenting social and sectarian divisions, ironically similar to the fractiousness of the country in current times:

> You have your Lebanon and I have mine. You have your Lebanon with ... its prejudices and struggles, and I have my Lebanon filled with dreams and serenity. Your Lebanon is a political knot, a national dilemma, a place of conflict and deception. My Lebanon is a place of beauty and dreams of enchanting valleys and splendid mountains .... Your Lebanon is empty and fleeting, whereas My Lebanon will endure forever.

With my closest friends in Lebanon, I shared a love of and a deep appreciation for Gibran's words and ideals, especially his rising above the pettiness of Lebanon's political factions, the divisive religious prejudices, and the corruption of its feudal families. In particular, Gibran transcended the Christian–Muslim divide, believing that people of all faiths were the children of one benevolent god and that national boundaries did not and should not constitute walls particularly between people of the same region. As a Lebanese, Gibran felt part of the Levant and the broader Arab world:

> I am Lebanese and proud to be so.
> I belong to a nation whose splendors I praise,
> but there is no state to which I might belong or where

I might find refuge.
I am a Christian and proud to be so.
But I love the Arab prophet and I appeal to
the greatness of his name;
I cherish the glory of Islam and fear lest it decay.
I am a Levantine and, although in exile,
I remain Levantine by temperament,
Syrian by inclination and Lebanese in feeling.

Like most Lebanese, we had our traditional home in a village in the mountains, Hammana in our case, where we spent every summer. In the winter, we lived in the northern city of Tripoli where my father worked for a British company called the Iraq Petroleum Company (IPC) and where I was actually born. In Hammana, almost all my friends and relatives were Christian. Biases among them against Muslims and Palestinians were commonly, if discretely, voiced. One exception was my cousin Shawki, with whom I shared a disdain for sectarianism. We have remained the closest of friends to this day.

Tripoli, however, had a large Muslim-Sunni population and many Palestinian families who had to leave their homes in the wake of the first Arab–Israeli war in 1948. My group of friends in primary school there included two Lebanese Muslims, a Lebanese-Christian, and two Palestinians. We were all classmates and went to the same British club and enjoyed the recreational facilities that were offered by the IPC to employees and their families. We couldn't be happier playing together and sharing adventures and stopping at one another's homes where we always felt welcome. It never occurred to us in those days that we came from different religious and national backgrounds. I would be surprised and offended later when I heard a Christian in my village denigrate Muslims or Palestinians. These comments were hurtful because they touched on friends I loved and because of the hypocrisy they revealed in those who made them. Later, as I grew more politically conscious, I realized how polarizing these attitudes were and how serious in light of the regional issues that surrounded Lebanon and threatened to split it apart.

By high school, my father had retired from his job in Tripoli and we moved to Beirut, a larger more cosmopolitan city with the added advantage of being much closer to Hammana. The National College of Choueifat, perched on the top of a hill outside the Beirut suburb of Choueifat, was one of the oldest private schools in the country and provided a well-appointed walled-in campus that offered an excellent learning environment. I quickly befriended another student by the name of George Baaklini who introduced me to other friends from his hometown, Dhour el-Shweir, and first among them was Mounir M'jaes. These two friends had a significant impact on my life and have remained friends throughout all our respective career changes and geographic moves. Roughly at the age of 16, we were unusually (for our age) engrossed in reading poetry, philosophy, and literature and loved intellectual discussions, things that led us to question all the prevailing religious, sectarian, and political divisiveness, biases, and attitudes in Lebanon.

The Deconstruction of State, Religion, and Moral Code

In essence, my friends and I grew alienated in our teens from the prevailing social and political codes that held Lebanon together—albeit in the way a torn but patched up rug is held together. We questioned religion on logical grounds and found it wanting, we questioned sectarianism on ethical grounds and found it abhorrent, and we questioned the conservative moral code that kept people imprisoned and afraid to express their natural tendencies and desires. In our state of alienation from the social, moral, and political values surrounding us, we felt alienated from the socio/political system in which we lived, but in Gibran Kahlil Gibran's writings, we felt a sense of elation in the belief that the future we believed in was better than the reality in which those around us seemed totally immersed. Gibran's first novel, *The Broken Wings*, was written in beautiful Arabic prose depicting a sad love story in which a young man loses the first woman he ever loved and the love of his life to a feudal clerical figure whose money and influence forced the father of the young woman to give her to him in marriage. The tragic ending describes the young man, upon hearing of his love's death, asking the grave digger where Salma Kramah was buried. The grave digger replies, "in this grave yonder, I buried her and with her, the infant baby on her chest." The young man ends with, "what strong arms you must have because here you also buried my heart," "as he collapsed on Salma's grave sobbing." The story was based on a real-life drama which typified the corruption of politicians and clerics alike and the impact that had on youthful dreams and true love. Social ills which revolted Gibran in the late nineteenth century revolted me and my friends almost a century later—nothing had changed and in the 1960s and 1970s, young lovers were still kept apart by the same prejudices and hypocrisies. In fact, my friend George and I defied the conservative mores of our school and the community surrounding it by daring to date young women in our school despite the regulations seeking to separate the sexes at least in their living quarters and after hour activities. My first love affair was with a Shia-Muslim classmate who risked serious harm from her family had they found out about us. I still recall that upon catching us kissing in a classroom after hours, a Muslim supervisor took her aside to reprimand her and she related to me in disbelief that his most bitter reprimand was "if you had to have a boyfriend, couldn't you have found a Muslim boy instead of this Christian?"

Violence by male family members against women in their family who dared to break with the conservative mores of their communities was still rampant in the sixties. I was struck like a thunderbolt one evening at home, while reading about the murder of a young girl by her father for precisely that offense, that her name was the same as my high-school sweetheart. I obviously could not call her house directly to check on her and had to wait till the next day to see if she was at school or not—I was only 16 and not a drinker, but I stayed up the whole night and drank a whole bottle of wine to deal with my anxiety. I was relieved the next day when I went to school totally hungover and disheveled to find out that it wasn't her after all—my fears were allayed—it was someone else with the same name, but I was still in shock the whole day over this crime and wrote an opinion piece for the school paper attacking the so-called crimes of honor, but of course it wasn't published.

Religious Belief

Religious belief does not, as a rule, stand the test of logic. Once an inquisitive mind starts asking questions about God and organized religion, once you study logic and philosophy, then religion doesn't stand a chance—you either believe simply as a matter of unquestioned faith or you don't. I recall reading a book for philosophy class by the early Islamic scholar al-Ghazali, a book called "al-Monqidh Min al-Dalal," literally the savior from ignorance, but has also been translated as "Deliverance from Error." In the book, Ghazali writes in refutation of philosophers who attacked religion by personalizing the experience. He describes how as a youth he had questioned religion and explored all its logical fallacies. He then questions all religious doctrine including the existence of God. At that point, Ghazali describes a state of personal crisis that completely paralyzed him. Since he had even rejected the laws of physics and nature, he could no longer undertake any action including going leaving his room in search of nourishment. "It is at that desperate point," he writes, "that God shone a light right into my heart which revealed his existence to me." From that starting point, Ghazali goes on to reconstruct religious, social, and physical laws on a logical basis which allows him to become functional again in the world of the living.

Whereas Ghazali's deconstruction and reconstruction of religion were works of art and of pure logic, in the end, his belief in God had nothing to do with rational thought but depended on that light in his heart, in other words, he took a leap of faith that allowed him to go back and use the philosophers' tools to reconstruct the rules and norms needed to make everyday life possible.

The state of desperation that Ghazali temporarily descended into was very close to that described by existentialist philosophers much later as a state of "total angst." Jean Paul Sartre indeed finds that questioning everything—an exercise required by intellectual honesty and rigor—leads to a state of paralysis. For Sartre, however, the answer was not faith in God but rather an immersion in the world and a commitment to fellow man. The conclusion that God does not exist and that the universe in a sense is unhinged does not logically and should not ethically lead to total paralysis. It could and should lead rather to a greater sense of responsibility toward the world in which injustice and suffering exist on a large scale. Since there is no God, according to Sartre, man is responsible for all the sins and faults committed by humanity and must therefore do something to help repair the injustice and alleviate the suffering.

Suffice it to say here that deliverance from darkness according to Sartre was more convincing than say, Feurbach in his, *The Essence of Christianity*, or indeed of al-Ghazali who simply injected God into his lost soul, logical or not, and proceeded as if the matter had been proven for convenience's sake.

The Clash of Ideologies

Lebanon was patched together by the French externally and a gentlemen's agreement internally between its Lebanese founding fathers known as the National Pact. The parties to the agreement included the main feudal families of Lebanon from the main sects: Christian, Sunni, Shia, and Druze. The sectarian consensus-based system had two founding principles: Make sure all religious sects are represented according to an agreed on quota system, and don't make any grand design changes or major decisions outside of a national consensus. In Lebanon, this agreement was a product of social and regional factors which prevailed in 1943 and the compromises it entailed made the republic of Lebanon possible. Christians, Maronites in particular, had to give up any intention to disassociate from their neighbors and hitch their futures to far-off European nations, while Muslims in return gave up on any plans to merge into Syria or the broader Arab region around them. For many years, this system prevented rebellions and defections from the union of its component parts. The National Pact arrangement broke down, however, in 1975, and has been wobbly ever since because the region has become increasingly complicated and national polarization now prevents consensus on even the most mundane of issues. This system frustrated independent-minded youth in my days and even more so today because it denies true citizenship to the Lebanese and forces them to think, act and vote parochially and along sectarian lines.

As a result of the limits of sectarian politics, political parties of all shades and colors thrived in Lebanon, reflecting in most cases regional trends. Hence, the Arab Nationalist party, Nasserism, Ba'thism, as well as a Communist party competed for the hearts and minds of Lebanese youth and politicians, seeking to curry favor with regional powers such as Syria, Iraq, and Egypt, sought to sell their wares in the Lebanese open market of ideas. Even as secular political ideas competed, however, sectarian feudal families still dominated and most parties were absorbed into one religious faction or another. Hence, Arab nationalist parties tended to be the domain of Sunni Lebanese, the socialist party was taken up by the Druze while Shia Muslims gravitated toward Iran. The dominant Christian parties stressed Lebanese independence but in reality gravitated toward western powers and, in the 1975 civil war, preferred an alliance with Israel over any accommodation with the Palestinians, led in Lebanon by the Palestine Liberation Organization at the time (PLO).

As a young man studying at the American university in Beirut, I definitely did not identify with any of the Christian parties because of their narrow focus on sectarian identity and their thriving on the sectarian fears and paranoia of their constituents. I also did not much care for the left-wing Arab nationalist parties because of the paucity of thought and the rabble-rousing nature of their organizations. One party which I did briefly admire was the Syrian Social Nationalist Party (SSNP). Its founder, Antoun Saadah, had written several books on the concept of nationhood, what constituted it, and the pre-Arab and Arab influences on Levantine cultures. He called for a nonsectarian state in Lebanon that looked beyond its narrow borders to the broader Levant, sometimes referred to as the fertile crescent or Greater Syria. I also liked his looking beyond his own Maronite identity to a broader sense of citizenship, titling one of his books: "Islam in Its Two Messages, Mohammedan and Christian." All serious intellectuals in Lebanon seeking freedom from the confines of sectarianism had at one time or another belonged to this party, to include men and women of letters, media, and theater. I was quickly disappointed, however, when I went to some party discussion groups to find that even with the relative intellectual depth of their party dogma, the party functionaries did not tolerate diversity of views or deal well with challenges to their adopted political philosophy.

Several violent clashes among students at the American University of Beirut in the late sixties confirmed my fears that all issues relating to needed reforms in the country were ultimately being hijacked by local political interests and that ideology and sectarianism in Lebanon blended in a dangerous way that portended ill for the country.

One incident in particular, in 1968, illustrated this dilemma. On December 28, 1968, Israeli forces stormed Beirut International

Airport and blew up 13 civilian planes sitting on the tarmac and belonging to Lebanon's Middle East Airlines and the all-cargo Trans-Mediterranean Airline. The raid was in retaliation for the hijacking two days earlier of and an El-Al plane by members of the Popular Front for the Liberation of Palestine (PFLP), a hijacking which was eventually resolved diplomatically by an exchange of the passengers for Palestinian prisoners held in Israeli jails. Many Lebanese felt the humiliation of their airport being struck so brazenly without so much as a gun being fired by Lebanon's armed forces against the attackers. I recall Lebanon's leading journalist at the time, Ghassan Tueini, writing an editorial in the daily An-Nahar entitled, "A House with No Roof." Students at AUB struck in an expression of anger at the authorities and demanded the government's resignation over the incident. The strike seemed to include students of all political colors for at least two weeks, until first the Christian right-wing students broke ranks and appealed to the army to come onto campus grounds to quash the strike. A few days later, the government did indeed resign and a new prime minister, from one of Tripoli's leading Sunni families, Rashid Karami, was chosen to replace him. At that point, one of the leaders of the strike, himself a Alawi from Tripoli, along with some Sunni supporters of Karami, also broke rank and the strike ended in anger and discord. The national organization the students had tried to build collapsed.

I recall being pressured by a Christian professor and an old friend of the family telling me I had to take sides (with his group of Christian students against Muslims and Palestinians). I never believed in the old Arab adage, "my brother and I against my cousin, my cousin and I against strangers." I recall debating it with my father one day and asking, "Why is it that one should side with one's brother, what if the brother was wrong (which in my experience was often the case)?" Adding, "and why is there no third option of mediating the conflict instead of jumping into the fray?" I recall my father smiling and saying to me, "that's why you are the diplomat in the family—" a prophetic statement on his part as it later turned out that I was indeed destined to become a diplomat.

The episode at the university left me with a foreboding regarding the violence I had witnessed between opposing student factions. I realized that Lebanese society was getting far too polarized to allow for a genuinely independent national reform movement and feared that such clashes would only get worse—those clashes and others were in fact a prelude to the civil war that started later in 1975. In 1971, I decided it was time to leave the country I loved in order to pursue my education and dreams elsewhere—it was quite natural for me, growing up bilingual and already at a young age influenced by American culture, to choose to pursue higher education in the United States.

CHAPTER 2

FROM ACADEME TO DIPLOMACY

Albany

Seek education even if it's in China, says an old Arab proverb. I knew from my high school year that I wanted to get to that ultimate point in formal education, a Ph.D., but I had no idea where that route might actually take me. Choosing Albany, New York, for pursuing a degree in political science was mere happenstance. My high-school friend George had gone there a year ahead because his older brother was a professor at the State University of New York at Albany (SUNY). I followed suit because I had never been to the United States and thought the company of friends I already knew and trusted was as good a reason as any when choosing where to live and study in a foreign environment. I was surprised however to find that I knew considerably more about New York and the United States in general than most of the Americans I met knew about Lebanon. From movies, songs, and books, nothing I saw in New York City amazed or even surprised me, to the disappointment of friends who took me there to impress me. I was surprised to see how small Albany was (a population of 200,000 at the time) and how cold it got in winter. Nonetheless, I grew to like Albany very much and to feel at home in its academic and small-city environment. Friends and their families received me warmly and, outside of some asking me to repeat my name several times and a few questions about where in the world Lebanon was, I found Americans to be generous, friendly, and open minded about my origins and the information I provided on the Middle East. The lack of familiarity with the Middle East on the part of many, at least in those days, was sometimes quite funny. On introducing myself to someone one time, and after I said my name as clearly as possible, the guy repeated with difficulty, "Knob eel? What do we call you for short?" I laughed as I told him, "it's already quite short, I don't know what I

13

can do to shorten it further." On another occasion, a woman I was dating came back from a family visit one weekend and proudly announced that her brother had just adopted a new dog and named it Nabeel in my honor. Surprised by the shock on my face, I explained, "we don't name dogs after people in the Arab world, it's not polite!" Her second surprise, "Oh, so Lebanon is an Arab country?" "Yep, afraid so," was my reply with a smile.

I had left Lebanon with a thousand dollars in my pocket, a gift from my father to get me started and I did not want to ask him for more, so I worked as a bartender for a few months, then as a fast food shift manager. The latter job left oil marks on my arms for years from the frying of fish in industrial-sized deep fryers. The friendships and insights I gained doing these jobs however were worth it. The young students trying to earn their way through college and working class men and women who had no other means of earning an income filled these minimum wage jobs. Their work ethic and warmth touched me and helped me get adjusted quickly to my new environment. Meeting women in the workplace was also a new experience. This was entirely different from dating young women from bourgeois Lebanese families whom I met at the elite American University of Beirut. To begin with, my first two girlfriends were Jewish—already a break from the phobia associated with anything touching Israel and anyone of the Jewish faith whom one rarely met in Lebanon even before the 1967 war when there was still a small Jewish community in the country. These women and their families were largely not observant Jews, did not follow Middle East politics very closely and were totally open to my being Arab. It was also a novel experience for me being approached by women who were not shy to express their interest in me. In fact, my first date was with someone who worked in a restaurant adjacent to where I worked and who, seeing me pace outside the store during my break, whistled in order to draw my attention. I covered up my surprise by saying "you interrupted my train of thought and now I'll have to start pacing all over again."

The second year, however, I received a teaching scholarship which offered a tuition waiver and a stipend of $220 a month in return for my teaching an introductory course in political science to undergraduates. I found teaching to be great fun—the Shakespeare buff in me had plenty of opportunity to walk into a classroom as if walking onto a stage and putting on an act. In fact, I sometimes began a class by quoting from Hamlet or Macbeth—to the surprise, if not always delight of the students. Teaching was hard work, but it helped my graduate studies as it forced me to read material I had not come across before and to debate issues with students related to U.S. government and the controversial role played by the United States on the world stage. Many were surprised that the United States was not always viewed as a benevolent force for the good by the rest of the world. Students, and teachers with left-wing leanings, however thought I was being too moderate in depicting a government that for them was actually a force for evil. This dichotomy of views was to remain a constant in my interactions with Americans in intellectual circles and in fact the contrast has only become sharper over the years. The fact that I also met my future wife, MargaretAnne, in one of these university classes made up for any frustrations at the social level and got me started on a family of my own, something I always wanted.

Five years breezed by quickly after that, amid taking graduate courses, preparing for exams, and writing my dissertation, with plenty of time for Tennis and swimming in between. My dissertation topic, "Islam and Modernization in the Middle East," seemed too esoteric in the 1970s, but it set the stage for my interest in political Islam, slated to become a much more salient subject in later years. I received my Ph.D. diploma in December 1976 and a job offer followed quickly after to teach at the University of Jordan in Amman. MargaretAnne had already visited Lebanon with me and loved it. We always assumed we'd go back to Lebanon to teach at the American University of Beirut and thought Jordan would put us a step closer to that goal. We got married and left to Jordan, arriving there at a time when Amman seemed like a small village which offered little by way of entertainment or lively intellectual environment.

News Flash: Jordan Is Not Palestine

Teaching mainly Jordanian and Palestinian students in Arabic presented challenges and insights. As usual in the Arab world, a university campus was generally a microcosm of its social and political environment. Palestinian students in Amman tended to be leftists and Arab nationalists. East Jordanians tended to be extremely chauvinist about being Jordanian and always suspicious of their Palestinian colleagues, even though they too were Jordanian citizens. Hiring new faculty invariably ended up in a tussle over the national identity (read ethnicity) of the person being interviewed rather than their academic competence. Older generation Palestinians, particularly those who were successful businessmen, tended to be more integrated into Jordanian society and stayed away from politics at least in their public life. The younger generation, particularly on university campuses, was another matter. Here, one sensed a deep frustration, a sense of being second-class citizens and an aspiration to think of the broader issues in the Arab world beyond the confines of Jordan.

After 3 years in Amman, I got tired of the high dose of politicization between Palestinians and Jordanians on campus and the policy divisions within the university as a result.

My wife was also driven to tears with sexism and male chauvinism which had her being treated like a second-class citizen in the country. There seemed to be no end in sight to the Lebanese civil war and MargaretAnne wanted desperately to go back to finish her law degree in Albany. She went back ahead of me and I followed from Beirut, this time arriving in the United States as an immigrant at the end of 1980. I became a U.S. citizen roughly 2 years later.

Back in Albany

Going back to teaching in Albany as an adjunct professor was a frustrating experience. Full-time tenured positions were hard to come by and universities and colleges tended to use adjuncts like slave labor—paying pittance per course and demanding a heavy load to boot. At first I taught as an adjunct at several universities in the greater Albany area, at one time teaching, and therefore commuting between four different universities until I found tenure- track Assistant Professorship at the College of Saint Rose. I loved teaching there and my long and roaming discussions with my lefty professor friends—over rounds of beer at our favorite pub—left me with life-long memories and friendships.

I routinely taught four courses per semester accepted speaking invitations in and out of town and started a Middle East studies center at Saint Rose. Being one of very few Middle Eastern professors in the area, I also became a valued commodity for the local media whenever something tragic happened in the region, as it inevitably did on a recurring basis. I recall commenting on the Sabra and Shatila massacre of Palestinians in Lebanon in 1982 and laying the blame on Israel for its occupation of south Lebanon and its encouragement of and support for the crazy right-wing Lebanese militias who actually carried out the killing. A Jewish friend with whom I regularly played Tennis and with whom I had never discussed politics became enraged and would not even listen to my explanations of the impact of Israel's occupation on Lebanon. He ended our brief discussion with "Arabs killed Arabs and the Jews are being blamed for it."

This was but one example of how difficult it was to have a rational discussion of Middle East events with the pro-Israel community in the area. I was bold enough to accept a speaking engagement at a local temple once, knowing that many in the audience were members of the American–Israel Public Affairs Committee (AI-PAC). As a precaution, I brought along my pregnant wife hoping

17

that that might soften the harshness of any opposition to my talk. I still recall to this day the retort from someone in the audience who, upon hearing my distinctions between moderates and radicals among Palestinian leaders said, "The difference between Gonorrhea and Syphilis is not that great my friend!"

During those years, I also dabbled in some activism on behalf of the Arab-American community, forming a local chapter of the American-Arab Anti-Discrimination Committee (ADC) in association with John Zogby who collaborated with his brother, Jim Zogby, in founding that association in Washington, DC. John and I had the able assistance of Alice Azzam, a prominent member of the Arab community in Albany at the time and who was a great friend and asset in our activism. We mainly tracked anti-Arab stories in the local media, wrote rebuttals, and often talked to local editors and journalists about adopting a fair tone in their coverage of the Middle East and avoiding in particular slurs against Arabs and Arab culture in general. Academically, I was interested in studying Arab-American lobbying in general and visited Washington, DC, to see how organizations like the ADC and the National Association of Arab-Americans (NAAA), which was doing good work at the time under the leadership of Khalil Jahshan. The five or so organizations that worked on a national level did a good job getting Americans of Arab origin engaged in local politics, the ADC fought discrimination and encouraged Arab-Americans to run for office. The Arab American Institute (AAI), founded by James Zogby in 1985, was and remains today an advocate of Arab-American engagement in national politics and participation in the electoral process at all levels. The NAAA was quite successful at tracking legislation that impacted Arabs in general and its bulletins and newsletters were quite useful in raising awareness of national and international issues. The various organizations did however suffer from lack of sufficient coordination among one another and some of them were too dependent on the personality and of their leader to last and become truly institutionalized. Funding was always a challenge as well. My paper, entitled *The Arab Lobby, Problems and Prospects,* appeared in the *Middle East Journal* in 1987.

Washington Bound

Eventually, the long hours of teaching, researching, and introducing Middle East courses and speakers to my students left me exhausted, especially when our first child arrived and I found that subsisting on the college's low wages was no longer adequate and commiserating with my fellow faculty on being part of the intellectual proletariat no longer amusing. When a friend in Washington, DC, suggested I take the Foreign Service exam I was curious and took it almost on a lark not expecting to be offered a job. After all, I was a recent immigrant from a troubled country and region and this was the Department of State, something which had long loomed as large, mysterious, and forbidding. I was surprised when I was invited to take the oral exam and surprised even more a few months later when I was actually offered a job. In between exam and job offer, I had to obtain the appropriate security clearance, and the visit of the investigator seemed like a cloak and dagger affair. He called, asked me to meet him in a room inside the observation tower at Albany airport. I was full of apprehension as to how that would go, but relaxed when the questions seemed routine and really irrelevant to what I thought should have been areas of concern. He asked about drinking habits, domestic violence, and smoking pot. I relaxed and almost suggested to him some questions about the civil war in Lebanon, the many factions involved, any personal involvement I might have had (none in reality)—but I avoided giving him too many ideas, in the interest of speeding things along.

The opportunity to ask such questions did not, however, elude one examiner during the oral part of the foreign service exam. A vivid memory from the oral part of the Foreign Service exam was when a member of the examining board asked me what I thought of Reagan's policy in Lebanon. My answer was almost immediate,

—Stupid. Would you like to know why?

—Please!

—Because he took sides in another country's civil war without understanding the complexity of it, he then placed a small number of marines in a geographically vulnerable position surrounded by the militias of the people he had taken sides against.

—You know Nabeel, I agree with everything you said, but if you work for us, you can't say that in public.

—I understand, and don't mind as long as I can say that to policy makers behind closed doors.

—You will be able to do that, that much I can promise.

In chatting with the person who asked me the question later, he further reassured me, "you know Nabeel, unless you wake up every morning wondering whether or not you'd made the right decision in joining the Foreign Service we will have made the wrong choice in offering you the job."

Frankly, one of the main reasons I was uncertain about joining the Foreign Service was my wondering how often I would be representing policies with which I disagreed. I would find out in later years that the best American diplomats and some of my favorite bosses and colleagues were those who were broad minded enough to tolerate criticism, invite alternate ideas and not insist on blindly following Washington's official line. To be sure, I came across the opposite kind of diplomats as well, those who were professional bureaucrats or narrow-minded political appointees who "drank the coolaid" heartily and insisted on nothing less from their colleagues and subordinates. I can safely say in reflection, however, that in 25 years of service, I never allowed anyone to put words in my mouth—I either got away with circumventing the bureaucrats or had influential higher-ups willing to defend me when I spoke or acted according to my conscience and not blindly toeing the official line.

On being told I was approved for the Foreign Service, I asked to defer a deployment to Riyadh which was the first post offered because I was in the middle of a teaching semester. I accepted the second offer, to start my second career as the Branch Public Affairs Officer (BPAO) in Alexandria, Egypt. As I wasn't sure the Foreign Service was for me, I took a leave of absence from teaching, something my colleagues at St. Rose strongly urged, not wanting me to sever ties with academe prematurely. My circle of friends at St. Rose were mostly left-wing academics, interested in Latin America and very critical of the role the United States had played there in the seventies in propping up dictators and opposing socialist movements and workers' rights. I was quite amused and a bit confused when they blurted out one evening after I'd announced my decision to join the Foreign Service, "Nabeel, you'd be joining the enemy!" My protests of, "What do you mean enemy, this is your government?" only elicited vehement views on the imperialist nature of U.S. policies, especially in Latin America and that a self-respecting academic (especially one coming from a third world country) should not lend himself to serve such a devious master. My protests that one should not generalize and that policies do change and evolve received no sympathy either. Years later, long after Latin America changed and U.S. policies did, at least in my estimation, evolve, albeit sometimes inconsistently, I still found that many left of center liberals and academics almost as a religious dogma refuse to see anything but conspiracy in U.S. policies throughout the world and dub the U.S. government as controlled by "the deep state," or "the permanent war state." I was determined to find out for myself if such conspiracies against the third world actually existed, how U.S. foreign policy was made, and whether or not someone like me could have an input into the policy process.

I therefore started my journey to discover what life in the U.S. foreign service was like and to see if the life of a diplomat was a good fit for someone who was not only interested in exploring how U.S. policy was made but who also wanted to delve deeper into Arab culture and politics as an Arab-American diplomat. I left my first posting in Alexandria after 3 years convinced that the life of a diplomat had much to offer, that indeed living and working as a diplomat in the Middle East provided valuable insights into the region, even if the U.S. foreign policy process remains baffling and frustrating even today, seemingly impenetrable for someone not part of the political or economic elite. I also left Alexandria with fond memories of Egypt, of foreign service colleagues, some of whom have remained friends to this day, and of Egyptian writers and artists who helped me better understand Egypt and the Egyptian people.

CHAPTER 3

EGYPT: WHAT WE GOT WRONG
WHAT WE GOT RIGHT

Alexandria

I was delighted to accept the assignment of Branch Public Affairs Officer (BPAO) for Alexandria and the surrounding Delta region because, for one, I had never been to the area and secondly, I had long had this romantic notion about the city and started to dream about the job I would be doing there. From the beginning, I had a feeling this would be more of a literary experience for me than a political one. It was both. A good friend recommended I read Lawrence Durrell's Alexandria Quartet, the classic tome full of depictions of relationships and intrigue lurking in every corner of the city. I chose, however, not to read about the city before arriving there to allow myself the experience of living there and forming my own impressions before appreciating what the literary giants had to say about it. When I finally read it, I found Durrell's narrative too complicated and unreflective of the true nature of the city. I appreciated instead Naguib Mahfouz and other Egyptian authors who better understood both the city and the country. I also enjoyed reading Constantine Cavafy's poetry, both for the love of adventure and the optimism about the journey ahead:

As you set out for Ithaka
hope your road is a long one,
full of adventure, full of discovery.

I also appreciated Cavafy for his expressions of love for the city and the sadness one feels after leaving a city like Alexandria. Cavafy's short poems struck me as much more evocative of the spirit and history of Alexandria and left more of an indelible mark on me than the often opaque Durrell. Cavafy's famous lines have remained with me ever since I first read them:

23

> There's no new land, my friend, no New sea;
> for the city will follow you
> In the same streets you'll wander endlessly ...

I was haunted by these lines in particular because they applied not only to Alexandria but to the city of one's childhood and cities after that where one has lived, loved, and left. I included Cavafy's lines, for example, in a farewell speech I gave before leaving The Moroccan city of Casablanca—a city that continues to live within me even though I have not even gone back for visit since I left it in 2002.

The American Cultural Center (ACC) on 3 Phara'na Street, a 2000 square meter property with a palatial old villa magnificently suited for art exhibits, musical concerts and intellectual roundtable discussions, not to mention a warm environment for scholarly work afforded by its small but well-stocked library. The property was bought by the U.S. Government in 1962 for a mere 35,500 Egyptian pounds deducted from the sale of U.S. agricultural products to Egypt at the time. The ACC opened in 1962, closed in 1967 because of angry demonstrations against the United States after the Arab–Israeli war that year, and reopened 12 years later to a much friendlier reception.

When relations returned to normal between the United States and Egypt in 1974, it was agreed that consular and cultural relations would recommence in Alexandria. The ACC renovation began in 1976 and the building officially reopened to the public in 1979. From then till 2001, and certainly during my tenure between 1987 and 1990, the ACC was very well received by the Alexandrian population, security around it was minimal and there was barely an incident until the mood changed again after September 11, 2001, and again more dramatically after the U.S. invasion of Iraq in 2003.

Standard cultural and educational exchanges between the United States and Egypt in those days contained the usual mix of art, music, and speaker programs, still in those days managed by the now defunct U.S. Information Agency. Part of the package, though bureaucratically one-step removed, was the Fulbright commission and the educational exchange programs managed by it. I certainly enjoyed organizing an Egyptian-American art exhibit in my first year in Alexandria to encourage communication between American artists and their Egyptian counterparts. Among the other fun events, I established a monthly literary forum and invited writers, journalists, and intellectuals to discuss books, articles, and topics of mutual interest.

The dominant and controversial political themes in Egypt in the years I was there were, **Arab nationalism, normalization of relations with Israel, and the status of the Muslim Brotherhood**. The first topic was controversial because president Sadat had, in the 1970s, turned the tables on Nasserism and, after his relative success in the 1973 Arab–Israeli war, turned away from the traditional hostility toward Israel and set Egypt on a course which ended in the two countries signing a peace treaty in 1979. Sadat was assassinated for his troubles in 1981 by a radical Islamist in what ominously foreshadowed the growth of religious extremism in the region. Nasserists, who had previously carried the mantle of Arab nationalism and resistance to Zionism, became a rare commodity and the debate over Egypt's foreign policy was carried on by two protagonist forces, Egyptian nationalists who believed in Sadat's path to peace and prosperity and Islamists who carried the torch for Palestine and believed that Egypt had betrayed its Arab/Islamist identity by breaking ranks with the Arab world and submitting to the dictates of Israel and the United States. The secular Arab left was lost in the middle between two right-wing forces, one narrowly nationalist and another a pan-Islamic force that wanted policy to be based on religious values of right and wrong rather than a secular view of the national interest.

I recall, during my third and last year in Egypt, a conversation on these topics over drinks at my house with friends I had made among the attendees of my intellectual forum. Between the ardent supporters of a go-it-alone policy for Egypt and the counter argument that Egypt ought to be an integral part of the broader Islamic world, I found myself arguing for the discredited middle ground, an Arab nationalist policy that coordinates peace and prosperity with other Arab countries and lead rather than defy them and ignore their views and interests. I also argued that it made no sense to coordinate with the broader non-Arab Islamic world since there was very little in common between say Egypt and Indonesia. One guest who had vehemently been arguing for an Egypt-first policy excitedly pointed at me and shouted, "I know you now, you are a Nasserist!"

I thought to myself, "Oh boy, I've been in Egypt too long and have lost my objectivity: an American diplomat, being called a Nasserist by an Egyptian must be a rare thing indeed!"

Normalization with Israel

The best phrase to describe Egyptian–Israeli relations in the late 1980s is a cold peace. At the official level, there were almost daily contacts that went beyond diplomatic representation to official high-level visits and almost daily military and intelligence exchanges. The two states had a common border and a vested interest in keeping it quiet. To that end, The Palestinian group Hamas, which officially came into being in 1987, was a cause for concern on both sides of the Gaza–Egyptian border. The Mubarak regime's relations with Hamas were troubled from the start. On the one hand, Egypt wanted to act as big brother to Palestinian leaders and help them negotiate peace with Israel; on the other hand, Hamas was viewed by the Egyptian regime as an offshoot of the hated Egyptian Muslim Brotherhood and Egyptian officials often felt more comfortable dealing with Israeli counterparts than with Hamas functionaries. There was also economic cooperation which, in the late eighties, included several agricultural joint projects between Egypt and Israel with hopes that this collaboration would grow. The popular level, however, was a different matter. For American media and for the average American, Anwar Sadat was a hero and a popular leader. The Egyptian president, as the first Arab leader to travel to Jerusalem and address the Israeli Knesset, breaking what he termed the "psychological wall" between the two countries, was a popular figure in the United States. To boot, he was at ease with American media and knew how to use it to develop his positive image in American eyes. What most Americans failed to understand, however, was the intensity of hatred for Sadat in his own country and particularly among Islamists and hold-over Arab nationalists. Certainly, the man had his supporters, not just in the military and Egypt's security establishment, but also among many wealthy Egyptians who wanted to end the cycle of violence with Israel and get on with the business of expanding the economy and commercial of the country. Sadat's anti-socialist policies certainly provided room for wealth accumulation, but for those already well to do. The average Egyptian, however, and particularly the poor, were disappointed that they never saw the peace dividend which only some rich businessmen and industrialists seemed to enjoy. Bread riots became a familiar scene in Egypt under Sadat and one famous slogan they chanted and carried in banners said, "Ya Batal al-Ubour Aynal Futour?" Meaning, "Oh hero of the crossing, where is our breakfast?" in reference to the Egyptian army crossing the Suez Canal and attacking the Israeli army in the Sinai in 1973.

Egyptians' sense of humor was in high gear in those days and served as a vehicle for venting. I recall an Egyptian journalist relating a joke from the Sadat era that clearly typified the resentment many still felt even after his death. Sadat, the joke went, asked his ministry of communications to issue a stamp commemorating the Camp David handshake between him and Israeli prime min-

27

ister, Menachem Begin. When the stamp wasn't forthcoming, Sadat prompted his minister and queried him as to the cause of the delay, only to be told that the stamp would not stick. "What do you mean it's not sticking, aren't you putting enough glue on the back of it," queried Sadat? "Yes, sir," replied the minister, "but the people are spitting on the face of it not the back!!"

Years after his death, Sadat was still a controversial figure both in Egypt and in the Arab world. His legacy, "al-Tatbei'" meaning normalization with Israel was an ongoing debate in the late eighties. Many of his critics felt that they appreciated not going to war with Israel but they didn't have to like the Israelis and welcome them into their homes. Naim Tekla, a Copt from Upper Egypt and a novelist, without ever confronting the issue directly, bucked the trend through his novels that portrayed Egyptian Jews and an era in which they lived in peaceful coexistence in Alexandria and Cairo. One particular novel, *Nahla,* featured an Egyptian young man who has a telephone romance with a Palestinian woman he never meets and who then moves with her family to Palestine without giving him an exact address. The hero then travels to Israel in search of his mysterious beloved, builds a friendship along the way with an Israeli family and has an affair with an Israeli woman on a Kibbutz and eventually comes back to Alexandria without having ever found his Palestinian love. Scathing reviews in the press lambasted Naim and accused him of seeking to encourage normalization of relations with Israel in his writing. I organized a roundtable for Naim at the American Cultural Center to help him face his critics and debate the book and the issue of normalization head-on. Naim insisted throughout the discussion that he simply wrote a fictional love story and had himself never been to Israel. His defense did not convince any of his critics, but in the process of discussing it, we debated normalization and the freedom of expression in Egypt. Playing agent provocateur, I posed the question, "what's wrong with an Arab writer imagining a love affair with an Israeli woman—isn't that what writers do, and isn't that idea, though anathema to many Egyptians at the time, that lay ahead in the future once peace really took hold in the region?"

Naim was an instant and a lasting friend until his early demise a few years after I left Alexandria. He succumbed to a brain tumor in 1996 and was only in his mid-40s at the time. Our conversations during walks along Alexandria's Corniche and over coffee and pastry at the famous Trianon Café took us from exchanging love stories to religious and political discussions and pondering the future of Egypt. In addition to his bold novels, Naim also wrote opinion pieces in the press about the rights of Copts and the officially sanctioned discrimination against them. Much as I agreed with him and supported his right to express his controversial ideas, I cautioned Naim to be careful and less confrontational in his discussions and writings. His participation in discussion sessions at the American Cultural Center were the subject of criticisms and accusations of betrayal of his country. After I left, he was subjected to a bitter attack on him after he participated in a discussion of war and peace in the literature, again at the ACC (April 1995). A leftist critic wrote in *Akhbar al-Adab*, a literary newspaper, that Naim was using his American connections to propagandize for peace with Israel, ignoring Israeli literature that vilified all Arabs and American media which portrayed the Arab as a murderer and terrorist. He had once confided to me that he had in fact received anonymous death threats and that his vilification in the press was partly the cause. Before I left Egypt, Naim introduced me to, Farag Fouda, a friend of his who was more directly political and confrontational than Naim and had debated and ridiculed Islamist writers and thinkers in the media and on panel discussions. Fouda was assassinated in Cairo in 1992, 2 years after I left my post in Alexandria.

Twixt Literature and Religious Extremism

One thing I will always remember Naim for is his introducing me to the Egyptian Nobel Laureate, **Naguib Mahfouz**, 2 years

29

before Mahfouz became the first Arab writer to win the prize. Mahfouz normally spent a month or two of each Summer in Alexandria and his wont was to walk to the Saint Stefano hotel by the beach and sip Turkish coffee and chat with friends, disciples and anyone who cared to stop by for a quick hello. Naim was one of his devoted friends and followers and rarely missed an evening with him when he was in town. Once I was officially introduced, I always accompanied him to these gatherings. These evenings with Naguib Bey—as he was fondly known to his friends and admirers—were totally relaxed and informal and the chats roamed easily from topic to topic without any agenda or format. It was what the Egyptians call "Dardasha" sometimes or "Tharthara" a word in the title of one of his books, translated as, "Chit-Chat on the Nile." A renaissance man, Mahfouz was equally comfortable discussing European existentialism as ancient Arab history or current politics. One of the main themes we often came back to with him was political Islam, or fundamentalism. Recall, this was before Jihadism became an international phenomenon and al-Qa'eda and ISIS became household words.

Religious extremism/zealotry was more than a passing interest for Mahfouz. One of his books, The Sons of Gebalawy, first published in 1959, was banned in Egypt and republished in Beirut in 1967. The book raised Islamist ire against him because the story in it was considered an allegory for the story of creation and its characters clearly mirrored the lives of the prophets. Starting with Adam and Eve in the Garden of Eden and down the line to Christ and Mohammed, the stories were all told in down to earth human terms. In the story, Gebalawy, the master of the garden who banishes his sons from it, dies in the end. Islamist hardliners considered the book blasphemous and accused Mahfouz of mocking the prophets and of depicting God as a human with a finite life. Mahfouz always maintained that he was just writing a fictional story and never intended anything religious or philosophical behind it. The title of the original Arabic version, "Awlad

Haritna," means the children of our neighborhood and perhaps should have carried the famous disclaimer "any resemblance to real or historical personalities is purely coincidental." Yet, I recall a conversation with Mahfouz after reading the book for the first time, in which I said, "the characters and stories are very reminiscent of the Bible and the Qur'an but they're all so human. If I had been taught religion that way when I was growing up I might still be religious today!" Mahfouz just smiled and nodded his head and didn't say anything to that. It's as if he had taken a vow never to discuss the book directly, never to admit to what his original intention was in writing it. For the record, he had stated in official newspapers that he was sorry the novel offended some people and that he was fine with the government's decision to ban it.

The subject of blasphemy versus freedom of expression came up very directly in our conversations one evening when discussing Salman Rushdi's Satanic Verses and the reaction to it worldwide and, in particular, the Khomeini Fatwa against Rushdi. Mahfouz complained that he was being asked by journalists for an opinion and could not honestly give one since he had not, indeed could not read the book because of his failing eyesight. I quickly obtained a copy and read the 700+ pages in one week, so I could summarize it for Naguib Bey. He, Naim, and I conspired one evening to meet at a different café so we could discuss the book in some privacy and not worry about every word and who was hearing it. I summarized the whole story for him in 15 minutes or so during which he was so mesmerized he never touched his coffee. When I finished, I ventured that I felt the book was more about Asian immigrants to the west, and London in particular, than about Islam or Muslims—had it not been for that one part where a character resembling the Prophet Mohammed named Mahmoud, whose 12 wives are depicted as prostitutes. Mahfouz agreed and wandered why that part was in there at all—that it almost had nothing to do with the general narrative. We debated the idea of going too far in humanizing the Prophet and whether or not that was possibly a useful thing for Muslims to do, whether south Asian or Middle Eastern. Mahfouz strongly felt that the point Rushdi wanted to make about the Prophet could have been made without the reference to 12 wives and to prostitution. "There's no point, I think, in going out of your way, whether you have the right or not, to insult and offend the beliefs of millions of people. It seems needlessly provocative."

After he won the Nobel prize, Naguib Bey came back to his coffee gatherings with friends as if nothing had happened. On his first evening back in Alexandria, I implored him to go to Stockholm to accept the prize in person, saying it was an honor not just for him but for Egypt and the whole Arab world. "You want me to die?!!" retorted Mahfouz, "Never been on a plane, never want to be." Indeed, Naguib ultimately sent his two loving daughters to accept the prize on his behalf—ideology had nothing to do with it, he was just intensely afraid of flying!

Mahfouz was genuinely humble about the prize, saying there were several Egyptian writers who deserved the prize more than he did. "My friends don't call me Nagib Mahzouz for nothing," jokingly making a pun on his name (Mahzouz means lucky in Arabic).

Another post-prize encounter with him took place at the Cairo Book fair in 1989. President Mubarak took Mahfouz in tow as he toured the fair, to show him off I suppose. I was one of the U.S. embassy officers staffing the American exhibit as Mubarak stopped by to look and chat briefly with us. I immediately noticed Mahfouz standing shyly behind the president so I left Mubarak to chat with one of my Egyptian colleagues showing him the exhibit and went straight to Naguib Bey—"Izzayak?" I asked him in Egyptian dialect (How do you feel)? And, "we miss you in Alexandria." Mahfouz immediately shot back in a loud voice, "This is a Mouled!" (a reference to the Prophet's birthday celebrations), adding more quietly, "I hate all this fuss it makes me dizzy!"

These were relatively calm times in Egypt and yet political Islam was certainly pervasive in the Muslim Brotherhood's slogans, social work, and occasional demonstrations in Alexandria and the poorer neighborhoods of Cairo. More radical organizations like the Gama'at al-Islamiyah and Jihad had also formed, advocating a more violent approach to the application of Sharia and eventual overthrow of the Mubarak regime in favor of a direct Islamist rule. Cairo's international book festival, a yearly event frequented by students, scholars, and intellectuals from all over the Arab world had an increasingly Islamist hew, seen in the titles on display and some of the panel discussions featured in its programs. The Egyptian government's policy on the issue was confusing. On the one hand, it banned the MB's political activities and jailed members of the Gama'at wherever it could find them; on the other hand, al-Azhar, whose Sheikh (president) was hand-picked and presumably heavily influenced by the government, was more often than not controlled by an MB faculty and management and spewed opinions that were not tolerant of secular thought or writers like Farag Fouda who risked and then lost his life challenging the Islamists and their views. The political and intellectual environment was in short inhospitable and intimidating to secular thinkers and writers and threatening Fatwas against them were not uncommon. The government generally did nothing to discourage intimidation or to help promote tolerance and secular thought and only intervened after acts of violence were perpetrated, particularly if these acts were against the state.

The Security Environment

My years in Alexandria coincided with the term in office of Egypt's notorious minister of interior, Zaki Badr, who served from 1986 to 1990. He was known for being a no-nonsense tough security official, feared by Islamists and the public in general for his extensive network of spies and informers who watched everyone. The problem was that no one knew quite what the redlines were for the security establishment. On the one hand, the ministry of interior harassed Islamist students on campuses and tried to deny them victories in student elections. On the other hand, any criticism of the regime from any quarter could land one in jail.

As diplomats in the field, we were critical of Egyptian authorities' violations of human rights but tended to soft-peddle our criticisms in order not to rock the boat of bilateral relations. Our attitude toward Islamists in particular was also complex and undefined. While we did not care for the values of the Muslim Brotherhood, we did not consider them to be a terrorist organization and felt it was important for us to understand their views, what motivated them and what were the limits of any common ground between us. I explored this personally when I invited the head of the MB in Alexandria to my roundtable discussions at the ACC. A brain surgeon, Nabil Hashem was a very gentle and reasonable sort with whom one could discuss almost any topic. He came to an event one time with visiting former Congressman Paul Findley and talked about American support for Israel, chances for the establishment of a Palestinian state, and seemed to very much enjoy the interaction without exhibiting any of the animus one associated with ideologues. I asked him later what would the MB want as a bottom line on Palestine and he answered quite simply, "Whatever the Palestinians are willing to accept would be fine by us."

I wrote memos to the Embassy about my meetings with Dr. Hashem, reflecting on his views on religion, politics, and society, memos which were appreciated by our political officers in Cairo who had not met MB leaders in as friendly a setting as I had. One time, Ambassador Frank Wisner, who was on very friendly terms with president Mubarak, related to me Mubarak's concern as to why the U.S. cultural attache in Alexandria was meeting with the MB? I asked the ambassador if he wanted me to stop seeing Nabil and He said, "no, keep doing what you're doing!"

The author with Paul Findley & Nabil Hashem.

Ironically, the brain surgeon developed a brain tumor and was bed-ridden for a couple of months before passing away. I visited him at his home during that period and we had long conversations about Islam and politics. I recall grilling him on the more fundamentalist views of Islam, particularly on the question of whether a Muslim was supposed to think of Christians and Jews as people of the book—as often referred to in the Qur'an—or as "Dhalleen" meaning those who had strayed from the correct faith? His answer was that there were different interpretations of the same verses in the Qur'an and Hadith on that matter and that sometimes the interpretation was adopted to fit a particular political view rather than the other way around. His own views were on the liberal side, but he admitted the ongoing debate on this and other issues in Islam meant that a definitive answer was hard to come by even among the MB members, let alone that an agreement could be found between them and the more hardline Islamists who, unlike the MB, believed in imposing their views on others. When Dr. Hashem passed away, I walked in his funeral procession.

I left Egypt in 1990 to assume another post, this time in Riyadh, Saudi Arabia. Despite his kindness, gentility, and refusal to provoke, Naguib Mahfouz was stabbed in the neck in 1994 by an Islamist fanatic as he was on his way to meet with his Cairo coffee gathering. He survived the attack after surgery and brief hospitalization. He had said in an interview before the attack that death threats didn't scare him, "I might be threatened today but die of natural causes tomorrow." After the stabbing, he described how his attacker had called out his name and that he had turned to him with a smile, assuming it was one of his fans wanting to shake his hand. Naguib Mahfouz died quietly at his Cairo home in 2006 surrounded only by his immediate family.

Farag Fouda, a dynamic forty-something writer when Naim Tekla and I had a drink with him at a hotel in Cairo in 1989, was by contrast deliberately confrontational and used every opportunity to challenge Islamists and call them out for illogical and, in his view, mistaken interpretations of Islam. "I can't believe how intimidated most Egyptians are by these people. They do not represent modern day Egypt, their views belong to the stone age and they should be told so to their faces over and over again." Fouda was assassinated in 1992. There is no easy path for secular-minded Arabs in dealing with the scourge of radical Jihadis.

There were plenty of opportunities for tourism during our 3 years in Egypt. MargaretAnne, having quit her law practice in Albany, devoted herself to family—in particular, our two children, Elysaar and Jibrahn, who thrived in their early years at the British School, which was within walking distance from our home on Kafr Abdo street. Among our closest friends in Egypt were David and Avtar and their kids. Together, children in tow, we toured the sites in Egypt and went on a memorable cruise to Greece. Among my closest personal friends in Egypt was Faukiya Morsi, a beautiful and very smart Egyptian woman who worked at the U.S. consulate's consular section at the time. She, Naim Tekla, and I often conversed about things great and small after our monthly intellectual forum sessions at the ACC. The last time I saw her and Naim together was during a visit in 1995. She survived Naim by only a couple of years and died in a tragic car accident on the Alexandria–Cairo highway. With the death of my two friends, followed by the demise of Neguib Mahfouz and, more recently, the return of military dictatorship to Egypt, I lost any incentive to revisit Egypt.

U.S. Policy

Back at the Department of State, my colleague from Alexandria days, Ron Schlicher, and I were on an Interagency Working Group (IWG) established in 1993 to help define the Department's policy on Political Islam. Robert Pelletreau, at the time Assistant Secretary for the Near East Area (NEA), tasked us with drafting a paper on the subject. The IWG took a few months to debate the meaning of Political Islam, the types of groups that possibly fit under that rubric and whether or not it made sense to generalize at all on the subject. Two good things came out in the final report presented to Pelletreau: A definition of terms, since various agencies and political officers used terms like fundamentalism, political Islam, religious extremism, and, inevitably, terrorism almost interchangeably. It was remarkable that an agreement was actually reached among the 20 or so interagency officers in as short a time as it did. Academics in fact are still debating basic definitions of terms while politicians often have no compunctions about proposing wide-ranging policies and responses to a phenomenon they don't even bother to define.

My recollection of the policy outline is as follows:

The United States has no policy on Islam, just as it has no policy on any other religion.

The United States has no policy on fundamentalism, that being a particular understanding of Islam that does not necessarily address itself to policy issues of interest to the U.S.

Political Islam, even though a political ideology, is also too broad and varied in its implementation to justify a standardized response. The values of political Islam are somewhat antithetical to the basic tenet of separation of church and state in the United States, but just because we disagree with that philosophy does not mean it should automatically be branded hostile to the U.S. national interest.

When it comes to specific groups that espouse political Islam, however, we begin to look at their attitude toward the United States and policies they advocate which may indeed be hostile to the U.S. national interest. In this regard, U.S. policy toward Islamists—specific individuals or groups with an Islamist philosophy and agenda—depends on their actions and general attitude toward the United States and toward violence. Ultimately, individuals and groups that are deemed dangerous get placed on a terrorism or supporters of terrorism list. With those, no dialogue is possible.

In terms of directives to diplomats in the field, the policy paper recommended that Foreign Service Officers be open to talking to anyone willing to have a dialogue with U.S. representatives so long as they did not advocate or practice violence as a means of achieving their political goals.

Over the years, our dialogue with moderate Islamists was always shy, awkward, and half-hearted, partly because the policy had never been stated clearly and partly because of the urge not to offend friendly regimes where these individuals or groups were considered banned opposition groups. In the wake of 9/11, presidents Bush, Clinton, and certainly Obama have publicly denounced Islamophobia and distinguished between radical Islamists/Jihadists and Islam and warned that we shouldn't let the acts of the few taint our attitudes toward the many believers who meant us no harm. No one at a policymaking level though makes the distinction between moderate and radical Islamists, even if in reality, it is U.S. policy to do so. Not many U.S. diplomats have gone out of their way to do it because of this ambiguity. As a result, trust was not established with Islamists who could have acted as a buffer between us, the regimes in the region, and the hard line Jihadists who began appearing in greater frequency by the turn of the twenty-first century.

When the Egyptian MB came to power after the 2011 uprising that toppled Housni Mubarak, U.S. government contacts and willingness to work with elected president Morsi came as a surprise to many in the region and confused everyone including the MB—who were not prepared to run a huge bureaucracy and did not have a clear roadmap for running the country's foreign policy or its economy. In Egypt, the ousted regime's supporters, including the military, assumed we had "let Mubarak fall" and were abandoning them; the secular youth—civil society leaders who had led the fight against Mubarak thought we were in bed with MB and had engineered their ascent to power. The MB didn't trust our friendly overtures either and thought we were no doubt plotting their downfall, something they felt was proven correct when they were overthrown by the military and Abdel-fattah al-Sisi was anointed president—never mind that president Obama was uncomfortable with Sisi and tried to press him for a timetable to restore civilian government in Egypt. The knack to confuse and offend everyone in the Middle East has been a U.S. specialty lately in the Middle East and largely a result of not honestly and openly taking the right position from the start and sticking to it. When Donald Trump came to the White House, he seemed to have an actual liking of dictators and authoritarian regimes—the idea of ruling unencumbered by any checks and balances appealed to him. As such, relations with Egypt under military rule have been gradually returning to normal and there has been no angst over whether or not we were on the right side of history—security arrangements and a favorable trade balance have trumped other considerations, for the time being at any rate.

CHAPTER 4

SAUDI ARABIA

Arriving in Riyadh

We arrived in Riyadh in August 1990, coming from Cairo, via a short stay in Washington, DC. I recall two immediate reactions upon exiting the airport: (1) The heat felt like you were standing behind the exhaust of an airplane and (2) Question popped into my head: Where did everybody go? We had just been living in Egypt with streets teeming with people, cars, motorbikes, and the occasional donkey cart. Riyadh streets by contrast seemed empty—just wide highways with a few speeding cars and occasional rows of residences hidden behind the high sandy-colored walls surrounding them. I would later have the same feeling only more so upon visiting the King Fahd Library, an amazing structure with over a million volumes back then all stored at the right temperature and humidity levels, with hi-tech shelves that separated on command from a computer in the reference section and a light to point you to the book you had asked for. Again, there were very few people actually using this magnificent facility. I couldn't help thinking of Egyptian university students crammed in dusty old building with no temperature controls and no hi-tech system to guide them to the books stacked on bowed metallic shelves. This would be a common theme in thinking about inter-Arab politics for me, the lack of coordination between populous but poor countries and rich but under-populated regions like the GCC countries.

August of 1990 just happened to mark the start of Desert Shield, the build-up phase that led to the actual war, Desert Storm, on January 17, 1991. After spending my first tour of duty in Egypt where I was able to spend the bulk of my time away from the office at home with my family, the Riyadh stint was quite different and perhaps portended other stints in dangerous environments

41

to come. After only one week of checking into the U.S. Embassy, a process barely finished when I was told to pack a small bag and head to Dhahran, where I was to work with a U.S. Information Agency (USIA) film crew on stories of Kuwaitis fleeing Saddam's occupation of their country. After one month away, I returned to Riyadh for a few weeks and worked with a military team preparing another video on the war effort, then went off again to work in Taif with U.S. ambassador to Kuwait, Edward (Skip) Gnehm and went with him from there directly to Kuwait as soon as the war was over. When I got back home this time, my son Jibrahn, barely 4 years old at the time, smiled broadly when he saw me and said, "Why you here?" He said it in a pleasantly surprised tone but it hit me that for him the norm was for me to be away. I also realized that working conditions in an Arab capital on a war footing were likely to be more the norm in the region than was the case in Egypt. As I had intended, my work in the Foreign Service was to remain focused on the Middle East.

Desert Shield

The trip with Worldnet's film crew took us first to Dahran where the United States maintained (and still does) a consulate, for interviews with Kuwaitis who had made it there after fleeing their country, then on to the border town of Hafr el-Batin in a C-130 military plane. While in Dahran, I took a side trip to view the desert surrounding the city and came upon a recruiting point for young Saudis wishing to join the fight against Saddam Hussein. A Saudi sergeant stood on the sidewalk near a parking lot with a desert backdrop behind him waiting for new recruits to file in. One new recruit parked and exited his large Mercedes car nearby, saluted and filed in, overweight, disheveled, and obviously unaware of what was expected of him. The sergeant started to brief the new recruits on the logistics and training schedule ahead of them as the sound of vehicles revving up behind him got louder and louder. My colleague and I moved around the sand dune behind the recruiting point to see what the ruckus was about and beheld quite a sight: Young Saudi men had gathered beneath a large sand dune with fancy four-wheel drive and sports cars and took turns seeing who could drive up to the top of the dune, make a U turn, and come back down without getting stuck in the sand or tumbling down as a few did when their vehicle reached the top and overturned, to the cheer and laughter of the crowd below. The lack of seriousness of the trainees and the fun-loving crowd with their sports vehicles against the background of a setting sun belied the drums of war beating just a few miles away as troops from over 30 countries arrived and took their positions along the Saudi–Kuwaiti and Iraqi borders.

The front was also nothing like I expected. Flying over it, we could see nothing for miles except sand, camel herds, and a few structures that looked like hangars clustered in a couple of places along the front. Those, we found out when we deplaned and went to be briefed, were Mobile Army Surgical Hospitals—but a far cry from the MASH 4077—one of my favorite TV comedies based on the Korean war of the 1950s. The Saudi version, and the Kingdom had supplied everything down to thousands of bottled water flown in from France and Lebanon, came equipped with the latest in medical technology and huge carpeted and air conditioned tents for patients, soldiers, and visitors to rest and watch the news on oversized screens—the atmosphere of a sports bar rather than the austere conditions one might expect being at the front of an impending war.

Saudi General Mohamed al-Shahry, second in command at the northern sector and in charge of logistics, told us it would be impossible to cover the full length of the Saudi–Iraqi borders but that the units being deployed were all quite mobile and capable of tracking the movement of Iraqi units and moving into position to confront them. He was personally anxious for the war to start and expressed concern that the Bush administration was taking all this time to launch military operations. I asked Egyptian and

Syrian officers at the front if they or their men had any reservations about fighting another Arab army, and under U.S. command no less. One officer replied, "we are here to defend Saudi Arabia and will execute any command given by our Generals and leaders back home." Another said his men felt strongly they were defending the holy sites from a possible invasion by Saddam's forces and hence had no qualms whatsoever in performing that duty.

These soldiers were well fed, rested, and seemed in high morale, in contrast to reports we were getting about Iraqi troops who, even though in occupation of luxurious villas in Kuwait, were poorly fed, not well organized and worried about an impending assault "by the Americans" to route them out of the tiny country. Indeed, upon entering liberated Kuwait at the end of the war, we would later see the pitiful shelters they had built around the city to defend against an American landing from the sea—the direction from which they most expected the invasion to be launched.

The Politics of It All

The case against Saddam Hussein in August 1990 was straight forward enough, having invaded and occupied an independent country recognized by the international community, but his motivation for the move against Kuwait was more complicated. Saddam had emerged from an 8-year war against Iran, partially funded (on a loan basis) by Saudi Arabia and Kuwait, and covertly supported by the United States. Saddam was furious after a long and very destructive war that Kuwait would not forgive his debt, reportedly amounting to $14 Billion, a debt he felt he had incurred while defending Arab Gulf interests not just his own. Saddam also accused Kuwaitis of having exploited the Rumayla oil field on the border between the two countries by way of slant drilling in violation of prior agreements. The attack on Kuwait, while not justified under any pretext, was certainly not sudden or unprovoked. Diplomacy could certainly have avoided this war.

Particularly controversial was American ambassador to Iraq, April Glaspie's meeting with Saddam a week before he invaded Kuwait. Glaspie, delivering the administration's talking points, had said that while the United States had no opinion on border disputes between two Arab countries, she did hope for a quick resolution of the conflict through the aegis of the Arab League or that of Egyptian president Mubarak—clearly indicating that the United States hoped for a peaceful mediated resolution of the conflict. This was widely credited in the media and within the administration with having given Saddam the impression that the United States would not stand in his way should he decide to invade Kuwait. Ambassador Glaspie took the fall for a possibly ambiguous U.S. position and for the failure of intelligence agencies to predict Saddam's decision to invade. Not many of us in the Foreign Service, at least not those of us who knew the ambassador, believed that she had in any way erred or single-handedly caused the outbreak of war. James Baker, U.S. Secretary of State at the time, was not known for giving his diplomats in the field much leeway and his assistant for Public Affairs, Margaret Tutwiler, was not one to mince words in conveying the Secretary's instructions. At any rate, Glaspie sent a cable to Washington reporting on her meeting with Saddam and did not receive any corrections or additional instructions. Further, once the United States and international build-up started, Saddam had six months to recant and withdraw his troops from Kuwait before the war started in January of the following year. If upwards of half a million troops on his borders and countless strongly worded UN resolutions did not change his policy, it is doubtful that a mere verbal warning from an ambassador would have deterred him. The man had clearly made up his mind to invade by the time he met with the U.S. ambassador, and was simply sending a message at that meeting to that effect, that he would be taking action against Kuwait. Once his troops marched into Kuwait, nothing dissuaded him from formally annexing it and declaring to the world that he had no intention of voluntarily withdrawing his troops.

April Glaspie, who had been a rising star and a leading Arabist in the State Department, took the fall, nonetheless, and was dispatched to a deputy's job at the U.S./UN Mission after which she was assigned as Consul General in Cape Town, South Africa, from which position she retired—in other words, she was quietly eased out of the Foreign Service.

Iraq annexed Kuwait formally on August 8. With a few exceptions, there wasn't much argument in the international community in defense of this occupation—despite the pro-Saddam positions taken by the leaders of Jordan, Yemen, and the Palestine Liberation Organization—positions for which Yemenis and Palestinians would later pay a heavy price. There were concerns nonetheless, over the U.S. going to war against an Arab country and one which was seen, at least in some corners of the Arab world, as having championed the Palestinian cause and of being a bulwark in the region against regional powers such as Iran and Israel. The Bush administration needed a carefully crafted campaign to convince the American public and the international community that military action needed to be taken. That the Iraq invasion violated the sovereignty of an internationally recognized country was evident enough. The argument, that 250,000 Iraqi troops were amassed on the Saudi borders and therefore threatened further expansion, a claim made by the administration, was never demonstrated. The domino theory was invoked nonetheless to convince reluctant members of Congress to support the U.S. going to war. Saddam certainly did not help his own cause by refusing multiple diplomatic efforts to dissuade him from the course he had chosen.

The war for the liberation of Kuwait was preceded by meticulous and patient diplomatic work on the part of Secretary Baker's State Department, carefully putting together a large international coalition to defeat Saddam. The Department of Defense also took its time in putting together the complex military machine, logistics and command structure required to coordinate a multi-nation military effort to drive Saddam's army out of Kuwait as efficiently and quickly as possible. Public Diplomacy was part of that effort. Desert Shield lasted from August 2, 1990, to January 17, 1991, when the next phase, Desert Storm, began.

The battle for hearts and minds in the United States but also in the Middle East and beyond was necessary for the war effort. In the United States, the Bush administration needed to convince the American public that the war was justified on economic, strategic, and humanitarian bases. The administration had to content itself with issuing official statements since the Smith–Mundt Act of 1948 (amended in 1987 and 2013) prohibited USIA from disseminating its material—meant for foreign media and audiences —for domestic use. The Kuwaiti government took on the task of a public campaign to win over U.S. public opinion by hiring Hill and Knowlton, a New York-based PR firm, to represent them in Washington and to help win public support for U.S. military action to liberate Kuwait. Garnering support from the Arab world was also important so the war wouldn't be seen as western armies lining up against an Arab/Muslim country. Diplomatically, Secretary of State, Jim Baker, mounted a well-organized campaign to compliment what Saudi Arabia and the GCC countries were doing. As a result of both campaigns, Morocco, Jordan, Syria, and Egypt all supported the war against Saddam and sent troops to join the coalition to foil his occupation of Kuwait.

USIA was charged with mounting a campaign to win the support of Arab publics. The goals were to explain the plight of Kuwaiti citizens living under or escaping from Iraqi occupation, to expose Saddam's brutality and to show a mighty international force being prepared to reverse the occupation of Kuwait.

One project I worked on in Dhahran was to help produce short interviews near the border between Saudi Arabia and Kuwait depicting the reactions and stories of Kuwaiti families fleeing the occupation and then airing their stories on Arab TV stations that were willing to show them or to broadcast them on Worldnet's closed-circuit TV shown to select audiences at U.S. embassies in the region. This was before the American-funded al-Hurra station was started. Using the material with Arab stations was meant to overcome the tendency of viewers to dismiss it as American propaganda if viewed on exclusively USG media. Of course, Arab media was not always inclined to accept USG made videos.

While the videos yielded nothing dramatic, they did generate a stock of stories that ordinary people told about their life under the brief occupation and a glimpse of a Kuwaiti resistance of sorts—not the shooting kind but a collection of neighborhood organizations that served to help people survive the occupation and evade being arrested and interrogated by Iraqi soldiers. Thus, assistance was provided surreptitiously to families that needed it and those known to be wanted by the Iraqis were offered help in evading arrest. One trick employed was to change the street signs around so when soldiers came with addresses for people on their list, they could never find the right person they were looking for. Such stories, however, were no match for the incubator story circulated during the first few weeks of the occupation by the Kuwaiti lobby, and which proved totally false afterwards.[1]

A Line in the Sand—video originally made by a PSYOPS (the army's psychological operations) team eventually edited and recast, replacing my original Arabic narration with a new Arab voice-over by USIS, never proved to have had much of an audience. The video depicted the world's reaction to the occupation of Kuwait, the nature and size of the international coalition against Saddam and the might of the military force assembled against him. The video was meant for Iraqi audiences since we were convinced that their state-controlled media was not giving

---

1   Briefly, a young woman claimed to be an eye-witness to Iraqi soldiers ripping new-born babies out incubators as part of stealing and vandalizing hospital equipment in Kuwait. The young woman was later outed as the daughter of Kuwait's ambassador to Washington who was not an employee of the hospital and could not possibly have witnessed such an event.

them the correct picture, and to Saddam himself who was also likely isolating himself from the reality outside his borders. In addition to being shown on Worldnet and some stations in the region that allowed it to be aired, the video was also beamed into Iraq by the military without actually knowing in advance who if anyone would be able to pick it up, given that there were very few satellite dishes inside Iraq at the time.

A Disinformation campaign was staffed by a fusion team at USIA headquarters back in DC, putting together CIA, military, and civilian personnel to respond to rumors and Iraqi propaganda on Worldnet—with its limited audiences at U.S. embassies overseas—and in any papers and news agencies that were willing to pick up and use these official retorts.

In the Limelight

In Jeddah with President Bush, 1990.

November 21, 1990: President George H. Bush came to the Kingdom of Saudi Arabia (KSA) to meet with King Fahd and with the Emir of Kuwait who was being hosted along with his family and cabinet by the KSA and were all staying in the city of Taif. Most of U.S. Embassy, Riyadh, had gone to Jeddah where the meetings were to take place. I was asked by our Public Affairs Officer to stay behind in Riyadh to "mind the fort." I never got the story straight, but the President came without his interpreter for some reason—something about the Saudi authorities not granting him a visa. In a last minute panic, someone from Washington told the traveling party they had a "cleared American" in Riyadh they could use as an interpreter for their high-level meetings. Hence, the call went out for Khoury—an American officer with top security clearance and who spoke Arabic fluently. I departed Riyadh post-haste to Jeddah.

In all, I sat in on three meetings: One was at a dinner hosted by King Fahd in honor of the visiting delegation, another was at a bilateral meeting with the Kuwaiti government, and a third at a press conference held jointly by President Bush and the Emir of Kuwait. In all cases, discussions revolved around the occupation of Kuwait and the impatience of the Kuwaiti government with the slow pace the war effort was taking. At dinner, Secretary Baker asked King Fahd if he wasn't concerned that military action against Saddam might lead to his overthrow and create a dangerous vacuum in Baghdad (rather prophetic on the part of Baker, given what happened in the wake of the 2003 invasion of Iraq). King Fahd replied in the negative. He said that the situation could be managed, that the risk of a void was minimal and that military action to remove Saddam from Kuwait was imperative regardless.

King Fahd did not elaborate on how any void created in Iraq might be filled and the only other conversation at dinner was him extolling the virtues of the Saudi dairy industry. He wanted Secretary Baker to taste the white goat cheese in particular and said that it was made for him (King Fahd) personally on a special farm and dedicated dairy facility. Baker was concerned about some of the food at the table and wanted to know if it was safe to consume. I assured him in an aside that it was.

At the meeting with the Kuwaiti government, the Emir went on and on about the suffering of his people under Iraqi occupation and his fear for the future of his small peaceful country, so brutally victimized by Saddam's army. He believed that Saddam would never leave voluntarily and had to be removed by force. He didn't understand why the decision to go to war had not yet been taken. At one point, the Emir smiled and wondered what Margaret Thatcher would've done in his place. President Bush was full of sympathy and reassurance that the occupation of Kuwait would not stand. Secretary Baker, a master strategist with endless patience, reminded the Emir and his cabinet that every chance was being given Saddam to see reason and leave Kuwait peaceably, but in the meantime, a huge armada was being amassed to force him out if it became necessary. Baker also wanted to make sure the U.N. approved any military action, and to that end, much diplomacy was being invested in obtaining unanimous support at the UNSC and, that if it came to war, the United States wanted to make sure Arab countries participated so it didn't look like the west ganging up on an Arab country.

At the end of the meeting with the Kuwaiti government, I briefed ambassador Edward (Skip) Gnehm on what was discussed. He asked me if I could accompany him to Taif, where the Kuwait government in exile was located and where a makeshift U.S. embassy functioned with Skip and a handful of foreign service personnel. Permission from Riyadh granted, I joined the ambassador and his small team, notably political officer and friend David Pearce and a couple of others, plus a small security contingent.

If there was ever a gilded cage within a gilded cage, Taif was it. Nestled in a mountainous region south west of Riyadh and on the road to Mecca, Taif presented a serene, if luxurious setting at an expansive Holiday Inn resort made available for the Kuwaiti royal family by the Saudi government. The small U.S. embassy staff mingled with only a few other foreign diplomats who moved

51

there temporarily to stay in touch with Kuwaiti officials. Embassy facilities were minimal and a total staff of 13 had only one computer to share between them, but had close contact with Kuwaiti officials and the time to chat, sometimes over sumptuous buffets offered three times a day. Compensating for the lack of any entertainment or family members, we did not miss a meal while in Taif. Meal time was the only distraction from work and the word would go out at snack time especially: Dessert Storm! Otherwise, jogging in idyllic countryside surroundings provided another pastime for those desiring some physical exercise to work off all those extra calories.

Authorized Departure

In the run-up to the war, U.S. policy was to support the Saudi government by not alarming the international community into quitting the Kingdom unnecessarily. The Saudi relationship with the international business community depended on confidence in the Kingdom's stability and security. As a result, and as Riyadh emptied of foreign embassies and communities, the U.S. embassy was practically the last one to consider a U.S. Gov't authorized departure of embassy families let alone embassy staff. I was asked to help staff the embassy's community liaison center phones set up to answer questions from the American community in Saudi Arabia. We received numerous calls daily from American citizens concerned about the approaching war, what the Embassy analysis was and why the United States had not yet ordered assisted departure of citizens from Riyadh when all the other western nations had done so for their people. I was patiently explaining the situation to one outraged woman about our view that it continued to be safe in Riyadh and finally said that my wife and two children were still there with me in the city. Exasperated, the woman then blurted out, "Is there anyone there I can talk to who isn't an Asshole?!!"

The war started before the embassy authorized families to depart Saudi Arabia or issued gas masks even after much fuss was made over Saddam's Scud rockets and possible chemical weapons on them. My family finally left, two weeks into the war along with other embassy families but only after we and the children watched scuds, looking like headlights coming at you, traversing the skies over Riyadh. The Saudi official announcements on TV were almost comical in their attempt not to offer too much detail, first bannering "danger is coming" on their screens when a Scud missile was known to have been launched at the Kingdom, then announcing "Danger has arrived" once the missile had impacted. It was only hours afterwards, usually during the evening news, that they would give some information on where the missile had landed and if it had caused any damage or casualties.

Another embarrassment was over gas masks. The children heard from other foreign classmates that their embassies had provided gas masks long before the U.S embassy provided any. The fact that other embassies had them and provided them to their employees and families eventually drove our embassy admin to suggest we could get them from allied embassies or directly from Saudi government offices inside the diplomatic quarter where we lived.

Kuwait after Liberation

I recall, before Desert Storm actually started, having a discussion about the war with the Embassy's political counselor. I had just come back from the front and said that in my opinion, the war should not take more than two weeks: One week of aerial bombardment and another week to flush out any Iraqi troops who had not yet run off from Kuwait. My colleague replied that I was underestimating Saddam and that it was likely to be a long and difficult war. In my view, the administration as well as it's political officers on the ground tended to overestimate or deliberately exaggerate Saddam's power.[2] True, his army had ballooned to a million strong after the war with Iran, but it was filled with poorly equipped and trained foot soldiers with diminished motivation after the long and exhausting war with Iran. Further, lacking the proper coordination between air, ground, and naval units, Saddam's military was no match for technologically advanced European and American forces, aided by tens of thousands of Arab foot soldiers. The war ended sooner than most expected, in three weeks and with almost negligible casualties for the coalition: 36 Americans died in total, more than half of those were killed by friendly fire in Khafje in northern Saudi Arabia.

The aerial and naval assault which constituted the first phase of the war began on 17 January 1991 and went on for five weeks. This was overkill by any measure as Iraqi troops were on the run practically from the first week. The bombardment targeted roads, bridges and factories all over Iraq with the purported goal of preventing reinforcements from reaching Iraqi troops in Kuwait, but in essence weakening Saddam's military for years to come. This phase was followed by a ground assault on 24 February. The coalition ceased its advance, and declared a ceasefire 100 hours after the ground campaign started.

U.S. ambassador to Kuwait, Gnehm, his political officer, and I, were cleared to go into Kuwait a week after the fighting ended. We had to mark sometime at Dhahran airport on the way while waiting for the Kuwaiti government to send in one of their officials ahead of us. The decision to delay on our part was to avoid the optics of the Americans going back first—the Emir of Kuwait having decided not to go in himself until the Americans had made sure Kuwait City was safe and his palace was rehabilitated for his and his family's use. We landed at the burnt out Kuwait international airport the day after the actual ceasefire was declared.

---

2   In a memo to the president, Secretary Baker had imparted that Margaret Thatcher had been "sobered" by his telling her to expect a long war with numerous casualties.

We then flew by helicopter and landed inside the U.S. Embassy compound.

Flying over the city, one could hardly tell it had been through a war of occupation followed by a war of liberation. It seemed largely intact. The worst damage of course was to the burning oil fields outside the city, to the barricades along the coast used by Iraqi soldiers to defend themselves against what they assumed would be a sea landing, and to the airport where an actual ground battle took place. The allied bombing deliberately avoided the city itself and Damage to the city from the occupation was minimal as Kuwaitis had not put up any resistance to advancing Iraqi forces. The Emir's palace was heavily damaged, along with some villas that showed signs of looting and burning, presumably to inflict an extra measure of humiliation on a monarchy that dared to defy Saddam.

The U.S. Embassy in Kuwait did suffer some damage and was under repair for the first few weeks after the return of ambassador and staff. The damage however was self-inflicted. U.S. special forces who had entered it first wanted to make sure the compound had not been taken over by Iraqi forces and bugged or booby-trapped. It had not, but in the process of finding that out some walls had been taken down, water pipes and electric wires exposed, etc.

The Diplomatic Mission ad-interim

The informality which typified embassy work, at least the first few weeks after the war, was a refreshing change from the usual formality of a large embassy like the missions in Riyadh or Cairo. War and its aftermath put embassy staff in an unusual and still dangerous circumstance and demanded unusual working hours. Dress code and diplomatic protocol were naturally relaxed. In Taif, Skip Gnehm would exercise on his stationary bike during odd hours of the day and we tended to hover around him for

55

updates and informal discussions of policy options as he was exercising. In Kuwait, a slightly larger staff and military officer intermingled and communicated around meal times, consisting mostly of military combat rations (MREs). Packages would be ripped open and contents exchanged as if in an old barter souk with some exchanging the meat they got for spaghetti (the only food item that required some heating) or those fond of dessert would trade a main course for other munchers' chocolate bars and biscuits. Plenty of water bottles, supplied during the war and after by the Saudi government, were a heaven-sent since there was no running water at first at the embassy or at the deserted and partially burnt Hilton across the street where we all stayed. We bathed with the bottles of mineral water after walking up to the higher floors which were not affected by the fire. Kuwait was basically safe, if scary, due to the lack of electricity and the fear that holdouts among Iraqi soldiers or intelligence operatives might still be lurking around to attack any American that came into the city. We used walkie-talkies to communicate with one another and we kept them always on to listen for any developments or instructions.

One night, just after turning in around midnight, a loud explosion rattled our windows. Chatter on the radios indicated a bomb of some sort had been tossed into the embassy compound. Minutes later somebody was found crouching inside a doorway in a dark alley not far from the embassy. The marines who caught the perpetrator asked on the radio if I could come down and help them question him in Arabic. I was half-way down the stairs before the call came to cancel the request. Between his broken English and the smattering of Arabic one of the RSO's staff had, it was decided that a lone Iraqi soldier had lost his way and stayed behind after his fellow soldiers had left. The grenade he tossed over the embassy wall was a concussion bomb, capable of producing a loud bang but little else. He offered himself up and pleaded for mercy. It was decided that a longer conversation could wait until the next day.

Going to meetings with the ambassador at night was scary because of the defensive driving required by regulations and necessitated by the need to avoid parked cars that looked like they might have been placed as booby traps on the road. I was generally sandwiched with the ambassador between two armed marines with their guns sticking out the windows while the lead and follow cars zigzagged around ours at every intersection, ready to block any car that attempted to ram us. The blocking tactics were no different from quarterbacks in a Football game, flanked by defenders who block any incoming tackle, except that I often felt more like the ball being tossed around rather than the quarterback running with it.

More often than not, my outings were with the political officer, David Pearce. We often started our days at 6:00 a.m., read what traffic we could get off of unclassified computers, decided what issues needed to be reported on that day and therefore who to go see by way of researching the issues. One such issue was to investigate reports of abuse conducted by returning Kuwaitis on Palestinian residents who had stayed behind during the occupation and allegedly collaborated with Iraqi troops and intelligence officers, pointing out Kuwaitis wanted by them.

We were able to document several cases of abuse, some at the hands of Kuwaiti police and others at the hands of ordinary citizens who would stop Palestinians in the streets sometimes and subject them to insults and beatings. We found that Lebanese living in Kuwait tended to display Lebanese and Kuwaiti flags on their cars so as to distinguish themselves from Palestinians who, like them, were considered foreigners in Kuwait but were more politically suspect than the Lebanese. One Palestinian took us to his home and introduced us to his brother who, he told us, had been arrested by Kuwaiti police and tortured then released without charge. The brother took off his shirt and showed us the bruises left by beatings and scars from cigarette butts extinguished on his body by the police. Another Palestinian family told us they were packing up to leave Kuwait, the father, a school teacher, having been fired from his job upon the liberation of Kuwait for no reason other than being a Palestinian. These stories were common enough that it was obvious that Arabs living in Kuwait, but particularly Palestinians (because Yasser Arafat had sided with Saddam during the occupation of Kuwait), were being subjected to random acts of violence and revenge with no proof being produced that they themselves had collaborated with the Iraqi occupation army.

A more pleasant issue we followed was a budding civil society organization among women. We attended a conference with Kuwaiti women leading discussions on women's rights and civil liberties. Besides the euphoria in those early days over the liberation of their country, the liberal–secular Kuwaitis were anxious to remind us that this was the right time for us to pressure the returning Kuwait government on granting democracy and women's rights to their citizens. They suggested that the U.S. government should make demands on the Emir, while the whole country was still in a thankful mood for the United States handing them their country back. While the United States never publicly castigated or pressured the Kuwaiti government to introduce democratic reforms, the State Department's human rights report made open mention of the restrictions on civil liberties and human rights abuses, especially those of minorities in the country. The Emir of Kuwait did promise liberal reforms but initially disappointed civil rights activists in the aftermath of liberation, claiming other more urgent priorities needed his attention. Eventually, though some reforms were undertaken. Women's right to vote, for example, was finally approved by parliament in 2005 and women voted and ran for seats in 2009, more than 18 years after the liberation of Kuwait.[3]

Kuwait is today ahead of other Gulf states in democratization measures and enjoys lively debates in parliament, though the in-

---

3   https://goo.gl/p836Bj.

58

stitution is still subject to being dismissed if it crosses the line and attacks the Emir or members of the royal family directly. Civil society organizations exist but are mainly labor-oriented or social and cultural in nature. Political and human rights NGOs still face restrictions which inhibit the institutionalization of comprehensive political rights.

Back in Riyadh: Women Drivers and Religious Police

A colleague (Matt Lussenhop) and I flew back to Riyadh after U.S. Embassy—Kuwait was up and running with its own staff and no longer needed our help. We joked about having come in to Kuwait like stowaways and were returning to our regular posts in style—flying back to Riyadh on General John Abizeid's personal Lear jet—life was beginning to return to normal in Riyadh and we could resume the cultural work we were sent to Riyadh to do in the first place.

Saudi Women

First question I received from colleagues in the Public Affairs section at the embassy when I arrived in 1990 as the new Cultural Affairs Officer was, "do you want your wife or your secretary to run the women's programs?" My answer was an instantaneous, "I'm the Cultural Attache, I'll do it." The standard attitude among American colleagues was that conservative social customs in Saudi Arabia were too strict to allow women to come to cultural events, even at a foreign diplomatic mission, where Saudi men were also in attendance. It was customary then to have women organize cultural events for women in order to put them at ease. I came to the embassy with the attitude that this segregation of the sexes was wrong and that since it wasn't part of the American culture, we shouldn't indulge and participate in it. The Arab in me was also a liberal one and rebelled against the extreme chauvinism of Saudi culture. My reply was, "there are those who are liberal enough to come and we should encourage and support them."

I had introduced while in Alexandria, Egypt, an intellectual forum, open to writers, journalists, and intellectuals interested in exploring cultural and political themes. One bureaucratic reason for doing this was to introduce American literature through translated works—translations that had been underwritten by USIA. My political reasoning however was that discussions of literary works are often a window on social and political ideas that people, particularly in closed societies, don't have the chance to broach directly. Indeed, such discussions have over the years provided opportunities to listen to and understand what the Arab literati were thinking and what issues they most considered to be important. This approach had yielded dividends in Egypt, where Islamists and Arab nationalists debated ideas across our table at the ACC. While my political officer colleagues spent most of their out-of-embassy time talking to government and business officials, I thought I would broaden the discussion and involve university professors, students, and authors, knowing that the latter in particular had their fingers on the pulse of the people and often expressed in a literary setting their own sentiment on a broader range of issues and indeed the sentiment of the broader community to which they belonged.

The group that came to my intellectual forum at the embassy in Riyadh was small, but generally included one female professor along with several of her male colleagues and one female graduate student. A woman artist also attended a few sessions. She was a painter with very liberal views and turned out to be one of the leaders of the women's driving rebellion of 1991.

The graduate student, a young woman in her 20s, met one of her male professors for the first time at the forum. In Saudi Arabia, women did not generally meet their male professors face to face. Professors lectured via a video link, written exams and papers were dropped in his mail box, which he corrected and sent back to the students. It was one of those special moments when Souad (not her real name) met her literature professor at the U.S. embassy. She recognized him of course from his video lectures and name, he recalled her name but had never seen her face. At the embassy, Souad wore her Abaya over her clothes but left her face uncovered—something she would not do out on the street or any public venue where men were present.

This small circle was perhaps not indicative of a large slice of Saudi society, but of a small group of liberal-minded Saudis not afraid of bucking the prevalent social norms and wanting to enjoy open discussions of the literature, culture, and occasionally politics. I recall that a discussion of Nathaniel Hawthorne's Scarlet Letter elicited a lively discussion, comparing seventeenth-century puritan America with medieval Europe and twentieth-century Saudi Arabia. The group, a liberal one to be sure, mused over the cultural exceptionalism argument of Saudi officials and conservative apologists—that Saudi culture is different and should not be compared to nor seek to emulate western cultures. While there was agreement that the latter should not be held up as a model for Saudi society, there was also agreement that there was nothing immutable about Saudi values and that they, of their own accord, were bound to evolve and perhaps change completely over time.

The group had been to my house once for dinner. All brought their spouses with them except for two unmarried participants. I pushed the envelope on another occasion by inviting them to view a video of the film Being There at my house. We had read the book by Jerzi Kosinski and instead of a discussion, I thought it would be fun to discuss the film in conjunction with the book. What had slipped my mind was a rather saucy scene in which Shirley McLaine, trying to seduce the main character, played by Peter Sellers, engages in masturbation in front of him. Once that scene started, it was too late to stop and reverse plans. The women in my living room looked at one another and one by one slipped into the kitchen and occupied themselves with tidying up, thus avoiding the embarrassment of watching a sex scene with men in their midst. They promptly returned when the scene was

61

over and no one ever mentioned that a very awkward moment had passed.

The women's driving rebellion of 1991 involved a small number of women (estimated between 30 and 40) who took the wheel from their husbands and/or drivers in order to protest the ban on women drivers, a ban that no other country in the world exercised, at least not in the final decade of the twentieth century. Two of the women were regular attendees of my cultural forum and, along with a third organizer, came to see me at the embassy the night before they drove. They wanted to alert me to their plans and to ask if I could make sure any American journalists in town knew about it in advance and were prepared to cover it for the international media. It was very short notice but my colleague, the press Attache, was able to get the word out to a few U.S. journalists in town. The event created a splash in-country of course mainly due to the government's over-reaction: As anticipated, the women were stopped by religious police, aided by regular gendarmes and taken to police stations. Husbands and/ or other male family members were called to come and get their women out of jail to avoid the provocation of keeping the women overnight—a contingency for which the stations in question were not prepared. These women were all highly educated and professional women and, while no prison sentences were issued, the participants had their passports confiscated and therefore unable to travel out of the country for a year, some (the professors among them) lost their jobs while others (my artist friend among them) had their studios ransacked and vandalized—all meant to put pressure on them and their families not to repeat such defiant behavior again.

Officially, the U.S. embassy made no comment on the issue, considering it an internal matter. Not surprising, since the embassy had not reacted earlier when U.S. troops were still in the country defending it from a possible Iraqi attack and an American woman in military uniform jogging alongside a male colleague was stopped by the religious police and the man beaten by them as he tried to defend his female companion from their harassment.

Conservatism in the media and entertainment industry sometimes seemed to go overboard even for Saudi Arabia. A Saudi journalist came to interview me at home once for a TV family show as part of a program on diplomatic families in Riyadh. The interview seemed benign indeed and included my reading to my son from Gibran Kahlil Gibran's book, the Prophet. When the program finally aired, I was surprised to see that the book-reading segment had been excised. Inquiring about that with the interviewer, I was told (in confidence) that reading from a Christian author like Gibran was frowned on by her management. It was incredible as I had never thought of Gibran as particularly Christian and had only chosen him to read from because my son had been named after him, though my wife and I spelled his name more phonetically, Jibrahn.

Another excess my wife and I noted while shopping for swimming suits for our children was that boxes containing the swimming suits had pictures of little children wearing them and incredibly had the legs of little girls censored out with black felt-tip pens. We mused on how perverted an exercise to have grown men spend hours blacking out little girls' legs from the photos on all the boxes on toy store shelves.

Eye on Political Islam

One of the issues that interested me personally during my time in The Magic Kingdom, as we often referred to Saudi Arabia in private conversations at the embassy, is the issue of fundamentalist preachers and the tolerance thereof by the official establishment in Riyadh. The war being over, I focused on cultural programs to better interact with the liberal community, while studying the impact of fundamentalist preachers. For that purpose, one of my assistants brought me books and cassette sermons by Islamist preachers and writers. It was common in those days for such preachers to display their recorded sermons and pamphlets at book fairs or kiosks near university campuses. Three such preachers were popular at such venues and their pamphlets, books, and taped sermons were apparently ubiquitous. I read, listened, and penned three cables to Washington titled, Eye on Political Islam.

Safar el-Hawalli, Ayed el-Qarni, and Salman al-Awdah were three influential Islamic scholars and, as it later turned out, were role models for the founder of al-Qa'eda, Ussama Bin Laden—who had studied at the University of Jeddah as a young man. One of his professors was Muhammed Qutub (brother of Sayed Qutub, the leading Egyptian fundamentalist Islamic theorist for the Muslim Brotherhood in the 1950s). Muhammed Qutub sought refuge in Saudi Arabia when his elder brother was executed by the Nasser regime—a regime known not only for its secularism but also for its hostility toward monarchies in the region led by Saudi Arabia. Qutub was therefore well known to the three preachers and teachers of influence on Bin Laden, particularly Safar al-Hawali who had defended his theses in front of Qutub and who would himself later be quoted by Bin Laden.

Bin Laden also quoted Safar and Awdah in particular when opposing the presence of U.S. troops in Saudi Arabia in 1991. They and Abdel Aziz Ibn Baz (later mufti of the Kingdom) were colleagues on a committee that considered how to return Saudi Arabia and the Arab/Islamic world to the fundamentals of Islam. Safar and Salman were imprisoned for anti-gov't activities in the late nineties, when Bin Baz had become Mufti and therefore more in line with the Saudi government's security policies. Bin laden wrote to Bin Baz when that happened suggesting it was wrong to imprison Hawali and Awdah and that he should use his influence to have them released.

Before security concerns led to the imprisonment of these preachers, however, the Saudi government not only tolerated but indeed lent support to their activities. The contents of the cassette sermons came from recordings of mosque sermons and university lectures, in other words, these were not unusual occurrences and certainly not circulated in secret. The anti-U.S. content was sharp and reflected not only policy preferences but also deep cultural bias against all western norms and education. They also reflected ignorance of and hostility toward western societies in general.

One example has stuck with me all these years and came from a sermon of a preacher traveling by air for the first time and railing against such modern means of transportation:

> There I was, hung somewhere between heaven and earth, not knowing whether we were facing east or west. How can those who fly often do this, spend so much time not knowing which direction to bow and pray to the Ka'bah?

Another preacher, on landing in Washington, decried what he saw as examples of depravity:

> We landed in Washington, the capital, and I couldn't believe my eyes: People were running naked in the streets and men and women were fornicating like dogs in public parks!

My cables were classified at the Confidential level at the time because of the political message in them, namely that in a country where freedom of speech was severely restricted these vile attacks against western culture and the United States were obviously allowed to contaminate the minds of the youth against the powers that were in the Kingdom to protect it from foreign invasion and which had just repelled precisely such an occupying force from neighboring Kuwait.

Sixteen or so years later, al-Qa'eda grew to be an international terrorist organization, attacking the U.S. homeland, establishing a home base in Afghanistan and harassing and killing American and international forces in Iraq. The Jihadi ideology of AQ metastasized into ISIS which reestablished an Islamic Caliphate—fashioned after their own prejudices—in the Levant and again threatened the region and the world with its terror, in this case turned mostly on the Syrian and Iraqi populations. Saudi Arabia's tolerance for such dangerous ideologies went unchallenged by the USG until after the fateful events in the region made it clear that such ideas when unchecked do in fact kill.

Trips to Abha and Taif were the most pleasurable in terms of a change in scenery and surroundings—more mountainous, less humid, and less congested with diplomats and government officials than either Riyadh or Jeddah. One interesting feature on the road south, however, and a reminder that one was still in Saudi Arabia, was a large exit sign on the American-style highway heading south saying, "Mecca, Non-Muslims Must Exit!"

In between war zones and cultural challenges, I somehow found the time for Scuba Diving lessons at the embassy swimming pool, with one deep-sea dive in the Red Sea off of Jeddah. Spectacular underwater reef and sea-life were definitely among the highlights of my visit.

Taekwondo lessons were also on offer with a Korean instructor and I and a couple of colleagues managed to partake in this activity together with our children, turning an otherwise violent sport into a family affair. One inside joke remained with us all these years is something the instructor said in his limited English about the need to be gentlemanly and not over react to provocations, but, demonstrating a simple but effective strike, the instructor added, "if bad talk keep coming, One Strike, Ma'essalamah!" Meaning, make one strike count and don't go in for long fights ...

U.S. Policy

There is no doubt that Saudi Arabia remains an important player in Middle East and world politics today and that the U.S. needs to maintain good relations with its people and rulers. That said, two caveats pertain: The relationship must be built on honesty and the ability of the United States to be critical where criticism is due and to oppose Saudi policies that may be detrimental to U.S. interests and values. Two, Saudi Arabia no longer has the same economic, political, and military value it used to bring to the table. The world is moving away from carbon-based energy sources, Saudi Arabia is not currently playing a stabilizing role in the Middle East and since the early nineties has not invited the United States to reestablish military bases on its soil. Unquestioned support by the United States, to the extent it ever was, is no longer justified.

Honesty dictates that when the Kingdom's rulers follow a discriminatory policy toward minorities and foreigners who belong to faiths other than Islam that they be reproached directly and openly. Speaking out for values we believe in is of primary concern of course, but in the world of political interests and calculated risks, national interest concerns are also involved. Dictators and authoritarian regimes can only suppress minorities and abuse the human rights of their citizens with impunity for so long. Ultimately, as we've seen in rebellions and revolutions worldwide, populations rebel and eventually succeed in overthrowing their abusive governments.

Shia Muslims, women and foreign workers were, and still are, treated as second-class subjects in the Kingdom. Even though the Department of State's annual human rights report mentions gender segregation, relative neglect of regions where Shia Saudis live and harsh treatment of foreign workers, the report is taken as a perfunctory exercise and does not get the diplomatic follow-up it deserves if one expects to have an impact. In 1990, Yemeni president, Ali Abdallah Saleh, took a position in support of Saddam Hussein after the latter invaded Kuwait. In retaliation, Saudi Arabia expelled an estimated one million Yemeni workers, many of whom had spent a lifetime in the Kingdom without acquiring citizenship. This was purely an act of revenge as there was no evidence that these Yemenis posed any security risk to the Kingdom. I was surprised to see our intellectual and liberal friends in Saudi Arabia at the time express complete support for that decision. I recall telling them angrily over an informal dinner one evening that it is difficult for me to support their right to freedom of expression when they did not even sympathize with the rights of the minorities among them and would not extend that courtesy to the Yemeni population which lived among them for years. Today, with war against the Houthis of Yemen raging for a fifth year, it is outrageous that the world is sitting idly by and watches the near total destruction of a nation and its population.

In March 2015, Saudi Arabia launched a war on Yemen's Houthi rebels—a Yemeni group which had seized the capital Sanaa in the aftermath of the uprising which forced the former president Ali Abdallah Saleh to leave his office and make way for his vice president to succeed him. President Hadi, installed with full support from the Gulf countries led by Saudi Arabia, was expelled from the capital by the Houthis. Ostensibly, the Saudis wanted to roll back the coup and hand back the territory gained by the Houthis to the newly elected government. As of this writing, however, Saudi aerial bombardment of Yemen has gone on for 4 years and has not been able to dislodge the rebels from Sanaa. The Yemeni factions on the ground, half of whom at least are being fully supported by Saudi Arabia and other GCC countries, have been fighting without any victory or peaceful end in sight. The United States, first under the Obama administration, and now under Trump, has gone along with the Saudi narrative—that Iran is to blame for Houthi excesses in Yemen—and has provided crucial logistical, intelligence, and other more direct assistance to the Saudi war effort, without ever questioning the justification for the war or the impact of the bombardment on the civilian population. The malnutrition and disease resulting from the almost total blockade imposed on the country have made Yemen one of the worst humanitarian crises in the world since the Second World War.

The value of Saudi Arabia to U.S. strategy has in fact been diminishing since the end of the cold war and the lessening dependence of the U.S. economy on imported oil. (https://goo.gl/N7r0YT) Beginning in the mid-2000s, U.S. imports of oil declined as its own production and export of oil was on the rise and in 2014, U.S. oil imports reached a 30-year low. Further, the search for alternate sources of energy accelerated in the past 10 years and, at least in theory, the U.S. and western economies are gradually weaning themselves away from oil as new less polluting sources of energy are adopted. All this to say that the economic value of Saudi Arabia depreciates as the need for oil decreases.

Militarily, the value of Saudi Arabia as a staging ground for U.S. military operations in the Middle East was significantly reduced with the withdrawal of all but small training contingents from the Kingdom. The withdrawal was partly due to rising objections from hardline religious Saudis as well as from Arab public opinion in general to the presence of non-Muslim troops near Islam's holiest shrines in Mecca and Medina. The United States has since had its air, land, and naval forces in the Middle East stationed at al-Odeid base in Qatar, in Kuwait, and in Bahrain respectively, obviating therefore the need for such facilities in Saudi Arabia. Talk of a pivot from the middle East to East Asia during the Obama administration, based on a vision of future U.S. engagements becoming more important in that region of the world, further projected diminishing need for a strong military presence in the Gulf region as a whole.

The alliance with Saudi Arabia was never about common values. An absolute monarchy without even a written constitution, the Kingdom's leaders, the founding and ruling family of Ibn Saud allied themselves historically with the conservative Wahabist movement and have never looked back from that association, prohibiting secular political parties and civil society organizations and leaving political space to the most conservative elements of society. Based on all the above, it makes more sense for

U.S. policies in the Middle East, especially in light of the Arab uprising of 2011 and the ensuing turmoil, to be more cautious in supporting Saudi policies that only aggravate regional tensions and encourage extremism and resentment of U.S. involvement in needlessly aggressive Saudi policies.

CHAPTER 5

RABAT

All Embassy officials, especially those with cultural and media responsibilities, are supposed to entertain or host representational functions in diplomatic parlance. As my contacts quickly found out, mine were not the typical diplomatic cocktail receptions. In addition to the bolder media personalities, I quickly gravitated toward the dissidents among writers and intellectuals and especially civil society leaders. We tended to sit around comfortable couches and cushions and listen to music and discuss democracy, free press, and revolution. It was not my intention to foment rebellion or foist American democracy on unsuspecting audiences, I simply discovered that that's what Moroccans of certain ilk discussed among one another and since I found that a fascinating insight into the hidden Morocco, if you will, I tended to let my friends talk about their favorite topics, to listen to music and to dance if the mood so struck them. I recall a businessman I befriended and invited to one of my dinner parties was totally taken aback when I introduced my friends to him, adding after they walked away, "this one spent 15 years in jail and was just released two years ago; that young beautiful woman was jailed and tortured for five years, her parents thought she was dead." He said, "Nabeel, your parties are something else, I never met any of these people and didn't even know about the life stories of those jailed under Hassan II."

It wasn't unusual for successful business people, especially those with palace connections, to be immersed in their own well-to-do circles and to be living almost a universe apart from the poor and the rebellious middle class. Another businessman friend while attending a play with me was unaware of the term "Yihraq," used in the play, literally meaning to burn something. The term is used in Moroccan dialect to mean someone who immigrates illegally to

71

Europe, burning all their identity papers so as to make it difficult for authorities to trace him, thus allowing him the chance to begin a new life in Europe. It is also used euphemistically to simply mean to leaving one's country and never looking back.

Beneath the veneer of gentility and wealth to which most foreign embassy staff were introduced lay another layer or two that were, and still are, worlds apart. A veritable tale of two cities unfolded as one went to the outskirts of large cities like Casablanca or if one traveled to the Rif countryside where the villages told another story—one of poverty, deprivation, and an underground trade in drugs and smuggled merchandise. Mohamed VI, upon acceding to the throne, made a serious effort to uproot poverty and build public housing for those who could not afford it on the open market. Ten years into his reign, however, the other Morocco still lived in ghettos referred to as "bidonvilles," literally tin cities, in reference to the tin shacks used as homes by the residents of the poverty belts.

Hassan the second, King of Morocco since 1961, was still very much in power during my tour as press Attache in Rabat, 1994–1997. A darling of the west for his urbane, westernized style (read clothing, hobnobbing with movie stars and speaking French and English fluently with European and American leaders). Beneath that air of modernization however the man ruled with an iron fist. Having survived coup attempts and rebellions, Hassan II was not a forgiving man, nor one to relinquish either economic or political power for the sake of democracy and human rights. From 1979, till Hassan's death in 1999, the King was assisted by an able and feared henchman, Driss Basri, who was his minister of interior for all 20 years, often known as the years of lead for the repression of dissidents in the 1960s and 1970s. University students who demonstrated against him and Communist party activists who plotted against the monarchy were harshly repressed and many were tortured, executed, or simply disappeared. It would not be till 1991 that the last of the political prisoners of earlier

72

decades were released from jail and not till his son, Mohammed VI, took the throne in 1999 that a partial list of the disappeared was made public and an official apology offered to the families of the victims.

Years of Lead

"The sea and nothing but the sea." A single seemingly simple phrase at the opening of **Khadija's novel** but one which looks to the sea as an outlet and open space, an escape from the confines of prison, imagined when behind locked gates and in underground dungeons, and a look beyond the confines of reality. Once out of jail, said one character in the book, "Never look back at prison gates so you don't end up back there, always look ahead."

Khadija Merouazi's book, *The Story of Ashes* (Arabic, *Sirat al-Ramad*), is a rare and unique look at life behind bars for the hundreds who disappeared in Morocco during the rule of Hassan II. It is more importantly about those who endured the long years of confinement and lived to tell the story. Written as a fictional novel, the book is nonetheless a look into the shattered lives of those who survived their confinement physically but limped through life emotionally in the years after their release. The heroin in the book returns from prison to her small apartment in Rabat as if visiting a place that doesn't belong to her anymore, shy to be again among familiar furniture and clothes, shy so meet the welcoming neighbors with their hugs, kisses, and children who couldn't stop jumping with excitement, and one in particular who remembered that she used to read him stories. The boy asks her to return to her old custom but she can't decide which story to tell, one about the dreary past, the fuzzy indeterminate present or the future which looks bright for a moment but turns scary at the thought that the future itself in the Arab world is still a prisoner of civil wars, oppressive rulers, and uncertain fortunes. Khadija's sensitive portrayal of the plight of former prisoners and her perspective on the needs of the poor in her country touched me deeply.

Politically, the disappeared all came from university student groups from the late seventies and early eighties, some of whom belonged to left-wing parties, while others were just individuals disgruntled with absolute monarchy and looking to communicate with other like-minded young people willing to demonstrate against the system. The authorities were alarmed when demonstrations spilled outside university campuses and made some connections with city workers and the poor who lived in ghetto areas surrounding the cities. Since most students had not technically committed any crimes, they were rounded up by plainclothes men and stashed away in secret prisons mostly without trial. Incarceration included torture (of both men and women) and humiliation in order to discover connections, organizational structures, and any broader networks that might be considered a threat to the regime of Hassan II.

Ironically, the years of lead, as they are commonly referred to, led to the birth of a vibrant civil society as the last of the political prisoners were released in the late eighties and early nineties. Those who did not perish or leave the country the first chance they had remained in the country and dedicated themselves to building civil society NGOs to help those that needed help and to build a fourth estate that could watchdog the government, so the abuses of the past could not be repeated with impunity.

Today, there are literally thousands of registered NGOs in Morocco, a majority of them consisting of a small number of activists working on social and economic issues. A small but very active number of them, however, work on democracy building and human rights issues with a focus on lobbying and raising awareness among the public as to civic rights and responsibilities. Here are some names of activists who came out of prison to become leaders in civil society organizations—In some cases, I'm only using first names, and/or fictitious ones to protect the individual's privacy:

Fatima (fictitious name), nabbed by plain clothes policemen, disappeared and was tortured and abused for several months then dumped in an empty lot outside city limits. Bleeding, hungry, and scared, she made it back to job, friends, and an unsuspecting family and never sought any help in rebuilding her life. She is now married, takes care of two children, holds down a job and volunteers tirelessly for an ombudsman-type organization and several human rights associations that cater to defenseless citizens, listening to their tales of woe and helping them find government and nongovernmental services to help meet their and their families' needs. Her activism is almost a remedy, not for what she personally endured but for the suffering of others, the burden of which she carries around constantly. She feels that the few months of torture she personally experienced were nothing in comparison to the suffering experienced by many others. In my years in Morocco, I met and was deeply impressed with many middle-class women who fit this profile and their activism and dedication gave me hope for the future, certainly of Morocco, but also of other Arab societies where civil society organizations are taking root.

Halima (also fictitious), kidnaped by the authorities from her university campus, disappeared and was imprisoned for 5 years—her family received no information from the authorities and never knew half of the vile things that happened to her while in secret custody. She now works for a human rights organization and joins almost every civil society activity she can find in search of things she can do to help others through their pain and perhaps in the process alleviate some of her own.

Idriss (Benzikri) went into prison a healthy young man and came out frail and ill—He spent 17 years in Hassan II's dungeons for having belonged to the communist party and having agitated for change in his country. When he was finally let out, he worked tirelessly in helping young Moroccan activists find the means to stay involved in social and political affairs without running afoul of the authorities. He was chosen by the families of the disappeared to lead a committee for reconciliation, based on knowing the truth about those who disappeared, compensating the families and then reconciling with their former jailers and kidnapers. After recovering from various illnesses he contracted while in jail, he succumbed to cancer and passed away 7 years after being released from jail at the age of 50. He was mourned by one and all in his special community of activists with a prison record and a new generation of human rights activists who looked up to him as a role model.

Abdelqader (real name) spent 15 years behind bars and was moved around from one secret jail to another. He worked on various artistic projects to keep himself busy and created an abstract collage with cloth his jailers allowed him to have. As a token of our friendship, he gave me this framed piece as a farewell gift as I was leaving Morocco. Today, 18 years later, the piece still hangs over the bed in my Washington home as a reminder not only of our friendship but also of what dictatorship in Morocco and the region has done to thousands of young men and women who dared to question their authority. He also authored several novels which under the guise of fiction tell the story of political aspirations, suffering, and the lost lives of those who survived physically but whose social and personal lives were torn asunder by their experience. Of great personal strength, Abdelqader recovered and rebuilt his life. Believing in Mohammed VI, he accepted a job with the government and is now a diplomat for his country in Latin America.

Sion Assidon (real name), a Moroccan Jew and a left-wing agitator in his youth, was the longest serving resident of King Hassan's prisons. He was freed in 1991 after 19 years in jail and heads a branch of Transparency International in Morocco, focusing on corruption and shedding light on the right of citizens to know how much wealth is accumulated by the political elite and what its being spent on. Sion is a tireless advocate of democracy and transparency in political and business life and extremely gregarious in his social life, almost as if anxious not to miss a moment of life after what seemed to him a lifetime behind bars.

The above individuals are but a few of the hundreds who were arrested, disappeared, or otherwise harshly treated by the authorities. I listed the few cases I had the privilege of knowing personally. The resilience of those who survived is demonstrated not only by their staying the course of rebuilding their lives and striving to serve their fellow Moroccans but also by often choosing to work with the regime of Mohammad VI, optimistically finding positive threads they could pull on to push for real change in the country. Fouad Abdelmoumni returned from two different stints in some of Morocco's worst prisons and dedicated himself to working on development projects, some of which were funded by USAID. He also continued to struggle for human rights in Morocco and the Sahara, working with the Moroccan Association of Human Rights (AMDH)—often thought of as being one of the more radical human rights organizations. Another case is that of El-Habib Belkouch who, after 5 years in jail, also came out to work on human rights, currently with the Moroccan government and various international organizations to protect the rights of minorities, to defend those arrested unjustly, and to fight against the use of torture in prison. El-Habib and Fouad continue to be my friends to this day and their friendship is one of the reasons I feel that my years in the foreign service have been worthwhile.

Some of the main human rights organizations, either established or staffed by those released from prison include Centre d'ecoute (listening center), staffed exclusively by women to deal with another large social problem in Morocco, that of domestic abuse and violence against women. Not allowed by law to offer overnight shelter, the center offers instead listening, legal advice and when requested, psychological counseling. I was able to obtain for the center a generous grant from the U.S. private sector to help with their work. I was lucky in this instance that the wife of our ambassador at the time, Ed Gabriel, was the vice president of the American company in question and was able to secure the grant.

The main Moroccan organizations for human rights were established in the seventies and eighties but came into their own as independent civil society organizations in the late nineties. The League for the Defense of Human Rights (LMDDH), was the first such organization to appear in 1972. It was part of al-Istiqlal party, one of the major parties at the time and often part of the government. As such LMDDh did not enjoy great autonomy. The Moroccan Association for Human Rights (AMDH) was founded in 1979 within the Socialist Union of Popular Forces (USFP), which was an opposition party until invited to form a government in 1989, roughly a year before Hassan II died. AMDH drifted before that toward the Socialist Vanguard Party, a more left of center party than USFP. The Moroccan Organization for Human Rights (OMDH) was established in 1988 outside the framework of political parties and has become the largest of the human rights groups in Morocco. There too, however, many OMDH members were part of the USFP. Most of the former prisoners and many of the younger activists and civil society leaders belong to one or all of these organizations—these groups have more that unites than divides them and they collaborate in pushing for a better observance by the government of the human rights of its citizens. The organizations, again staffed largely by the victims of oppression, include many able lawyers, academics, and activists who work with or outside of political parties and contribute to the political and social development of Morocco—they now collaborate with the government—particularly since the government established a Consultative Council for Human Rights and the government of Mohamed VI apologized for the excesses of the past and started prison reform and established new laws governing police arrests. These organizations nevertheless still stand in opposition to the "Makhzen" as the deep state is known in Morocco—a security and corrupt business cabal that survived Hassan II and continues to be quite corrupt and powerful today despite the progress made under Mohammed VI.

Other civil society organizations include Bayti (My home), an organization for homeless children, is led by Najat Mjid, a pediatrician by training who skillfully manages this shelter, school, and rehab center for kids who are either neglected orphans or children whose parents are too poor or irresponsible to care for them. As Consul General in Casablanca at the time, I was privileged to be fully briefed on the work of this wonderful organization and allowed to witness for one evening how its staff walked the streets of the big city at night seeking out these children, befriending and convincing them to seek help at Bayti. These youngsters were sometimes peddling drugs for adults, often using the drugs themselves or just hanging out on street corners very much past the bedtime of children their age. Conversations with these kids sometimes lasted for days or weeks in order to assess the needs of each particular child before deciding what type of help was needed and could legally be offered. In some cases, where parents were available and could be reached, reconciling the children with their parents was the most appropriate course of action, while at other times offering the children shelter and schooling was the way to go. I was happy to find a USG grant to offer Dr. Mjid which she used to write a book about Bayti's goals and methodology in order to share her experience in dealing with a significant social problem in Morocco.

Aicha Echenna, another brave and enterprising woman, tackles the problem of young women driven to prostitution by poverty and neglect. Following a similar street approach to the one followed by Bayti, her organization invites the women who are ready and willing to be helped to shelter at her facilities, learn to read and write and perhaps a craft to help them make a living without resorting to the sale of their bodies on the street. We sponsored a day at Aicha's facility for consulate staff and friends to visit with these women and buy some of their handicrafts and to encourage and publicize Aicha's work.

Questioning the monarchy's attachment to the western Sahara as Moroccan territory was and still is one of the three taboos in the country. Not many Moroccans question this policy in any case—whether out of love or fear is often hard to tell. Sahrawis have however questioned and resisted what they considered to be the occupation of their territory by Moroccan soldiers. Human rights organizations, and with good reason, have expanded their concerns and involvement to the Sahara because of legitimate complaints of ill treatment from Sahrawi residents at the hands of either Moroccan military or police officials. One case that came to my attention during my second tour in Morocco involved two Sahrawi women who had been tortured by having their bodies flooded with water via power hoses inserted through their genitalia. A Moroccan friend who trusted me enough informed me that the two women—wives of members of the Polisario—were in a Casablanca hospital for annual treatments they were receiving years after the torture, thanks to the work of human rights activists. I put together some food and supplies and drove with my friend, a young woman and human rights activist, to the hospital. My friend turned out to be much tougher than me and I let her go in alone with the supplies because as she was relating to me exactly what happened to these women during their captivity I lost control of my emotions and was afraid I would break down once I saw the two women and cause a scandal.

Songs of Rebellion

Morocco has always been, however, too diverse and rebellious to be ruled as a total dictatorship. Political Parties, elections, parliament, and a relatively free press existed side by side with Hassan's authoritarian rule—during the years I was there, everything was open for discussion in the media as long as one didn't touch critically on Islam and the Western Sahara—Oh, and any unauthorized mention of the royal family was off limits, of course!

While direct criticism of the King and his policies were clamped down on till the very end, Moroccans found outlets other than the media in which to express themselves—notably jokes and rebellious songs. Thanks to my dissident friends and helpful staff, I was made aware of both. One joke about minister of interior Driss Basri went like this: Basri's son was at fault in a car accident; always in a hurry, he left his father's business card instead of his with the other driver and promised that compensation would be paid. Having tried and failed to make contact, the frustrated driver finally got the father on the phone and complained loudly about that his car was still unfixed and someone had to pay. Basri said, "do you know who I am?," driver said, "No." Upon learning who he was speaking to, the driver then quickly asked, "and do you know who I am?" Basri said, "No, I don't." Driver replied, "Thank Goodness," and quickly hung up.

Another joke touched on the corruption of the King and related to the grand Hassan II mosque in Casablanca, reportedly costing over a billion dollars, much of which was extorted as taxation from the citizenry. In return for citizens' "contributions," they were reportedly offered a certificate of appreciation from "the commander of the faithful" as Hassan liked to be referred to. His supporters told the tax payers that this guaranteed them a place in heaven. Upon being turned back at the Pearly Gate, one angry soul produced the piece of paper as proof of his entitlement. Saint Peter is then said to have checked the signatory and said, "Oh, Hassan II, you'll find him at the seventh level down below!"

The cruelty of Hassan II and his regime were the subject of jokes because it was scary to directly and seriously express dissent. Songs were another way of expressing it.

81

I first met L'arbi Batma at a book signing in 1995. Intrigued by his words and the songs he and his Nas al-Ghiwan band were known for, I asked a trusted Moroccan colleague to arrange a visit to the singer's home. In preparation, I listened to many of the group's songs, making sure to get a translation from the Moroccan dialect used in the lyrics.

A cable I sent to Washington that year began with "to the beat of an African banjo and an Arab drum, Nas al-Ghiwan's lead singer al-Arbi Batma sings the plight of the average downtrodden Moroccan ...." It was an unusual starting paragraph for a press Attache to send but I liked to convey mood and flavor in my cables and I thought the description was the next best thing to sending an audio tape of the song.

Nas al-Ghiwan songs, when political, are always couched in ambiguity to avoid incurring the authorities' wrath. Coded messages are nevertheless understood by the group's devoted followers. Hence, a reference to a wolf, accompanied by thieves, guiding the sheep to their own fleecing and destruction is understood by fans to mean the King and the wealthy cronies around him, and songs referring to things being so tight that can lead people into doing stupid things—meaning if people are pushed to a corner acts of violence could follow. I recall several evenings with friends from civil society exchanging jokes and singing songs of rebellion over beer or wine to chase away the blues. One evening at my residence in Casablanca, a Palestinian friend was visiting and enjoying the company of my Moroccan friends. When we found out that he played the Oud (lute) I ran over to fetch mine, which was badly out of tune from lack of use (by anyone with talent anyway). Before the music, I had had to translate from Moroccan dialect to eastern Arabic so both sides could communicate. Once my Palestinian friend starting playing, music and song flowed and everybody joined in songs of rebellion from both sides of the Mediterranean and interpretation was no longer necessary.

My two tours of duty in Morocco, first as the U.S. press attache in Rabat and second as Consul General in Casablanca, left me with the stories of many broken hearts and shattered lives, but also with the enduring friendship of brave men and women who have dedicated their lives to trying to make sure others don't suffer what they suffered and that their country progresses toward a democracy that respected the lives and rights of its citizens. Theirs were ultimately stories of courage and love. I can safely say that, over 15 years after leaving Morocco, I have gotten over the pain they shared with me but I have not gotten over the love.

Morocco's Islamists

I made it a point at every foreign service posting to ferret out Islamists and talk to them. This was partly professional and partly personal. From a U.S. policy point of view, it was important to know what Islamists really thought about the regime they lived under, its relationship with the United States and what their hopes were for the future of their country and region. After all, the authoritarian regimes had a strong bias against these groups and there was no reason for foreign diplomats to take the local government's narrative at face value. It was important to know, I thought, how far their hatred of western values went and how genuine their professed tolerance of Christians around them, whether domestic or foreign. I wanted to assess for myself what the impact might be on the region if such groups came to power or were allowed to play a legitimate role in their respective countries' political life. From a personal point of view, I had written a Ph.D. thesis on the subject of Islam and modernization in the Middle East, positing that a liberal interpretation of Islam was not incompatible with western values. I wanted to test those ideas on the Islamists I met to better assess the intellectual dynamics within these movements.

At the time, the main Islamists parties in Morocco were the Justice and Development Party (PJD) and the Justice and Charity

Organization (JCO)—both quite public in their posture and appeal, and therefore easy to meet. Independent Islamists of various types existed of course, including some recruiting agents for al-Qa'eda but those were underground and beyond the pail for the purposes of any form of diplomacy.

One of my initiatives in Rabat, 1994–1997, was an intellectual forum convened monthly to discuss issues of the day with the journalists and Moroccan literati of various specialties—a way of deepening the dialogue beyond Washington's main political agenda and talking points. One of the sessions was dedicated to the discussion of the role of women in Islam. I invited, among others, Fatima Mernissi, Morocco's premier feminist at the time and an outspoken critic of Islamists. On the opposite side, I invited Abdelilah BenKiran, head of the PJD, who had issued a statement on Mernissi accusing her of having abandoned her faith—a sin for which the more radical Islamists considered capital punishment to be mandated under Sharia law.

The discussion went into all the key questions of the rights of women in Islam, the meaning of equality of the sexes and who had the authority in Islam to rule whether or not a Muslim had left the faith and if apostasy truly merited capital punishment according to Sharia law. In moderating such discussions, I was motivated to see if middle ground could be found between moderate Islamists and the more secular-minded Muslims. At least for that particular encounter there was. BenKirane stood up at the end of the discussion and thanked me in front of the audience for hosting it, saying to those assembled around the table, "until today I had considered Mernissi to be my enemy but sitting around this table with her I don't find the gap between us to be so wide." I recall in 2012 during a briefing I provided to Hillary Clinton on political Islam that I told her this story in advance of a trip she had planned to Morocco, ending it with "and the Islamist in question is now the prime minister of Morocco!" the Secretary of State grinned widely and said, "Quite a story

Nabeel, I will remind Benkirane of that when I meet him in Rabat next week."

The PJD was traditionally considered the more moderate of Morocco's two Islamist parties.

Abdelilah Benkirane told me in private conversation, reiterated in later years in public when his party won a plurality of seats in parliament, that he was not interested in dictating people's private lives—to include a dress code for women. From the various Islamists I met in Morocco, Benkirane seemed less concerned with Islamist social mores than with his political chances at the polls. I was told by friends that he was a cynic (if not a total hypocrite) and that he secretly loved to drink and paid only lip service to Sharia's prohibitions and warnings about the dangers of alcohol.

The main difference between the PJD and the JCO has mostly revolved around the issue of political engagement. Whereas the former believed, at least since 1997, in using any opening to engage in Morocco's political life and in fact run for office, the JCO believed, and still does, that it is a mistake to engage in a corrupt system, lending it legitimacy and likely becoming corrupted by it. In my dealings with members of both parties, I found the JCO more honest and more consistent in marrying their values to their behavior than the more opportunistic PJD.

Sheikh Yassin, the founder of the JCO, was kept under house arrest for many years by Hassan II for challenging the King's authority in religious, or indeed in political matters. In an open letter to the King in 1974, Yassin questioned the King's right to call himself Amir al-Mu'mineen (Commander of the faithful), a title Hassan II decided was appropriate for him since his family, the Alaouis, consider themselves descendants of the Prophet through his daughter Fatima Zohra. Since Yassin was under house arrest in the mid-nineties, I decided on the next best person to meet, his daughter Nadia who was active in civil society circles, was very well spoken and had no qualms about meeting with westerners.

Nadia Yassin is not your typical Islamist leader's daughter, to the extent, there is such a thing. Far from being a docile conservative woman, Nadia took the lead in her father's organization while he was in jail, spoke in public for the party and joined secular women in calling for women's rights in education, jobs, and healthcare. She received me, along with my assistant Fatima-Zohra Salah (FZ), in her living room—unlike in many conservative Muslim homes where the man of the house receives guests while his wife remains unseen (if the guests are male). Nadia received and engaged us in conversation while her husband, not involved in party work, did not even come out to greet or join in the conversation. Nadia was dynamic, quite comfortable in discussing any and all issues related to the party, the monarchy, women's rights, and the United States. In her mind, whereas she has common cause with her secular sisters in calling for more jobs and education for women, she differs in her overall view that imitating western culture is not for Moroccans or indeed for the Arab/Islamic world. Islam, when properly interpreted and applied, grants women all the rights they need to study, work, lead civil society organizations, all while still being mothers and wives. For Nadia, a male chauvinist culture was responsible for putting women down not Islamic values. "Men have been historically abusive regardless of culture and religion," I recall her saying—"this is as true in western secular cultures as in Islamic ones and women must always fight for their rightful place in society regardless of where they live or what religion they believe in."

I met with Islamists on a fairly regular basis during my tours of duty in Rabat and in Casablanca. I considered them part and parcel of political life in the country and wanted to contribute to Washington's understanding of who these people were and whether or not we should consider them dangerous. During the years I was in Morocco, I did not assess any of the Islamists I met to be a threat to Americans. Because Moroccan authorities were suspicious of their long-term goals and of U.S. contacts with opposition parties in general, I tended to meet with Islamists in public, usually over coffee at sidewalk cafes and sometimes at my home where I was sure all my visitors were fully monitored coming in or out by Moroccan authorities. I wanted to convey the message that I had nothing to hide and was not conspiring against the government behind closed doors. During my last week before leaving Morocco for the second time, I was invited to a farewell lunch by the minister of interior and the only other guest was the head of Morocco's military intelligence. As the conversation steered toward Islamists, I told my hosts that I personally trusted the JCO, the party banned officially, over the PJD which was fully legalized. "We know," said the director of intelligence, but your embassy always courts the other guys and invites them to meetings and receptions."

My impression of the Islamists was that neither party was in a rush and considered time to be on their side. The JCO was more open about its hostility to the monarchy and in that vein had more in common with left-wing parties and activists, calling for democracy, an end to corruption and the implementation of human rights for all. To be sure, the Islamist version of democracy differed from that of their secular colleagues. Whereas secular oppositionists demanded abiding by international human rights standards as a reference point, the Islamists would only accept Islam as a reference and guide. This was a matter of principle rather than a difference regarding individual rights. Individuals in both Islamist parties, for example, asserted the rights of individuals and minorities to respect and protection. They insisted however on finding the source of such a code in Islam and not in a secular code of law, believing the latter could drag them on other matters into agreeing to things that might be prohibited in Islam.

Sex and the Fundamentalist Sheikh: Another surprising Islamist was Abldelaziz Bin al-Siddiq, purportedly a radical fundamentalist sheikh who was imprisoned by Hassan II for the offense of publishing a public letter addressed to the king telling him that he had no right to call himself the commander of the faithful—a title reserved in Islam to the early Caliphs who succeeded the prophet—consensus having been lost after them as to who if any had the right in modern days to walk in the prophet's shoes as it were. Bin al-Siddiq was allowed to leave prison in 1991 with the proviso that he refrain from making any public political commentary. FZ and I visited the sheikh in his home in Tangier expecting to discuss his contretemp with the King. True to his promise not to discuss the king, he refused to discuss the matter, saying only "May God forgive him and all of us for our sins." I turned instead to social and religious issues and asked him about a column he wrote in a tangier newspaper called *al-Khadra al-Jadidah* along the lines of a Dear Abbey column. That subject proved more pleasant for him and he expanded on his ideas, starting with "Westerners have a false image of Islamists as conservative and narrow minded on sexual issues," said the sheikh, "this couldn't be further from the truth. We are the liberals in the real sense of the word but we don't engage in show and tell like you do in your magazines and your pornography. The west has the reputation, but we wrote the original sexual textbooks." Debunking the secondary status of women in Islam concept, the sheikh blamed outdated traditions and pronouncements for the mistaken image of Islam in the west. "Women's equality starts in the bedroom," said Bin al-Siddiq shockingly (I had only seen such a phrase in print in the poetry of Nizar Qabbani, a total libertine in such matters, and someone who believed that in order to liberate Arab societies one had to start by liberating women. "God orders us to enjoy what life has to offer and therefore a man and woman, within the sanctity of marriage, are at complete liberty to do whatever is mutually enjoyable. "We have no complexes in this regard whatsoever."

Indeed, when I checked various issues of the advice column al-Siddiq had penned, I was both amazed and amused and sent a cable to Washington on this topic entitled Sex and the Fundamentalist Sheikh. In answers to wives either forlorn or confused, Siddiq goes into detail as to what indeed is allowed and asserts, in print, that a man must not leave his wife's desires unattended to, selfishly obtaining his pleasure quickly and not bothering to ensure she attains hers. He goes into the necessity of foreplay and the need to wait until a woman is physically and emotionally ready before commencing with intercourse. Just as a man's sexual satisfaction is one way to ensure his fidelity, so is a woman's. Asked by a woman who says her husband watches Spanish television and then demands positions and acts from her that he watched western couples perform—she, alarmed that perhaps these things were not allowed in Islam, is reassured by the sheikh that nothing is Haram (forbidden) in the bedroom, provided it is done for mutual pleasure. The sheikh even says there is no clear prohibition against sodomy, even though he admits this is controversial in Islam and that scholars have differed in interpreting text and tradition in this regard.

I was told by colleagues in Washington that my cable on this subject was the most popular item by far that week and that it was read by one and all—regardless of whether or not they thought it relevant to any Morocco-policy matter or broader Middle East issues.

Mohamed VI Honored me with the Alaouite Medal before I left Morocco the second time, this time out of Casablanca. I was packing during what was to be my last week in the country when our DCM called me from Rabat and asked me to extend a week in order to receive the medal. Our ambassador at the time was Margaret Tutwiler, a political appointee by the Bush administration and not one to brook gratuitous advice from anyone. As someone who was on his seventh year in Morocco, I apparently overstepped in offering her my insights, which led to a tense relationship between us. She asked her deputy to call me with the news of my having been chosen for this honor—normally reserved for distinguished Moroccan scientists and foreign diplomats, rarely anyone below the rank of ambassador. Tutwiler barely spoke a word to me at the ceremonies held at the royal palace in Tangier. I was told by the Wali (Governor) of Casablanca that he and the minister of interior had nominated me and that the King was personally aware of the work I had done with Moroccan civil society and the media and felt the country owed me a debt of gratitude. I still recall the King's kind words as he put the medal around my neck. He said in English, "I hear you'll be leaving us soon." I replied in the affirmative in Arabic and added that I will miss Morocco. He said in Moroccan dialect, "This is your home, you will be welcome here anytime you want, anytime!"

U.S. Policy

Despite the overall friendliness of Moroccans and openness to dialogue, there was an unmistakable and deep-rooted skepticism among ordinary Moroccans and civil society leaders of U.S. foreign policy that began with the abiding support the United States gave to Israel, its insensitivity to Palestinian rights and its flouting of international laws whenever it suited the United States and Israel. I recall sending another cable to Washington— one which was a little less well received than the one on sex and Islam—explaining why a poem written in the late nineties by the Syrian poet Nizar Qabbani, entitled Children with stones, was more popular than any speech King Hassan, or indeed any Arab ruler, might have given. The poem was in support of Palestinians who pelted Israeli soldiers with stones on the West Bank despite the risk they took of being beaten, arrested, or even shot and killed. The poem was published in pan-Arab newspapers and was as widely read in Morocco as it was in the Levant where Qabbani was most popular. My cable, entitled, Poetry and Politics in the Arab World, explained the importance of poets in Arab culture going back to ancient times, and Qabbani in the contemporary age, who better expressed the feelings of the masses than did the kings and presidents of the Arab world. The pro-Palestinian sentiment, I explained, was just as strong in far-away Morocco as it was in the Levant, Egypt, and Yemen and that the opinions expressed and positions taken by their leaders should not put the west at ease regarding the acceptability of their pro-Israel policies in the region. While government officials rarely raised a fuss, the sense of the injustice of U.S. policies among the general public was pervasive. Pro-democracy friends who demonstrated in support of Palestinian rights, for example, always linked the U.S. to Israeli policies and even though they were against all authoritarian rule in the Arab world, they were not happy in 2003 to have the United States invade Iraq in order the change the regime there. A friend told me, "I would never demonstrate on behalf of Saddam or defend him under any circumstance, but I have to admit the sight of American troops in Baghdad knots up my stomach!"

I was made starkly and alarmingly aware of these feelings in 2001 when the 9/11 attacks took place in New York. I recall being called out of a meeting with Moroccan women civil society leaders to take an urgent call from the embassy. The DCM was online, said that the World Trade Center had just been attacked and that I should return immediately to the Consulate to review security procedures and coordinate as needed with the embassy's regional security officer. The next day, I received a phone call while at work from a wealthy, westernized, and well-connected Moroccan businessman who was one of my closest friends in the country. After offering condolences for the lives lost and expressing understanding of the shock that I and my family must feel, he proceeded to say, "but Nabeel, you must realize that you guys deserved this!" He started to explain that U.S. policies in the region were the cause and that the anger they generated was universally felt, but I cut him off and said "you should give me a week or so to digest the shock over what happened before you start criticizing U.S. policy. There will be time for a rational dialogue on this later, but this week is not it!"

One could argue that over the years of unconditional U.S. support for Israel, the Arab world had not exacted a heavy price from the United States and that the U.S. interests in the Middle East had not suffered greatly. Aside from the 1973 oil embargo, Arab governments had continued to do business with the U.S. government and with American companies, albeit with some notable exceptions, and Arab parents continued to send their children to study in American universities and the youth in general continued to look for work opportunities and immigration possibilities. Partly due to the lack of democracy in the Arab world, popular opinion—heavily stacked against U.S. policy in the region—did not manifest itself except in occasional popular demonstrations which did not take too violent a form—until the late nineties when Islamist extremism provided an outlet for those angry enough with the west and with Arab governments. Radical Islamist groups brought serious violence to bear against U.S. embassies and facilities in the region, starting in 1998, in Dar Essalam and Nairobi (the attack against the embassy in Beirut occurred first in 1983 but was a direct response to the presence of U.S. troops which were first sent to separate Israeli soldiers from the PLO and West Beirut, but then instructed by president Reagan to actually help one side of Lebanese civil war against another).

In Morocco, Islamists were generally not radicalized against the U.S. or western interests and even after the formation of al-Qa'eda, acts of violence against foreigners were indeed rare. Indeed, despite the occasional expression of anger at U.S. policies, the rejection of violence and terrorism as unacceptable forms of retaliation was almost universal. The U.S. embassy in fact organized an event, suggested to us by King Mohammed VI, advocating interfaith dialogue. The event was held in a church with Christian, Muslim, and Jewish clergy praying for the souls of those lost in the attack on the World Trade Center and was attended by a large number of diplomats, local dignitaries, and the general public.

The Limits of Democratization in Morocco

Moroccan royalty and the business elites are expert at wining and dining guests and foreign diplomats. The country is beautiful and some of the guest houses and palaces at different locations are just gorgeous. To boot, U.S.–Moroccan bilateral ties are the oldest on the books and Morocco is always touted as a friend and ally. During much of the cold war, Morocco was considered an asset for the United States, granting military and naval bases on both the Atlantic and the Mediterranean shores of the country, and denying the same access to the Soviet Union. All this to say, American diplomats have traditionally had a hard time speaking sternly to their hosts about corruption, abuse of power and respect for human rights, whether of their regular citizenry or those of the western Sahara—all of which problems are plentiful in Morocco and deserving of at least some frank discussion among friends and allies. But such topics were considered sensitive and put Moroccan officials on the defensive. The other subject that was almost impossible to discuss objectively with our hosts was the Western Sahara and Morocco's possession of most of the territory and its refusal to contemplate Sahrawi independence. U.S. ambassadors to Morocco have historically been political appointees, i.e. not drawn from career foreign service officers. As such, these ambassadors often found it harder to absorb the State Department culture which encouraged going outside the official circle of contacts and befriending civil society activists and journalists. An exception during my years in Morocco was Ed Gabriel, who was ambassador from 1987 to 2001. Like myself, a Lebanese-American, Ed found it easier than some of his fellow political appointees to make friends at all social and political levels and in fact used his friendship with members of the royal family to talk to them frankly about sensitive issues such as corruption, human rights violations, and the western Sahara.

I always felt that our best allies in Morocco were the young civil society leaders, the ones I introduced to Hillary Clinton when she first came to Morocco as First Lady in (1999). I believed that, as in the rest of the Arab world, absolute monarchy was anachronistic at the opening of the twenty-first century and that the future belonged to the youth and the advocates of secular democracy in the region. I was excited when my idea of organizing a roundtable for Mrs. Clinton with a select group of NGO leaders in the lovely city of Fez was accepted. I felt she would like them and get to understand the problems and prospects for democracy in Morocco through them. I also felt they would be energized by her interest in them and see that despite their criticism of U.S. foreign policy that we had a lot in common with them on democracy and civil rights issues and that it would be a bridge. We have not always been consistent in behaving according to the values we cherish, knowing full well that foreign policy is always a difficult balance between pragmatism (dealing with undemocratic regimes for immediate security interests) and idealism (supporting democratic forces around the world because of shared values). Secretary Clinton supported civil society at the State Department, both with funding programs of the Middle East Partnership Initiative (MEPI) and by receiving women of the world delegations and individual women of distinction. Secretary Clinton, along with others in government, however tended to also be impressed with Morocco in general and to think it was a model for development and progress in the region. They were not totally wrong. Morocco was by comparison to the rest of north Africa and the broader Middle East doing very well in terms of gradual progress and stability and it was deserving of our encouragement.

Despite words of praise heaped on Morocco, however, and genuine positive expectations upon the assumption to the throne by Mohamed VI, events of 2011 and 2017 pointed to the limits of progress in Morocco and the continued existence of a repressive state underneath the veneer of a seemingly gentler regime inspired by the personality of Mohamed VI. U.S. policy once again failed to demonstrate full support, even if only verbal and diplomatic, to our pro-democracy civil society friends.

In Morocco with First Lady Hillary Clinton, 1999.

Hassan II's notorious minister of interior, Driss Basri, was dismissed by Mohamed VI a few months after the latter began his reign. This in itself gave rise to expectations that police repression would soon become a thing of the past. There was also a genuine affection for the young king in the country and a feeling of trust that he had the best interests of his people at heart. With the demonstrations during the Arab uprising of 2011 however, police repression returned—albeit in a lesser form than under the years of Hassan II, and definitely not resorting to the harsh tactics used in Libya, Egypt, Yemen, and Syria—all of which experienced far more serious consequences of the rebellions than did Morocco. Restrictions on freedom of the press however did come back in the form of paper closures, arrests of journalists and editors. Corruption, never seriously uprooted, was still evidenced by the continued large land and business holdings of the royal family and the business elites.

In 2017, violence in al-Hoceima in the northern Rif region of Morocco brought back not only the rebellious past of that region, but also memories among Moroccans of Hassan II's repressive years—the so-called years of lead. Moroccans of the Rif demonstrated against the police brutality which resulted in the death of a fishmonger named Mohcine Fikri—crushed to death in a garbage truck's compactor. The seeming insensitivity of the state to his fate, and indeed to the fate of the entire region enraged people across the country. Moroccans from various regions demonstrated in solidarity with their brothers in the north, expressing their disappointment in the state's reaction to events there. Civil society leaders, many of whom had suffered under Hassan II's harsh suppression of student demonstrations in the late seventies and early eighties, had come to think favorably of his son and heir Mohammed VI. Indeed, many former political prisoners felt positive enough about the young king's reforms early in his rule that they took up government jobs or helped in the human rights field by coordinating their NGO work with that of the ministry of human rights. The 2017 events caused at least those most sympathetic to the February 20 movement and who had counseled the new young rebels in 2011 to moderate their actions are turning to a darker view of the monarchy. The Moroccan Organization for Human Rights (OMDH) called for solidarity with the demands of the youth in the north and the Moroccan Association for Human Rights (AMDH) at one point led a 24-hour hunger strike calling for the release of those detained for demonstrating.

As with the infamous 2011 events in Tunisia, sparked by a peddler named Bouazizi immolating himself, it is the underlying poverty and sense of humiliation of a wide swath of Rif dwellers that has fuelled this more recent uprising. Civil society leaders are warning that after an initial period of political and economic reform the monarchy (or to be precise the deep state referred to as al-Makhzen in Morocco) is again turning defensive and resorting to repression and putting the brakes on steps toward democratization.

Politically, the positive step taken by the King after 2011, accepting to name a prime minister from the party that won the most seats in parliament, led to the appointment of the country's first Islamist prime minister, head of the opposition Party of Justice and Development (PJD). Abdelillah BenKirane, prime minister until April 2017, was able to stay as long as he did in this post by toning down his Islamist rhetoric and accepting in advance the King's veto power over any and all decisions made by him. In effect, the King remained the real power counseled by the same close advisors he had since acceding to power while BenKirane appeared, most of all to his supporters, as a paper Islamist and ineffective opposition leader.

Economically, Morocco retains a low ranking on indices of development, corruption, democracy, and youth employment. Classified as partly free on the Freedom House democracy index, at 41 percent, the country remained in the lower half of the ranked world countries for 2016. Transparency International's corruption perceptions index gave Morocco a score of 37 out of a possible score of 100 for 2016. On the human development index for the same year, Morocco was ranked 123 (out of 188) on the United Nation's human development index (a composite of life expectancy, education, and income per capita data). This puts Morocco in the lowest third of world economies, behind Palestine and the Philippines. World bank prognosis for the year ahead projects a healthy 3.8 percent growth, but given the level of corruption and dominance by a powerful business elite, the report [1]concludes "Morocco's already low labor participation rate keeps declining. Looking forward, Morocco continues to face the paramount challenges of promoting stronger private-sector-led growth and job creation, and increasing shared prosperity."

---

1   https://www.andaluspress.com/%D8%AD%D8%B1%D8%A7%D
9%83-%D8%A7%D9%84%D8%B1%D9%8A%D9%81-%D8%A
C%D9%85%D8%B9%D9%8A%D8%A7%D8%AA-%D8%
AA%D9%86%D9%88%D9%87-%D8%A8%D9%82%D8%B
1%D8%A7%D8%B1-%D8%A7%D9%84%D8%AD%D9%
88%D9%85%D8%A9-%D8%A5/

Morocco's years of lead ended with the release of remaining political prisoners in 1991. There followed a period of optimism, with the King allowing the formation of civil society groups, granting more political freedoms, and the formation of the country's first opposition government in 1998. Another era of optimism began after Hassan II's death and the ascendency to the throne of his son Mohammed VI in 1999. The sense of optimism was palpable as opposition leaders and former political prisoners spoke freely of a new era in Morocco and praised the young king for being "quite different from his father."

To be sure, Morocco can never go back to the dark days of the years of lead. Political opposition is now too entrenched in the institutions of government, the courts are not totally under the thumb of the regime and civil society organizations are too active on social media to allow for disappearances and torture to go unnoticed, not just by Moroccans, but by the whole world. That said, recent events in Hoceima and prison sentences handed down against those who led the demonstrations there highlight the limits of progress in civil liberties and human rights and the disappointment of human rights activists after their initial optimism in the ability of Mohammed VI to bring about lasting positive change. The dilemma of U.S. policy remains to this day one of not being able to genuinely invest in a kinder gentler future for all and nudge a friend and ally toward it.

CHAPTER 6

FROM LONDON TO BAGHDAD

In Harm's Way

The young man coming toward me on the sidewalk was chatting with a female companion but stopped all of a sudden, recognizing me apparently from frequent appearances on Arab television, pointed a finger at me and said loudly, "You! You work for that criminal Bush, You'd best watch yourself here!" The incident is etched in my memory because it was the first direct threat I had received since joining the Foreign Service and it was on Oxford Street in London! I would receive another similar one in a supermarket a few weeks later when another Londoner, obviously of Arab origin, recognized and followed me from aisle to aisle in the market cursing and denouncing me and my government. This was 2003 a few months after the invasion of Iraq and I had just come back to London from a month at Central Command in Doha during the war and four months in Baghdad just after the war.

I was posted in London in 2002 to assist in the establishment of the Media Outreach Center (MOC) at the U.S. embassy there. The idea was a result of discussions among a small group of USIA officers—Chris Ross chief among them, Mark Hambley and I as vocal supporters, and approved by Charlotte Beers who was Assistant Secretary for Public Diplomacy at the time. The logic of establishing the MOC in London, I and Mark Hambley argued, was the presence of much of the pan-Arab media there, particularly al-Jazeera, which was skewering the U.S. motives and methods in the Middle East without giving U.S. spokespeople a chance to respond or explain U.S. policy from their perspective. To be quite fair, U.S. spokesmen and women were being too timid and stuck too closely to the wooden language of talking points to be effective in rebutting strong Arab nationalist, let alone ex-

99

tremist rhetoric. The idea of the MOC was to establish good personal relations with Middle East journalists and to be available to them 24/7 to answer their questions and provide information and live interviews. In addition to the satellite TV stations, the main print newspapers were also headquartered there: Al-Hayat, al-sharq al-Awsat, and al-Quds al-Arabi, among others. Personally, I wished for a genuine dialogue with the Arab media and saw it as a challenge rather than an occasion to justify U.S. policies that in my mind were often wrong-headed.

Before social media swept the globe around the end of the first decade of the twenty-first century, pan-Arab media, and in particular Arab satellite TV, became a huge phenomenon in the Arab world, both representing Arab public opinion and sometimes acting on and helping to shape it. Brash, dynamic and opinionated, the al-Jazeera satellite network (AJ) burst onto the scene in 1996 and quickly acquired a large audience in the region, estimated in its early years around 45 million viewers, excluding those in Europe and the United States—all while becoming a thorn in the side of many Arab regimes and western governments alike, particularly the United States whose policies in the Middle East were lambasted daily by correspondents, anchors, and talk show hosts and guests. From my perch as deputy director of the MOC, and thus a spokesperson for the Department of State, I sent a cable to Washington in 2003 advising policymakers and media watchers of the merits and demerits of al-Jazeera and pointing out that the network represented both challenges and opportunities for us.

With a lively interactive and dynamic style, the station appealed to the young and to the disaffected in the Arab world as a breath of fresh air for audiences used to endure the wooden language and stiff presentations of government-owned and controlled channels. Borrowing some of its methods from western TV, Jazeera featured news anchors who talked and joked with one another on air, talk shows introduced bold topics and controversial guests and, perhaps more importantly, this station dared to have an opinion. AJ newscasters offered up the news with an attitude and had an opinion on the events they covered and were not afraid to express it. Unfortunately for the United States, these opinions tended to be hostile to American policies and perceived goals in the Middle East. The main criticism of U.S. policy was its responsibility for creating and sustaining Israel as an enemy and a western agent in the heart of the region. In addition, the United States was described as hostile to the Arab/Islamic world, focused mainly on its economic interests and insensitive to the needs and aspirations of the Arab/Islamic masses. As for Arab regimes, and despite the fact that the station was funded mainly by Qatar's foreign minister, the station touched on most of the taboos in the region, the unrepresentative nature of Arab regimes, the flaunting of human rights of citizens by repressive governments, and the gap between rhetorical support for Palestinian rights and the collaboration with the United States and the west in order to sustain their security. It's only redline was to never criticize the Emir of Qatar and to not directly insult Arab leaders by name.

From an official American point of view, the problem with the station's demeanor, certainly in its early years, was a constant focus on negative imagery, not giving a full airing of the U.S. point of view or indeed of opinions of independent scholars with balanced views on U.S. foreign policy. The station's management also resorted to "sneaky" ways whereby an American official being interviewed would be shown on a split screen with images of war-torn Iraq and victims of war on the other side, something the guest would not see when connecting from a remote location and would not therefore be able to respond. Prior to the Iraq war, Osama Ben Laden's taped messages would be aired in full several times a day, hence giving al-Qa'eda a platform from which to appeal to its followers and potential recruits. Personally, I understood the feelings of Arab journalists witnessing foreign forces marching into an Arab country but it was my job to get them to at least give U.S. diplomats a fair hearing, while promising that their points of view would be conveyed to policymakers in Washington.

During a visit to the Station's headquarters in Doha, I met with the then executive director Jassem al-Ali to get to know him and his staff and to present and explain American complaints against the station. I started with the positive by showing appreciation of what the station had accomplished so quickly by way of coverage of important issues and attracting such wide viewership with its dynamic presentations. I said, however, that the biases of the journalists reflected badly on management and that from an American point of view, we didn't appreciate the deliberate casting of the U.S. as a constant villain, why correspondents from the field mixed their own (or indeed the station's) biases in with their reports instead of just presenting the facts—"a point of view could legitimately be expressed in an editorial or commentary but a correspondent reporting on a battle or on the status of forces in the field need not describe fighters in the field as good guys and bad guys." I added that the reporters were not doing their viewers any favors, opining, for example, that the Americans were facing stiff resistance from the heroic Iraqi soldiers and predicting that the U.S. invasion would fail, when in fact there was hardly any resistance being put up by Saddam's forces and while Baghdad itself was on the verge of falling. "What happens afterwards is another matter and anyone's guess," I added," but the viewers are entitled to an accurate description of what's happening on the ground and an objective assessment of the balance of forces, not emotions and wishful thinking."

Unbeknownst to me, a young man who came in and filmed our conversation was not doing it for the Station's record of the visit but was actually recording it for a film he was making about how the war in Iraq was being covered. As a result, the visit is now featured in Control Room, a documentary of precisely the issues involved in covering a controversial war—along with reporters and other spokespersons who were interviewed for the film. In my case, my balanced approach to al-Jazeera was contrasted with a tape of Donald Rumsfeld dressing down the station and accusing them of lying. Guy Berliner wrote in a review of the film:

"Nabil Khoury, spokesman for the State Department, acknowledges a grudging respect for al-Jazeera. He says that, while the network has been highly critical of the US, it has also been quite open to US officials to present the American side. Consequently, because of its high prestige and viewership in the Arab world, he says, the State Department has considered it important to engage Al Jazeera respectfully." And, "Khoury's remarks contrast humorously with the agitated, flailing attacks against the network by US Defense Secretary Donald Rumsfeld, which are also interspersed at various points in the film. In one scene in the film which evoked extended laughter from the theater audience, Rumsfeld insists that "people who lie repeatedly in the media, sooner or later, will be discredited."[1]

Despite my best efforts to bridge the gap and make friends among the al-Jazeera staff, the overall relationship during the Iraq war was bumpy at best and often rift with hostility and mutual suspicion.

Death of a Reporter

Al-Jazeera reporter—Tariq Ayoub, a Jordanian—was reporting on the Iraq war from the roof of the station's offices in Baghdad when the building was hit by two air to surface missiles, according to al-Jazeera officials. The incident was partially aired as Ayoub was reporting live at the time on American forces entering Baghdad. On the same day, the Palestine Hotel nearby was hit by American tank fire and a Spanish reporter was killed. I was in Doha and reported to work at the U.S. Central Command (Centcom) media center that morning only to find dead silence and pale faces. U.S. officials, military and civilian, seemed stunned by

---

1   http://www.tvguide.com/movies/control-room/cast/137471/

the news and didn't know what to say to the media gathered there for their daily briefings and interviews. I immediately told my assistant and the U.S. embassy rep there that I would talk directly to the al-Jazeera camera. The embassy officer tried to dissuade me, saying that we had no talking points, and after a phone call to the U.S. embassy, he informed me that the ambassador to Doha did not want me to go on air. I replied that I worked for Washington not for the U.S. embassy in Doha and that my bosses always allowed me to be the judge of who to talk to and what to say.

My insistence on talking to AJ right away was to offer condolences, an important part of Arab culture—not to mention just common decency—to recognize other peoples' pain and to commiserate on the death of a loved one. The al-Jazeera staff I had met in Doha behaved like a family and supported one another affectionately. The death of one of their colleagues while covering a war was deeply felt by one and all. American insensitivity and silence would have been interpreted as guilt. I immediately offered condolences on air, said that I had met the deceased journalist and indeed many of his colleagues at AJ offices in London and Doha. I asked that condolences be conveyed to his family in Jordan on my behalf and on behalf of the U.S. government. The anchor predictably started to question me on U.S. culpability and said, "isn't it obvious that the hit on AJ offices was intentional?" I pleaded that it was too early to analyze and come to any conclusions when the facts were not yet known. "I promise you one thing," I said, "there will be an investigation and when that's done I will come back to report to you the results." I added, "I cannot believe that this was intentional, I do not work for a government that kills journalists!"

It would be three years before I could see the actual report on the two incidents involving journalist casualties in Baghdad. The report on the death of the Spanish journalist was three pages long and seemed to make sense (the reporter was lying flat on his stomach and carried a large camera that was mistaken for a shoulder-fired missile by U.S. troops). There was only one paragraph on the death of Tareq Ayoub. My initial impression was to believe the report which stated that the Jazeera offices were in the line of fire between tanks crossing the bridge in Baghdad and the ministry of interior behind the offices, where some Iraqi troops were still holding out and resisting U.S. entry into the city. The brevity of the report however and the hostility often expressed by U.S. officials toward al-Jazeera left me with serious doubts.

I recall two incidents in Baghdad which later fed those doubts. One evening in the summer of 2003 Al and I were chatting in the green room—the strategic communications room, better known as Stratcom—when a lt. Col working for the front office came over to discuss a problem: a man and a woman working for al-Jazeera had just been stopped at a checkpoint in the aftermath of an explosion where an American had died. They were suspected of having set up their camera in advance of the shooting allegedly in order to film the wounded American soldiers and use the tape for anti-U.S. propaganda. The woman was seen handing a tape to a boy before she was arrested hence smuggling the evidence out. One problem that immediately presented itself was the U.S. holding an Iraqi woman journalist overnight, which was sure to cause anger and consternation in her community. In a meeting with the military, I asked for some time to find out what happened. I called an American office manager working for the AJ office in Baghdad and explained that I needed to have the tape in hand to see if I could help the journalists. The office manager agreed and we rendezvoused in one of the parking lots around Saddam's Palace. It felt like the office manager and I were spies in a mystery movie, meeting in dark parking lot and passing off a smuggled tape.

Back at the Palace, I viewed the tape along with the military lawyer at the embassy and we found no evidence that the camera had been set up in advance. Rather, it showed the team had arrived shortly after the explosion and set up quickly to show the scene and stayed a bit to see if anyone would talk to them about it. Based on our recommendation, the two journalists were then duly released overnight.

The other incident involved Secretary of Defense, Donald Rumsfeld. He had arrived in Baghdad for meetings and we set up an interview for him with Dan Rather, if I recall correctly. As he finished and got off the set, I introduced myself to him and said that I was the one who "did on-air battles with al-Jazeera for a living." "al-Jazeera?!!" yelled Rumsfeld, "Pow Pow," as he struck his right fist against his left palm. It was a childish gesture to be sure, but it was also indicative of an alarming mindset at senior leadership levels.

At another meeting and unrelated to this incident, ambassador Paul Bremer called his principal military and civilian advisors to consider the request by Iraq's Governing Council to close down the offices of al-Jazeera. He conveyed the wish of Iraqi leaders to close down the office because of constant attacks on members of the IGC, constantly referring to them as "stooges" of the Americans, and on to CPA as an occupation authority, all while making heroes out of al-Qa'eda terrorists. Bremer asked if we could/ should close them down. The military lawyer said yes, because under international law, CPA was in charge of Iraq and could accredit or deny accreditation to any media organization. Political counselors suggested that since the Iraqis requested it, there would be no political blowback. Others explained how we might carry out the closure. I sat there quietly until Bremer turned to me last saying, "Nabeel what do you think?" I said, "Of course we could shut them down, after all we have the big guns, but they have a bigger mouth! Closing them down in Baghdad does not shut them up from their offices anywhere from Doha to Rabat, not forgetting London—and they would surely bad mouth us even worse than they're doing now." Secondly, I said, "how would it look for us, coming here ostensibly to set up a democracy in place of Saddam when one of our first acts is to shut down a media network?"

Bremer said, "and that's the opinion I'm most influenced by, let's keep them open." Silence around the room and some dirty looks in my direction, but the offices remained open until the IGC had the authority to close them on their own. As an interim measure, the Iraqi "interim government" in September 2003, suspended Al-Jazeera and Al-Arabiya (Saudi owned) from reporting on official government activities for two weeks for what it said was support of attacks on Iraqi government members and U.S. forces. Al-Arabiya later reopened but al-Jazeera remained closed—though the measure did not stop them from reporting on Iraq events, often with taped reports sent to them from the field.

Al-Arabiya was less controversial for most—but certainly not all Iraqis and, presumably because of its Saudi ownership, it was also considered less hostile toward the USG. My own interactions with al-Arabiya journalists and management were mostly free of disagreements. I interviewed with their office in Baghdad on a regular basis and found one particular program called "Min al-Iraq" (From Iraq), particularly interesting and useful as a platform for discussion. On several trips to Dubai, where they were headquartered, I interviewed from their studios and became friends with several of their journalists and news producers.

I twice had the occasion to meet with the station owner and director general of the broader Middle East Broadcasting Corporation (MBC), Waleed al-Ibrahim, a wealthy businessman and son in-law to the late King Fahd. Sheikh Waleed, as he is most commonly referred to by employees and friends alike, invited me out to dinner with several al-Arabiya anchors and talk-show hosts which helped cement long-term relationships with some of them. The after dinner party at his hotel suite however included only some of his VIP visitors and a bevy of beautiful young women from Europe, the Ukraine with possibly some Russians among them. Some of the women were foreign airline hostesses but I couldn't guess at the professions of most of the others. His journalists and anchors were not invited to this event, replete with alcohol, music, and dancing.

Sheikh Walid struck me as always jovial and someone who loved the good life without any compunctions or inhibitions. At other times, however, he was all business and dead serious about the success of his media empire. On another visit to Dubai, he invited me to give a press roundtable to his anchors and news editors and surprised me during the middle of it by walking in with a Saudi prince who was high up the chain of Saudi intelligence. After introductions, I carried on with my discussion with the journalists and the prince sat there poker-faced and left after 10 minutes or so with not a single word, nod, or indication that he liked or disliked what he had heard.

Baghdad Blues

Al and Chad laughed their asses off as soon as we were back safe and sound inside the Green Zone and at our HQ, Saddam's old palace. We had just come back from a speaking engagement I had in town and Chad was riding shotgun in the back as usual but Al, instead of driving sat next to me in front and let me drive per my suggestion. I answered a phone call on my cell, never a good idea while driving, especially in a war zone. I slowed down on the highway as I talked and merely looked up when the shooting started and asked where the shooting was coming from. Al and Chad started yelling at me, "Step on it, Go, go, go!" It took me a few seconds to respond in what seemed like an eternity to my colleagues. The shooting came from a car passing us on the other side of the highway and didn't last long but Al later said there were masked men in another car following us but they backed off when Al and Chad stuck their guns out the window to shoot back. "That's the last time I'm letting you drive," is all Al could bring himself to say amidst laughter and both of them imitating me as I held the phone in one hand and steered with the other, calmly asking, "where's the shooting coming from?"

Al (Alaa-eldin elsadr) was at the time a contractor with DOD. I found him sitting behind a desk-top computer at the Strategic

Communications center, otherwise known as the green room in Saddam's old palace. He was tracking Arab media and when he found out I was sent to be a spokesperson for the State Department and to connect with Iraqi media in particular, he started sharing what he knew about the media scene in Baghdad. Al struck me as very knowledgeable and low key. Between his Egyptian sense of humor, my Lebanese jokes and our mutual interest in Arab media, we hit it off instantly. We found that we shared the same goals and believed in the same method to achieve them—that of befriending rather than antagonizing Arab media and exchanging their giving us a platform with our helping them with access to press briefings and training opportunities. Al helped me get oriented to Baghdad and the Green Zone and worked closely with me, helping me ferret out Iraqi journalists around town and connect with the broader Arab media in Baghdad. He was the sole point of light in that dark place and his friendship will always be the one solid gain from my Iraq experience.

Chad Beuhring, an army Lt. Colonel assigned to U.S. Central Command and forwarded to Baghdad to work with Stratcom, was a friend and colleague from the start of our acquaintance. I recall he always had a photo of his two young boys on his desk and was kind and attentive to an Iraqi colleague's children when she had to bring them to work with her. He volunteered to ride shotgun with me and Al whenever we went out of the GZ on missions we decided on and for which no formal protection was offered. In any case, the bureaucracy for requesting a convoy were too cumbersome and driving around Baghdad with military cars around you was a sure way of drawing the wrong kind of attention and scaring off the reporters we wanted to meet. I still recall how impressed Chad was with the hospitality and friendliness shown us by al-Jazeera reporters when we went downtown to their offices late one night for a meeting. They insisted on us sharing their dinner before leaving around midnight. Chad at first stood shyly by the door saying he would stand guard, but they laughed and said that we were all safe where we were and insisted he sit on the floor and join the rest of us for Masqouf, the famous Iraqi dish of barbecued Carp.

Chad was killed on October 26, the only fatality when the al-Rasheed hotel where we all stayed was shelled with Katyousha rockets. I was awakened by the sound of shells striking the concrete building and slid between the bed and the wall at the far end of the room until all of 26 shells were fired (apparently from an automatic rocket launcher). One of them hit just above the room next to mine where a female colleague was staying. I heard her screaming in the hallway and ran out in my underwear only see her on the floor yelling for someone to get her out of the building and several colleagues already tending to her. A slab of concrete had fallen on her as she slept and broke her shoulder. She was lucky to survive. Chad on the other hand had apparently jumped to the window when the shelling started in order to fire back at the attackers. A rocket slammed right into his room through the window where he stood. We found his gun on the windowsill and his body slumped on the couch beneath it. Al told me later he had to go identify his body at the hospital from what was left of his face. I cried almost non-stop for three days afterwards and the lone group therapy session offered by the Army to those of us who had worked in the same room with Chad did nothing to help. It is now 15 years later and his memory and the memory of that day still choke me up.

The Perils of Intervention

If my work with the Arab media earned me some notoriety and security risks during the first couple of years of the Iraq war, it also afforded me a chance to debate the issue with journalists and explore the potential impact the war would have on the region and on U.S.–Arab relations in the years ahead.

The following is extracted from an interview with me, published by the *Los Angeles Times*: [2]

> From an office inside what used to be the kitchen in Saddam Hussein's palace, Nabeel Khoury takes the heat in one of the toughest political jobs in Baghdad: defending America in the Arab media.

So began the article investigating U.S. public diplomacy in the Arab world and my role in it as a spokesperson for the State Department in Baghdad.

Although I was personally against the Bush administration's decision to go into Iraq in 2003, it was my job to explain it, if not outright defend it to a largely hostile Arab audience. This was my second experience with U.S. intervention in the region, having witnessed the ouster of Saddam from Kuwait in 1991. As an intellectual, and an Arab-American, I used press conferences and conversations with journalists to debate the issue, often at length, rather than to just spout Washington's official line. In this effort, I was partly trying to convince myself that something good could come out of this travesty. I made up my own arguments and what-ifs, more like a professor rather than a diplomat. Thinking as an Arab, I suggested that Saddam, and indeed all Arab autocracies, were anachronistic. Sooner or later, the region needs to join the community of democracies if it is to meet the economic and political needs of its people. Sure, I agreed with my critics, democracy should come as a result of people of the region demanding and bringing it about with their own activism, but what chance did they stand against a determined and brutal dictator? Indeed, Saddam looked very secure in the saddle before the war and, with two young sons around him, Iraq could have been looking at several more decades of the same regime and its brutality, more so perhaps under the sons once they inherited their father's rule.

---

2   http://articles.latimes.com/2003/sep/12/world/fg-image12n

My critics kept saying, "Look around you, nothing but death, destruction and chaos, Is this democracy?" To which my retort was, "Nope, this is certainly not democracy, but you have to factor in the chaos that normally follows any violent transition. Study the revolutions in Europe, none of them arrived at democracy without blood letting, chaos and incompetent governments that usually follow fallen dictators."

If This Be Governance

The Coalition Provisional Authority (CPA) was a chaotic place. Established to actually govern Iraq for the first year, in between the fall of Saddam and Iraqis getting ready to set up their own government, it was not a U.S. embassy in the traditional sense of the word nor was it an actual government—since it represented a coalition of governments, a situation which made it difficult to establish a clear line of authority. In political, military, and public affairs matters, it was hard to figure out from day to day what the policy was and who was supervising whom. To be sure, ambassador Paul Bremer was overall in charge. It being Iraq, however, he had Donald Rumsfeld and Dick Cheney looking closely over his shoulders from Washington, and dozens of their minions sent to Baghdad in one capacity or another to be their eyes and ears on the ground. The State Department played a secondary role in Baghdad and it was not a comfortable situation for career FSOs like myself to be in the midst of all this.

To begin with, media work was being done patchwork style. No one explained to me when I arrived what if any hierarchy existed. Dan Senor was, while he was there at any rate, the Bush administration's point man on public affairs, and he sometimes came into the Stratcom room to brief on what the administration's talking points were, but he was often traveling and one never knew when he was in Baghdad and when he wasn't. A British colleague had been there several weeks before me and would go off and brief the international media on his own without coordinating with anyone else at Stratcom. When I started to brief the Iraqi and Arab media, once a week to his daily briefings, he took exception to that and wanted to brief the Arab media himself even though his Arabic was not good enough and his mandate to do that was not at all clear. He was also jealous of my having Al's assistance and told me I was using an office resource without coordinating with him. It so happened on the day he confronted me on that I had just received word of my promotion to the senior ranks of the foreign service. As an Officer Counselor (OC), I now had the equivalent rank of a one-star General. Feeling full of myself, I told Sir Charles, as Al and I used to call him, that I worked for Washington not for him and that I would gladly coordinate with him once he started being more transparent about what the hell he was doing day in day out.

On matters of policy, things were as confusing to the Iraqis as it was to us working inside CPA. My press briefings to Iraqi and Arab journalists and frequent appearances on Arab TV had made me a public figure with whom Iraqis could easily identify, so I often became a point of contact for those who had questions they could not figure out the appropriate jurisdiction for. Beyond journalists, Iraqis of various political shades and interests also occasionally came to me saying, "we don't know who else to talk to."

On one occasion, a small delegation belonging to Muqtada al-Sadr's movement came to see me at the Rashid hotel. Muqtada, a very controversial black-turbaned Shia cleric (signifying he was a descendent of the Prophet) and a firebrand reputed to have personally killed fellow cleric Abdelmajid al-Khoei in Najaf, wanted to be a player in Iraq's interim government but was generally shunned by the members of the IGC. His advisors who came to see me wanted to know if we would support him becoming a member of the IGC, or at least for playing a role of some sort in return for assurances of moderation of attitude toward the U.S. presence in Iraq. The first occasion I had to see our political counselor after that was at a meeting I accompanied him to at Iyad

Allawi's office. Iyad was one of the opposition figures who came back from exile to become one of the leading members of the IGC. A Shia but with very enlightened views on Sunnis and on the need not to tarnish them all with Saddam's legacy. The subject of Muqtada came up in the discussion. It was probably not the right time for me to bring up my meeting, but I thought I should balance any strong denunciations of Muqtada and hardened positions toward him with the request I had received. I also thought having an Iraqi like Allawi there would allow him to weigh in directly on the subject. We also had one of our military officers with us, and there was stunned silence when I relayed that Muqtada had sent a message to see if he could come in from the cold, as it were. I passed on his assistants' suggestion that a meeting with him could be arranged. Later I was told that it was a strange thing for me to bring it up when extreme measures were being considered against the man. "We don't want to talk to him, we want to kill him." I was told. My only retort was, "if this is indeed policy then someone should've informed us spokespeople, and by the way, if you really want to do away with the man why haven't you done it yet?" To my amazement, the reply was, "we can't seem to find the guy whenever we go looking for him ..."

Bad Boys with Guns

"Book 'em Danno!" This was the title of a message I sent to Washington, via open email as we didn't have secure State computers yet at CPA. I had just assisted in an arrest of a very unconventional nature. Someone (Let's call him Mohamed) sought me out at al-Rashid hotel and begged me to help him find his father. His story, which sadly turned out to be true, was that U.S. soldiers had come to his home seeking to arrest him because he had worked for Saddam and was apparently on a wanted list. "When they didn't find me they took a computer, several thousand dollars in cash from my home and arrested my father—they took him as hostage!" The man showed me a note he found when he returned home saying, "Your father and the material we took from your home will be returned if you give yourself up!"

"Who do I give myself up to?" was the question Mohamed asked me—and one which seemed surreal even in Baghdad. "I'm quite willing to give myself up and answer any questions they ask of me, they can even keep the money they took, I just want my father back!"

The note was signed by someone with the rank of Captain, followed by the name of his unit. My first reaction was to go to what was our prison authority person who incredibly had only hand-written entries in very large notebooks and could not, via manual search, find the name of the person I gave him. He also had no idea who the person was whose name appeared on the note saying he had taken this man into custody. Finally, just asking around regular GIs we knew, we hit on someone who knew the unit and the Captain's name. I got a phone number and called—the person who answered at first pretended to be confused by my question, then when I told him the story he told me the Captain would call me back. Sure enough the Captain called and confirmed the story was correct and that if Mohamed truly wanted to give himself up then we could arrange the exchange on one of the bridges between the Green Zone and the city proper. On the designated day, Al and I drove with Mohamed to the agreed spot, the Captain arrived with several armored Humvees and I walked over to see him and walked back to confirm to Mohamed that his father was indeed in one of the Humvees. Mohamed seemed remarkably calm about being handed over to our military officers; I was not so calm and hated to be a part of this James Bond scene. The two men met half-way between our car and the convoy, they hugged and chatted a bit, tears flowing—I was a mess watching this. Mohamed got what he wanted, his father out of jail. We drove the father back to where he could take a taxi home. I never heard from or about Mohamed again even though I checked to see if his name was added to those in custody. It was not.

Al and I discussed the whole thing over a drink at the al-Rashid afterwards. I was shocked that our military would act this way, taking an old man hostage to make sure the son surrendered. Al was less surprised. He said this was a black-box unit, a shadowy group not formally under the normal military hierarchy and that they had their own methods of getting the job done. No one scrutinized their methods. I was losing my innocence. I would notice after that, waiting in the lobby before leaving for work in the morning, sundry and various military men with gear I had never seen before which made them look like aliens from outer space. In fact, not only were their units unknown but sometimes their nationality—I detected a South African accent one time when we picked up two GIs on our way to the Palace. They didn't like being asked, but they admitted to indeed being South African. Ghurka units were also deployed to Baghdad, originally Nepalese but largely attached to British forces, they guarded the Palace grounds among other duties. Their gentility belied a fierce fighting tradition and they generally kept to themselves on the compound.

Blackwater, perhaps because it's a known American company, typifies the problem with mercenary forces in Iraq. Essentially an armed militia on contract with the U.S. government, its units guarded CPA leadership and VIP visitors, but also ran patrols throughout Baghdad. Their behavior showed the perils of relying on contractors who were not directly under DOD hierarchy. Nominally, such contractors were under the Regional Security Officer (RSO), who worked for the Department of State—This supervision would be fictional even under normal embassy conditions, and conditions in Baghdad in 2003 were certainly not normal. A small contingent of diplomatic security personnel cannot supervise a mercenary force in a war zone. Blackwater is most infamous for the incident in 2007 where their patrol in downtown Baghdad shot and killed 17 Iraqi civilians, purportedly because they saw someone in the crowd with a gun pointed at them. Regular U.S. soldiers certainly make mistakes and sometimes commit crimes in war zones, but at least they are governed by laws and regulations and adequately supervised so that course-correction could be taken when incidents like that occur. The overall occupation of Iraq however did not give one any confidence that even the regular military was properly supervised.

U.S. Policy

Perhaps one of the worst signs of a confused policy in the early days of the occupation was the dismissal of Saddam's army in toto, instead of rehabilitating at least the rank and file and merging them into new units for the "new Iraq." This left a large number of angry men with guns and the training to use them but no salaries or benefits with which to ameliorate their anger. Many of those discharged would eventually join the ranks of al-Qa'eda or the Ba'thist resistance to the occupation, organized in the early going under Saddam's former top General, Izzat Ibrahim al-Douri. He was number one on the deck of cards, a gimmick devised by the military in lieu of an old-fashioned list of those wanted on charges of terrorism and/or attacks against the U.S. military. He was reported killed several times, only to reappear on video later to deny the rumors. He was never captured.

De-Ba'thification was the second blunder. It was a code word for routing out old regime stalwarts—an idea strongly recommended by the late Ahmed al-Chalabi, one of the most influential Iraqis with the Bush administration, particularly in convincing Donald Rumsfeld of the presence of WMD in Iraq and of the need to remove Saddam by force. Chalabi was a strong advocate of setting up a McCarthy-style inquisition and of going after old regime figures with only a vague notion of transitional justice. The USG went along with that and the unfortunate result was the victimization of hundreds if not thousands of relatively low-level old regime functionaries and sometimes even school teachers who were rank and file members of the Ba'th party—membership hardly anyone under Saddam dared refuse. The long term effects of this policy went beyond the victimization of many innocent people to making reconciliation among Iraqis a very difficult proposition.

I had first met Chalabi in London during a 2002 meeting between Zalmazy Khalilzad and the Iraqi opposition in exile. Colleagues and I from the U.S. embassy assisted at those meeting. I still recall Chalabi coming to the first meeting fashionably late—making an entrance and a statement by strutting in, camel hair coat slung over his shoulders like a cape and looking very much like he owned the place. He was told by an Iraqi colleague that the discussion was already underway as to who should cover the cost of the hotel where they were all staying and meeting, as the Iraqi delegation was already over its budget and they needed $20,000 to cover their expenses. Chalabi looked at Khalilazad and said, "Zal, you pay for it, just cover it for us." Far from an opposition figure speaking to his benefactor, Chalabi addressed the envoy of the Bush administration like one would address one of his employees.

Two alternate reasons were given for justifying the invasion of Iraq in 2003:

One involved the weapons of mass destruction (WMD); another, less public one, was the belief that the removal of an Arab dictator and replacing his regime with a democratic system would set in motion a domino effect leading to the spread of democracy throughout the Middle East.

After 1 year of the war and the search for WMD in Iraq, it became obvious that not only were those weapons nowhere to be found but also that there was something wrong with the intelligence that was used to assert their existence in the first place. The National Intelligence Estimate (NIE) that presented the evidence and conclusion to Congress that Iraq was indeed working on and stockpiling WMD cherry-picked the relevant information, thereby skewing the conclusions—reason which led INR, the bureau I joined later in my career, to dissent from the report. This was noted in a footnote #1, the number proudly displayed in later years on an INR baseball cap issued to commemorate the fact that INR got it right. My work with INR gave me a better perspective on the intelligence assessment process. Suffice it to say, raw intelligence, especially that which comes from human sources, spans the spectrum of credibility from the rumor level all the way to 100 percent certainty. INR assessed that the level of credibility of the WMD information used by the Bush administration to justify the war on Iraq was of very low credibility—and not corroborated enough by separate intel methods to justify the conclusions reached in the NIE.

The invasion of Iraq had a tremendous human cost and it unleashed dark forces that are still wreaking havoc in the entire region. For the United States, it left the impression with large swaths of the Arab/Islamic world that their lives don't matter and, worse, that the United States was possibly conniving to achieve exactly the chaos and destruction that resulted. President Bush stated very clearly in a speech before the Philadelphia World Affairs Council in 2005 that one of the goals of the invasion was the installation of democracy in place of dictatorship: "Besides the defeat of terrorists and the training of Iraqi security forces to keep fighting them, a vital element of our strategy [in Iraq] is our effort to help the Iraqi people build a lasting democracy in the heart of the Middle East." I believed then, and still believe now, that the promotion of democracy in the Middle East is in both the long-term interest of the region and the U.S. national interest. I did not believe however that the promotion needed to be done by force or that the architects of the invasion knew what they were doing. They were deaf to the advice offered them by people who understood the region far better than they did; they were also callous to the suffering that their actions generated.

The removal of Saddam Hussein's regime from power in Baghdad certainly cleared the way for the construction of something new in its place but it was never a sure bet what exactly that might be. Inside Iraq, Saddam's ouster unleashed sectarian and extremist forces that the Iraqi dictator had hitherto suppressed and/or prevented from entering the country. No one inside or outside the country was ready for dealing with such forces. The attempt to build a democratic system led ultimately to a new constitution, but also to the institutionalization of political forces that had not had the opportunity to participate in the country's political life before 2003. The rivalry, as well as the occasional collaboration between all these new forces became part of the new and complicated political dynamic that followed the fall of Saddam. Democracy in Iraq remains today work in progress.

Regional powers, primarily Iran, Syria, and Turkey, were sucked into the vacuum left by the ouster of Saddam—and this created a new regional dynamic that has become part of life inside Iraq. What happens in Iraq, the past decade has shown, does not stay in Iraq. Conversely, what happens in the region now flows directly into Iraq and becomes a part of its political reality. ISIS, which grew out of al-Qa'eda in Iraq, went first to Syria then came back strengthened to Iraq, occupying Ramadi, Iraq's largest Sunni region, and Mosul, Iraq's second largest city. The toppling of dictators throughout history has never been easy in any part of the world, and Europe's middle ages present 300 years of precedent as to what happens when absolute monarchs are toppled.

One of the unfortunate results from the war, the occupation and the unleashing of Sunni radical groups was the appearance on the scene of Shia radical groups, aided and abetted by Iran. Hence, while the defeat of al-Qa'eda and ISIS in Iraq has been accomplished—albeit not definitely and at great cost—the absorption or the demilitarization of Shia forces like Asa'eb Ahl al-Haq (AAH) and Kata'eb Hezbollah will be tougher. These militias were trained and equipped by Iran with the assistance of Lebanese Hezbollah and they continue at this writing playing a more or less independent role inside the country. The United States cannot interfere in this process without getting involved yet again in Iraqi internal affairs or possibly needing to send in a large force. Merely saying to the Iraqi government "make it so" won't do the trick. The challenge will be for the government of Iraq and for secular forces in the country to manage this internal complication politically and delicately. Today, and after several trial and error attempts to rebuild, the Iraqi military, especially their counterterrorism unit are much more professional and organized than they were after the departure of the bulk of American forces.

Baghdad 2016. Talking to Iraqi special forces.

Thomas Freidman came to Baghdad while I was there and I arranged for him to meet with Iyad Jamal Eddine, a black-turbaned Iraqi friend who was, and still is, one of the most secular political thinkers and activists in the country. Iyad invited us to dinner and introduced us to a surprise guest that evening, Hassan Khomeini, the grandson of none other than Imam Khomeini, the founder of the Iranian Islamic revolution. Hassan is practically persona non-grata with the clerical regime in his country and spends most of his time with fellow secularists in Iraq. The four of us had a lovely dinner and conversation in Iyad's house and talked about Islamism, future of Iran, and the future of Iraq. On his return to Washington, Tom posted an op-ed entitled, "Dinner with the Mullahs," in which he briefly described the conversation and concluded that talking to such secular-minded clerics gave him hope for the future of Iraq. It may well be frustratingly slow in coming, but I too have a feeling that Iraqis will eventually work out all the complex internal and regional problems they continue to face today.

The French revolution oscillated from absolute monarchy to the Jacobins' reign of terror and back to Napoleon's empire and the restoration of monarchy before it finally set the country on a republican path and the march toward their current democracy. Iraq, after less than two decades of experimenting with democracy, is neither stable nor fully democratic, but its chances, theoretically at least, are only as good as the ability of the Shia majority parties to forgo exclusivity and adopt a comprehensive reconciliation plan with their Kurdish and Sunni Arab minorities and move on pragmatically to forge a new social contract.

CHAPTER 7

YEMEN

"La Budda Min Sanaa Wa Law Tala Azzaman"
(One must return to Sanaa no matter
how long the separation)

—*from a poem by Abdelaziz al-Maqaleh*

"There is no denying it, Ali Abdullah Saleh's death has left a vacuum in Yemen and he will be missed."[1] I wrote this at the opening of a farewell message, an obituary of sorts, upon hearing of the death of the former president of Yemen on December 4, 2017, at the hands of his Houthi allies. As Deputy Chief of Mission at the U.S. embassy in Sanaa, 2004–2007, I had frequent dealings with Saleh and had mixed feelings about the man. Crafty to a fault, he was killed by the Houthi rebels after breaking an alliance he had forged with them in 2014 in order to help them take over Sanaa and put himself in a position to regain the presidency he was forced to resign in 2012.

A combination of the Godfather and George Carlin, Saleh was corrupt, often ruthless, an autocrat with a fierce desire to hold on to power—but a charming host and an unpredictable interlocutor who loved to surprise and amuse, if not outright ambush and outfox his guests. Though a partisan at the end of his life, he had always displayed the capacity to lead and to convince people to follow. His demise put Yemenis at a quandary as the rest of the country's leading figures, smaller in stature, and less sure about their goals and strategies seemed ill-placed to lead Yemen out of its quagmire and into a more stable future.

---

1   http://www.aljazeera.com/indepth/spotlight/yemen/2011/02/2011
    22812118938648.html

First, his faults, and yes, there were a few.

Saleh's ascent to power in 1978 and his election to the presidency in 1982 left in its wake a trail of intrigue and assassinations—starting with the demise of his predecessors, Presidents Hamdi and al-Ghashmi—with which plots he was at least associated, if not a central figure. His 33-year rule saw a ruthless leader who, while not committing any massacres along the lines of Saddam Hussein or Bashar al-Assad[2], was nevertheless not loath to intimidate, threaten, and on occasion have opponents disappeared when neither cajoling nor threatening worked. His control over Yemen was demonstrated when he first united the two Yemens in 1990 and then quickly crushed the southern secessionist rebellion in 1994, thus avoiding a prolonged and bloody civil war. In 2011, worried about being unseated by the Arab uprising, he was unsympathetic to the demands of the youth and sent his troops to disperse them by force from Taghyir Square, as the downtown Sanaa area they took over was dubbed. Dozens of civilian casualties and the split this caused within army ranks led to the GCC intervention and the deal which resulted in his resignation from the presidency.

Saleh presided over a regime in which corruption started at the top with graft, bribery, and a constant hand in the till. Ministers and associates were constantly demanding kickbacks for contracts with foreign companies and bribes to license domestic industry and businesses. Saleh himself was not shy about demanding his own cut and was notably known to have received oil-for-food coupons from Saddam Hussein in the nineties. Arms smuggling and trafficking, long a tradition in Yemen, was not only tolerated by Saleh, but a business in which he actively participated via Yemeni arms merchants who were close friends and associates of his. Through his longtime friend and top general, Ali

---

2   http://www.aljazeera.com/news/middleeast/2007/07/2008525185 14154964.html

Mohsen, Saleh was not averse to dealing with al-Qaeda-affiliated fighters in Yemen, ostensibly to maintain contacts and avoid terrorism on Yemeni soil. [3]

To his credit, much of the money he controlled was used to buy off rebellious tribes and dole out favors to maintain a favorable balance of power between Sanaa and the outlying regions. He certainly lived in relative luxury compared with the average Yemeni, but the opulence of his home and presidential palace paled in comparison to those of his oil-rich neighbors. He did not own palaces and yachts abroad and was not fond of taking extended vacations overseas. Money was always about power and greasing the wheels to keep the vehicle of state going.

Always willing to consider his options, Saleh took the side of Saddam in the first Gulf war and paid a heavy price in loss of income from the Gulf and the deportation of close to a million Yemeni workers from Saudi Arabia. He switched positions later in the 1990s, but kept on profiting from the boycott against Iraq via the oil-for-food program—reportedly receiving oil coupons from Saddam which he then sold on the international market while offering kickbacks to Saddam. In 2003, his switch was formalized when he sided with the international coalition against Saddam. Many of his Yemeni critics wished he had done the opposite and supported Kuwait in 1990 and Saddam in 2003—in either case, Saleh's position had nothing to do with political correctness and everything to do with profit. Regardless of his move to the western camp, Yemenis were among the highest numbers of foreign fighters who joined the ranks of al-Qaeda in Iraq during the American occupation.

Throwing in with the United States in the wake of the 2000 attack on the USS Cole, he allowed the FBI to investigate the bombing of the Cole in Aden's port in 2000, and later supported the CIA in going after terrorists in Yemen.

---

3   https://www.aljazeera.com/news/2019/08/al-qaeda-launches-deadly-attack-army-base-southern-yemen-190802081549242.html

Saleh's major tactical mistakes included returning to Yemen after his hospitalization in Riyadh in 2012 and allying himself with the Houthis in 2014 in hopes of getting back into power. I had tried to weigh in on his decision by sending him a message with his ambassador and son-in-law Abdelwahab al-Hajry, to the effect of "You don't need to do this, you can go anywhere in the world and enjoy life in retirement with your family and friends." I was touched when upon his return to Sanaa he mentioned me indirectly, saying "I was advised by a friend from a great power not to return to Yemen, but how can I stay away? I'm the president of a country not a tourist!"

Knowing the Houthis had never forgiven him for the death of Hussein al-Houthi in 2004 and that they sought power for themselves, he overestimated his maneuvering powers and his ability to outwit them. Having failed to take the upper hand in his alliance, the timing and planning of his revolt against them in 2017 were seriously flawed. His forces were surrounded in and around Sanaa and any Gulf-supported forces that might have tried to come in to help him were nowhere near the capital. His betting on the tribes around Sanaa to support him in fleeing to his hometown of Sanhan proved a fatal gamble.

Ambassador Thomas Krajeski and I usually saw Saleh together, but I also went on my own to see him when Tom was out of town. I particularly enjoyed bantering with him and offering him advice, which he willingly took from me when he would scorn it from other foreign diplomats. He was surprisingly responsive to our suggestions on fighting corruption and arms smuggling, but for those efforts to yield results, we would have had to hold his hands to the fire and keep up international pressure. He was a master at making a complete turnaround as soon as no one was looking, and in those two cases, he did!

He loved poking his guests in the ribs, figuratively, and sometimes literally, to throw them off guard. If he was caught at it and his bluff was called, he laughed and moved on to other issues. His demise left a power vacuum, certainly within his party, the General Peoples' Congress (GPC), but also in Yemen as no other leader has emerged with even the potential to rally nation-wide supporters, keep the country united, and perhaps stitch the right alliances to end the war that currently still consumes Yemen.

With President Saleh at Ma'asheeq in Aden.

Farewell call on President Saleh.

127

The 6-Year War

It was my first week on the job as Deputy Chief of Mission at the U.S. embassy in Sanaa and Outgoing ambassador Edmund Hull had finished briefing me on our main issues of concern in Yemen since I was going to take charge of the embassy after his departure, pending the arrival of the new ambassador to Yemen, Tom Krajeski. During a reception in my honor organized that evening by the embassy, Ambassador Hull and I were told that our presence was being requested by Yemen's Minister of Interior (MOI).

Upon arrival at the MOI, we were ushered into the ministry's operations center, introduced to president' Saleh's nephew, Yahya Saleh, at the time commander of Yemen's Counter Terrorism Unit (CTU), a force being trained by U.S. and U.K. military officers. Col. Yahya and other military officers preceded to brief us on the fighting that had just started in the north between the government of Yemen forces and the Houthis—a little known northern Zaidi tribe at the time. Without going into details as to what had started the fighting, he simply noted that this was a rebellion against the central government, that it was being supported by Iran and that our help might be needed in putting it down. For the duration of my tour of duty in Yemen, we would receive several such reports and requests for assistance. Search as we might we never found any evidence of Iran's alleged interference between 2004 and 2007. While I was there, the embassy never asked Washington to support the central government's requests for assistance in that war which, to the best of our judgment, was a domestic affair that could and should have been settled peacefully. In fact, that's exactly what I told General Abizaid, Centcom commander when he visited Yemen in 2005 and asked me while we were waiting to see Saleh, "What's this war with Houthis about, is it something we should get involved in?" I was very clear that in our estimation, this had nothing to do with international terrorism and that the only way for us to get involved was through diplomatic and economic assistance.

That meeting at the MOI marked, nonetheless, the start of an excellent working relationship between us and Minister Rashad Allimi. With a Ph.D. in sociology and a fondness for Tennis, Allimi, while intensely loyal to president Saleh, was a reluctant warrior in that he was at times visibly uncomfortable with passing on to us his boss's arguments and talking points. His requests for assistance in materiel would often be accompanied with a qualification, "even if we put aside the war in Saadah, we would still need this equipment for training and general upgrading of the capability of our armed forces." Allimi was also someone I could always call on his cell phone for an immediate response to a security issue or concern or to pass a message to the president and know it would definitely be delivered. I was saddened to learn in June 2011 that Allimi was among those seriously injured in the blast at the mosque inside the presidential palace and, along with president Saleh, evacuated to Saudi Arabia for treatment. It took several years of continued treatment for both men to recover from their injuries.

The Sa'dah War, launched by president Saleh against the Houthi tribe in the Sa'dah region, would consume a fair amount of our time for the duration of our 3-year term in Yemen. The war started when Saleh, on a visit to the region, was booed and heckled by locals attending a speech he gave there. The slogans raised were Houthi standard, "Death to America, Death to the Jews, Victory for Islam." Saleh was branded an agent of the west. Upon his return to Sanaa, Saleh summoned the elder of the family, Badreddine al-Houthi to Sanaa. The old man would not go and refused to send his son, Hussein, in his place. Saleh then sent a small force to bring the elder Houthi to Sanaa. The force was fired on and had to retreat. The escalation that followed was definitely Saleh's decision and more a matter of personal pride than a question of necessity. Even though Saleh often bluffed "I'm fighting this war on your behalf, these guys hate all Americans," we never felt directly threatened by the Houthis in any way. The war also did not

129

adversely affect security conditions throughout Yemen, which was lucky for me as it allowed me the chance to travel throughout the country, except the Sa'dah region itself.

Travels in Dictionary Land

I was introduced to Tim Mackintosh-Smith, author of the book, *Yemen: Travels in Dictionary Land*, at his home in the old city in Sanaa in 2006, by a dear friend who worked for the British Council. Tim is one of those westerners who study Arabic, fall in love with the language and, seeing Yemen as perhaps the most authentically Arab, fall in love with the country, its people and its culture. He received us in a native "fouta," the traditional sarong-like skirt worn by men, a tradition which most likely came originally from India, Indonesia and perhaps Malaysia. Tim spoke of his love for Yemen and had written how it was the spoken language that drew him, being the closest dialect to classical Arabic. Indeed, he had chosen it over his professor's recommendation of a "more respectable city." Tim decided that "Cairo was drowning in smog and smugness, Amman was reportedly boring and Tunis, well, complexée" the latter in reference to French influence on both language and culture in Tunisia. Indeed, I too found very little pretentiousness in Yemen—the people were very open, looked you straight in the eye and told you exactly what they thought with total lack of self-consciousness. I, like Tim, found it a very refreshing change from other Arab countries I had visited and served in as a diplomat, particularly Yemen's northern Gulf neighbors.

Today, over 10 years after leaving Yemen, I find myself still totally immersed in Yemeni events, totally opposed to the Saudi-led war strangling the country, heartbroken over the suffering of its people and frustrated with America's immoral support for the Saudi war effort. The memories I have of Yemen are all beautiful, of its mountains, villages, and the people with their incredible hospitality and openness. The 2004–2007 were good years for traveling around Yemen. Security conditions were good but whereas foreign diplomats were generally allowed to travel without a police escort throughout the country, U.S. embassy employees were required to ask for Yemeni security to accompany them on out of town trips. There was also a general restriction on anyone going up north to the Sa'dah region.

As DCM, I always had embassy security accompanying me, except on weekends and for personal travel when I did not request their assistance. In fact, I did not even request Yemeni security on visits to the countryside beyond Sanaa in order to be able to visit with friends and meet with local villagers freely without telegraphing embassy status every time I moved around the country. For that purpose, I drove my personal car in Sanaa on the weekends and for out of Sanaa trips.

Cahil, a Village on the Edge of a Cliff

Cahil.

Walking down a mountain path toward the village of Cahil, we came across a gaunt man sitting under a tree twirling a stick. We walked up to him and started chatting—a very natural thing in

131

Yemen, to walk up to a total stranger and strike up a conversation. Turns out Abu Bashir had recently been discharged from military duty because of an injury he sustained during the Sa'dah war. He had broken a thigh bone while running away from gunfire and the surgeon in Sanaa had done a bad job fixing it. He couldn't walk without pain. His tale highlighted not only the bad conditions and neglect in a large public hospital in Yemen, but also the lack of commitment of the government to its veteran soldiers once they got injured and faced perhaps a lifetime of disability.

Abu Bashir enjoyed the conversation and promptly invited us to tea with his family. I was surprised to see his wife and four daughters join us in the one main room in their modest house, all unveiled and all not at all shy to jump into the conversation. Yemeni women and girls in the countryside worked in the field, fetched water from distant wells and tended cattle—not functions one could easily perform wearing the black robes and veils typically worn by women in the city.

Cahil consisted of 30 or 40 homes, generally three or four stories high, arranged by order of first arrival building right at the tip of the rock jutting out at the edge of the mountain, with other residents building right under the first in order of arrival. Abu Bashir was probably one of the poorest in the village, his home consisting of only one floor, a room to the left as you walked in the corridor was dedicated to the family's lone cow, the second to the right was a large living room with matts covering the dirt floor and cushions all around doubling as a sitting room during the day and a family bedroom at night. The corridor ended in a kitchen with a wood-burning stove and stairs that went up a small bedroom and a roof.

Life in Cahil consisted of small-scale agriculture, a few cows to tend and perhaps a few goats. Some of the men would go down to the nearby city (Manakha) and drive taxicabs they did not own and receive a day's wages for the days they drove. Schooling, if at all, consisted of up to 6 years of primary education and involved walking 3 or 4 miles to the nearest school.

Our hikes took us to the mountains around San'aa and to the south, driving on the road that spirals down all the way to the Tihama valley to walk there, or, depending on which road you take, to Taiz and Hodeida. Once, while resting from a walk in the heat in Tihama, we spotted a woman walking by with a big bushel of twigs and tree branches; 10 feet behind her, a young man was walking leisurely twirling a stick in his hand. I walked up to him and struck up a conversation in Arabic, introducing myself simply by my name, leaving out my affiliation. After a few generalities, I asked if the woman walking ahead was his wife, and upon his answering in the affirmative, I said, "Why aren't you helping her, it looks like she's carrying a heavy load on her head?" The man looked at me for a few seconds before replying with a question of his own, "You're not from around here are you?"

Whiskey and Guns

Driving south with a group of British friends on our way to spending the weekend in Cahil, Adam, driving the car ahead of us, pulls into an unpaved parking lot in front of a small two floor building with a hand-written sign on the wall that said, "Youth sporting club."

Saying we needed to pick up some supplies for the weekend, Adam pushes open the door and we walk into a large unpaved room filled wall to wall with hundreds of bottles of alcohol. The first question, after Ahlan Wa Sahlan, was "are you looking for brown or white?" The owner was referring to choices of Whiskey and beer, or Gin and Vodka. Beer from all over the world was an impressive sight.

The owner then motions to me to follow him upstairs and there, arranged in no particular order, was a large collection of all types of guns, from pistols to machine guns and RPGs. "Take your time, look around and, if you don't see it here just ask, I can get it for you!!"

Smuggling is an old tradition and source of livelihood in Yemen: Generally, Qat, grown in abundance in Yemen, crosses the borders in the north into Saudi Arabia while booze and electronics, available at relatively cheap prices in Saudi, cross the borders into Yemen. Consumables, however, are not the only goods smuggled in and out of the country. Weapons of all types and all origins make their way into Yemen on a regular basis. One statistic we enjoyed musing about at the embassy was that there were on average three guns for every Yemeni man, woman, and child—and this is excluding heavy weapons and rifle-propelled grenades.

In August 2004, **Lincoln Bloomfield**, Assistant Secretary for military Affairs, visited Yemen on a not-so-secret mission to buy-back MANPADS, shoulder-fired missiles that could destroy a tank or bring down an aircraft. These missiles, particularly a variety known as Strela II, had found their way from governments to private hands in the wake of the Afghan war and the fear was that in the wrong hands, they could be used in acts of terrorism against civilian aviation. A/S Bloomfield was authorized to pay $10,000 for each still-functional missile. Then president Saleh, eager to cash in on the opportunity (the market price of each was roughly $2000), and get credit for cooperating with a U.S. counterterrorism project, was happy to receive, and to negotiate with Bloomfield. Saleh listened as Bloomfield explained the danger of these missiles in the wrong hands, likely spread after being used against the Soviets in Afghanistan, and now accessible to al-Qa'eda and other terrorists. Saleh indicated his willingness to cooperate adding, "in anticipation of your visit, we have already purchased of hundreds of these missiles back from the tribes in Yemen, but I want 1 million dollars for each!" Saleh explained that he had to negotiate with the tribes that had them and paid a heavy price politically in addition to the money he had to lay out.

Taken aback, Bloomfield said "I'm afraid the U.S. government has set a fixed price to buy these back and the price is not negotiable." Saleh laughed and said, "OK, OK, have your people take a look at them, we have them in a warehouse just out of town, we can negotiate something later!"

Over dinner with Saleh's nephews, Amar Saleh reiterated the one million-dollar request and I told him that was just not possible and that we were willing to leave the missiles behind if they insisted. I then personally went with our Acting Defense Attache, David Alley, to the warehouse the next day to look over the hundreds of shoulder-fired missiles stored there. We were particularly worried about the Strelas and David and an assistant gathered them in one corner and proceeded to bust the headlights on them, apparently rendering them useless without a guidance mechanism. Many of the weapons assembled were RPGs, which were not considered as dangerous because they had limited range and no guidance system. In the final meeting between Blooomfield and Saleh, a price was worked out, the deal sealed, and the only thing extra that Saleh got was a promise by Bloomfield to look into providing the spare parts Saleh wanted for old F-5 U.S. jets, leftover from the Vietnam era and no longer flight-worthy.

Arms Merchants and the State

Wondering how these missiles found their way to Yemen in the first place, and whether or not they had really been in the hands of various tribes or that the government had had them all along, I went about inquiring from those in the know. Unique about Yemen is the fact that Yemenis speak their minds and criticize their leaders unabashedly. Unlike others in the region, even officials will answer a question directly without bothering with official talking points. A member of Saleh's own government and an opposition member of parliament separately told me the story: there were eight or ten prominent arms merchant families in Yemen. Those most connected to the State had a deal with the government (read with president Saleh and his ministry of defense): The ministry would give them a certificate authorizing them to buy weapons, mostly from eastern Europe as it turned out, but they could use it anywhere that would accept it; they would then buy weapons by the shipload, ostensibly for the Yemeni armed forces, and pay for it with their own money. Upon arrival in Yemen, roughly 25 percent of the load would be given to the president, to the ministry of defense, or the ministry of interior, as the case may be, and the rest of the weapons would be theirs to sell on the black market—mostly inside Yemen or to customers overseas—say in east Africa. When I mentioned this to our DA and CIA folks, they were fascinated as they had had no clue about these transactions.

Once sure of the story, I went to president Saleh and explained to him what I had found out—without revealing my sources of course. "It's a pretty good game where everybody goes home happy, and I understand why historically things were done this way, but it's a dangerous game now with al-Qa'eda in the picture and in the market for these weapons." "Well, yes" Saleh retorted, "we do depend on these arms merchants, what do you expect me to do?" I said, "you should get rid of the middle man. Your MOD officials should be buying the weapons directly and using their own budget. We don't mind your army receiving the weapons they need and we do have a program to help you buy weapons officially but we cannot overlook this deal that leaves large caches of weapons out on the market for anyone to buy."

Incredulously, Saleh called out to one of his assistants and dictated a memo on the spot to the MOI and MOD: "Henceforth you shall buy the weapons you need directly from the countries that sell them to us, you will no longer rely on arms merchants to be the middle men for these transactions."

Knowing that Saleh was not beyond fooling his foreign visitors with a fake memo, I gave the matter a week and then arranged visits to both MOI and MOD. Indeed, they both produced the memo they had received and said they'd already issued instructions to their staff to start buying their weapons directly from the source.

Here's where Saleh's wile never stops working. Although MOD and MOI did indeed switch to buying their own weapons, we found out a few months later, it was all a switch and bate technique. The GOY was indeed doing the buying, but it was doing so with arms merchants' funds and then sharing the arms on the basis of the same 25/75 split. The GOY had switched from using arms merchants as middle-men to becoming itself the middle-man for the arms merchants!

Corruption

Corruption is endemic in Yemen, and always has been. From small bribes to large, everyone takes it for granted that they have to grease someone's palm before they can get anything done. This is not unlike other countries in the region. Certainly, in Lebanon, this is almost always the case or, as the French ambassador to Yemen told a group of us once over dinner, "Why do you Americans harp on corruption and bribery here, look north of the border and see the levels of corruption there." We were discussing, along with other European diplomats, the means of fighting corruption in Yemen. My retort to our French colleague was, "The Saudi officials certainly abuse public funds for private use, but unlike Yemen, they're rich and no matter how much they steal enough remains for building their infrastructure, providing public services and developing their economy. In Yemen, when the elite steal there's hardly anything left for the poor."

U.S. assistance programs of course included advice and help in implementing anti-corruption drives, provided of course the local government was willing to engage in such efforts, and in Yemen, we had received approval to suggest ideas. We did indeed initiate in partnership with the ministry of planning a public information campaign against corruption. This mostly involved brochures and billboards warning of the evils of corruption and the rights of citizens to demand services without bribery. We also offered public accountability remedies through transparency, but these campaigns were of limited value. The hidden corruption was in the large contracts for public projects such as roads, port upgrades, and infrastructure. Large corporations, foreign and domestic, offered bribes to ministers and sometimes directly to the president in order to win publicly announced bids. There was no way to stop such abuse of public funds unless there was approval from the top to monitor and stop under the table deals.

With ambassador Krajeski's approval, I devised a plan to address the issue through the introduction of foreign observers to the board of investment—a body that oversaw the bidding for large projects and granted contracts, especially to foreign companies. The idea was to allow international experts from the World Bank or other international financial institutions, to sit on the board and observe how large contracts are bid and accepted and recommend ways of streamlining the process to protect it from graft. I also recommended that we get our European allies and friends to join us in lobbying the president to adopt the plan. The French ambassador of course begged out, "Fine idea, Leave me out of it!" The British, German and Dutch ambassadors agreed to go along, and after a couple of meetings to hammer out the details of the proposal, we agreed to proceed and asked for an appointment to see president Saleh.

It was decided that the British ambassador, Michael Gifford, would read/present the demarche—a tactical error perhaps since Saleh would normally take advice better coming from the United States. The British, German, Dutch, and U.S. ambassadors gathered in the gazebo in the presidential palace gardens, which is where Saleh chose to meet us. "Khair" said Saleh as he walked in (Meaning what brings you all here)? Mike, not one to extemporize, took out the paper we had all agreed on and bravely ploughed through the introductory paragraph—which suggested the addition of an international observer to Yemen's board of foreign investments. Before he could go on to the reasons for our suggestion, Saleh frowned and said, "Stop, stop, what is it with you British, do you think you still rule this country?!!" He then abruptly stood up and walked out of the gazebo thus ending the meeting. The interpreter, Muhammad Sudam, grew pale and looked to me for an explanation, saying "Nabeel, did I make a mistake in interpreting what was being said?" I replied in the negative, telling him it wasn't his fault. Around the room, jaws dropped and Mike Gifford in particular looked crestfallen. The group was at a loss as to what to do in a situation like that.

Tom, in favor of taking a tougher line with Saleh's theatrics, said, "Well if he's not coming back we might as well leave." Feeling responsible since I had initiated this whole idea of ganging up on Saleh, I suggested that we needed to fix things and should not leave on this sour note. I noticed Saleh at the other end of the garden apparently briefing a group of his staff on what had transpired, so I walked up and listened to his explanations. I shook my head in disagreement. Noticing that, Saleh said, "Nabeel doesn't agree apparently." He then came out of the crowd around him put his arm on my shoulder and said, let's walk. I explained to him that I thought he was unfair to the British ambassador, "he was speaking for all of us." I said, "Look, you have a problem with corruption and it affects your dealings world-side; you did tell us you would accept our help in fighting it, so here we are offering to help." "The idea of international observers," I continued, "was to suggest reform steps, observe them being implemented and then tell the world that Yemen's economy was on the right path." It's just like the Palestinian elections (2006), I added, we didn't like the result but had to admit the election was free and fair because the Carter commission was there observing and reporting on it.

139

Saleh looked at me wide-eyed and said, "Why didn't he (Gifford) explain it that way?" I said, "Because you didn't give him a chance!" He then turned around and called out to Mike Gifford and said, "give me that paper you were reading from, Nabeel explained it to me and it's fine!"

In leaving the presidential palace, Mike said, "Nabeel, thank you for intervening, I was beginning to consider how I would tell my wife we were going to be leaving Yemen sooner than expected!"

But Saleh was like that, impulsive, quick tempered (not to mention theatrical), but also quick to laugh, make up, and allow himself to be convinced (if only temporarily). Procrastination on his part and lack of follow-up on ours meant that the placing of international experts on Yemen's board of investors never happened.

Terrorism and Security Cooperation

Ever since the bombing of the USS Cole in October 2000, president Saleh had allowed the FBI and the CIA to assist in identifying and tracking those who planned and executed the attack. Perhaps the first fruit of this collaboration was the killing of Abu ali al-Harithi, the planner of the attack on the USS Cole, by a drone strike in 2002. It was the first such strike in Yemen and a precursor to numerous strikes that followed toward the end of the decade, as al-Qa'eda in the Arabian Peninsula (AQAP) grew in presence and strength in Yemen. This cooperation, undertaken with the Central Security Force (CSF), quickly turned into counterterrorism collaboration via the creation and training of a counterterrorism unit (CTU) within the ministry of interior's CSF. Brits and Americans collaborated in equipping and training this force, led by president Saleh's nephew Yahya. Though small, this unit became the country's elite force, accepted and used our gift of a computerized inventory system and allowed surprise inspections (to make sure the gifted weapons were in their warehouse and not being sold out on the black market). The CTU also established the country's first all-female unit and I had the pleasure of officiating at their first graduation ceremony.

We much preferred funding and training the CTU to Yemen's regular military because it functioned largely as it was supposed to and lived up to the professional standards we had hoped for it. My one regret was that it played a role in the Sa'dah war and was sent during the first year of that war into the mountains to conduct a series of raids that ended up with the killing of Hussein al-Houthi, the older brother of the current Houthi leader Abdelmalek, among others in leadership circles. A senior officer from the MOI, generally known as one of the more cultured of our interlocutors, took pride one evening in pulling me aside at a diplomatic reception to show me the gruesome pictures from the raid on a Houthi hideout and the victims' corpses it left behind. I was disgusted and told him in no uncertain terms it was a revolting thing in which to take pride and that the attack looked more like a war crime to me!

My disappointment was twofold: that a unit we funded, trained, and trusted it would be used against terrorists infiltrating the country had in fact been used in an internal conflict that could and should have been settled diplomatically. In Sa'dah, the CTU was not fighting a terrorist organization committing acts of violence against random civilian institutions; it was rather fighting a tribal and political movement that had not at that point taken any ac-tion against the state. Second, that this unit, or indeed any unit of Yemen's military, had behaved in a barbaric fashion toward individual fighters resisting their advance on their region was likely in violation of congressional mandate that the use of U.S. equipment be subject to scrutiny regarding possible violations of the laws of war.

The Great Escape

In February 2006, 23 al-Qa'eda members incarcerated at Sanaa's central prison, also known as their maximum security facility, escaped by tunneling under the prison to a nearby mosque. This naturally raised alarms in Washington, all the more that several prisoners associated with the bombing of the USS Cole were among them. The ambassador, station chief, and myself went to see the president. PSO chief General al-Gamash (known to westerners as Gamish) was there with downcast eyes; the expression on his face was somewhere between shame and fear. He explained to us what happened. We told Saleh that we obviously had to see this for ourselves; otherwise, Washington might not believe it was a genuine escape. He gave orders right away for our visit to be arranged. Station chief and I went there right after the meeting so as not to give time for anyone to change the scene.

Even to my untrained eye, this prison did not look like a maximum security facility. Surrounded by residences without sufficient setback from nearby roads and two sleepy soldiers guarding the entrance: Alcatraz it was not! We were ushered to the special section from which the 23 escapees tunneled out. Much like a separate suite in a hotel, the section had several adjoined rooms and a bathroom set off from the rest of the prison by a door which, while unlocked, did block off vision of guards milling about outside what in essence was the AQ suite. We asked why the 23 AQ detainees were put together and were told they had asked to be near their companions (brothers in arms)!

In one of the inner rooms, adjoining a bathroom, a manhole in the middle of the small room was surrounded by soil and pebbles that had been dug out of the ground beneath the prison. We took photos of the hole (I actually posed for one of them) and then took a peek inside the tunnel. It was indeed makeshift but functional, and lit by a couple of single light bulbs with a wire extended from the prison cell. The walls were not buttressed except perhaps toward the middle but the mud and gravel walls were well patted down so as not to crumble. The tunnel extended about 40 yards and connected to the women's bathroom in the mosque next to the prison. The prisoners had used spoons, plates, and pieces of wood to dig out the dirt piled around the walls of the cell. General Ghaleb (el Gamash), head of the PSO, looked genuinely distraught when we visited him in his office. He was shaken, almost in tears. He said he couldn't believe that after a long and distinguished career in the service of his country that he had allowed something like that to happen. It was likely a mix of shame and fear of what Saleh might do to him, or what we might ask Saleh to do.

My colleague and I conferred when we got back to the embassy and decided it was a credible enough escape, given the shabby conditions at the prison and the lackadaisical way in which the guards seemed to go about their duties. Our report back to Washington was partly to indicate our assessment that it was a credible escape and not, as some in Washington suspected, a state facilitated release made to look like an escape. The deputy director of the prison and one of his assistants were eventually charged with criminal negligence, demoted, and imprisoned. Gamish, after being taken to the woodshed and indeed left "wondering in the woods" for a few months, returned unharmed to his duties. The escaped prisoners were hunted down and some were killed, while others were captured and returned to jail.

Jamal Ahmed Mohammed el Badawi, likely the most prominent of the escapees, was recaptured in Aden in October 2007—actually an agreement with his tribe had him give himself up, only to then be released again as part of an agreement with his tribe that he never again be engaged in terrorism. Washington was furious but the MOI explained that an agreement with Badawi's father and the tribe was an ironclad guarantee, and the plea from a tribal sheikh was not one the government could easily ignore.

FBI special agent **Ali Soufan** was the last USG official to visit the prison before the break-out and had reported on Badawi and his other AQ comrades in 2004. He was the lead FBI investigator on the attack on the USS Cole in 2000 and had been to Yemen several times before when Barbara Bodine was the U.S. ambassador to Yemen. I met him in 2004, when I was the Charge at the U.S. embassy and he was back to continue interrogating AQ convicts in Sanaa's central prison. A fellow Lebanese-American, Ali and I had much in common: birthplace for one, Tripoli, Lebanon, a pride in our heritage, to include a fondness for the Arabic language, and pride in having made the United States our home and decided to work for the U.S. government. The written and oral briefings I received from Ali on AQ convicts in Sanaa Central were the best I had ever seen or heard. He had a very straightforward style and his reports reflected an excellent understanding of the big picture, a family tree so to speak, of al-Qa'eda affiliated operatives and their modus operandi. His verbal briefs were devoid of bluster or political posturing—Only the facts!

He described conditions of the convicts, their state of mind, the stories they told about their families, all of which appealed to the human being behind the terrorist profile. Ali's approach to interrogations was far from a stiff formal one. He tried and succeeded in establishing rapport with those he interviewed, even brought them pizza and therefore shared bread with them, putting them at ease and succeeding in getting them to reveal linkages and admit to roles in terrorist attacks. His easy yet professional manner succeeded both in prison and at the embassy. His early retirement from the FBI has allowed him time to reflect on his experience on the U.S. national security's hottest issues and to write two excellent books, Black Banners and Anatomy of Terror. His TSC Intel Brief (The Soufan Center Intelligence Brief) is now a must-go-to source on social media for a quick and reliable recap of conflicts around the globe, with a succinct analysis in particular of Middle East security issues.

Why Is Nabeel Acting Like a General?

In 2005, we saw the seeds of al-Qa'eda in the Arabian Peninsula (AQAP) in the merger between al-Qa'eda returnees from Iraq and the earlier returnees from Afghanistan—something that would eventually become the strongest branch, and still the most vibrant AQ satellite organization. I was the Charge (CDA) at the time, with ambassador Krajeski on a trip to Dubai. The station chief asked for an urgent meeting and brought over intercepted correspondence between an Iraq returnee and al-Qa'eda in Iraq (AQI) leadership in Baghdad. The returnee was apparently sent back to Yemen with a mission to start an AQ chapter there, with the proviso to take his time and focus on ground work to build the infrastructure needed for the long term. At some point, however, the gentleman in question got restless, especially when a shipment of C4 explosive material arrived along with instructions on how to use it. A message from him telling his Iraqi handlers that he felt ready for an "operation" against the Americans reached us at the Embassy and after convening the security committee and reviewing the information we decided it was credible enough that we had to take action.

The security committee included besides myself, intel reps (CIA, DIA and NSA), The RSO (regional security officer), and POL (Political Counselor), and our Legal Attache (FBI). We judged the Embassy to be the most likely target and decided to offer embassy officers and their families voluntary departure—only two family members decided to take this option. All embassy staff decided to stay. Secondly, we decided to share the information with Yemen's intel folks (PSO and NSB) so they could try to track down this threat. In this regard, we also asked Langley to send a team of experts at tracking down such persons. I called the Ambassador right away to let him know what was going on and to let him know that he would be stuck in Dubai for the duration once we implemented an authorized departure plan. He agreed that I should take any measures I deemed necessary to protect the embassy and not to worry about him.

Our defense attache and my friend, David Alley, stopped by my office on the second day of this discovery to let me know that a team special forces (12) had arrived in Sanaa to train the CTU but found that the CTU had deployed to the north to help in the fight against the Houthis. "They're staying at the Hilton across the road with absolutely nothing to do until a special plane comes to take them back to Djibouti." David and I decided that it made sense to invite them over to the embassy to help defend it in the case of an attack. I asked David to check first with their commander in Djibouti and ask if that would be alright with him. David came back a few hours later to say the commander said, "Absolutely!"

We invited the troops to move into the Ambassadors residence, putting them up in a large living room (a Diwan or Mafraj—a room in most Yemeni homes with a lot of ventilation and natural sunlight) equipped with large cushions along the walls—thus doubling as sitting room and sleeping quarters. The room also had easy access to the roof where the force could deploy with a view of all sides of embassy walls. We then sent a message to Washington to inform them of the measures taken. Typical of Washington bureaucracy, the first thing I heard back was not concern for our safety but rather surprise at why I was taking measures that appeared military in nature .... In addition to a confused and confusing cable from Washington, I received a phone call from my colleague Alan Misenheimer, who was Acting Deputy Assistant Secretary at the time. It went like this:

- Allan: Nabeel, you have raised a lot of eyebrows here, at State and at the NSC. Folks are saying why is Nabeel acting like a General, deploying military personnel on the roof, etc, can you see the optics of this?

- Me: Sure Allan, I can see the optics but can you see the reverse, in case we waited for Washington to react and we were attacked in the interim? I'd like to see how those folks whose eyebrows were raised would explain to Congress why they didn't do anything in time and didn't allow us to defend ourselves when we had the means ....

146

- I added that there was nothing in concrete, we had merely invited the special force, with permission from their commander to stay on embassy grounds instead of sunning themselves at the swimming pool at the Hilton. "Of course, if you'd like to order us to reverse this step it can be easily done," I added.

- Alan promised to convey my message to the NSC and get back to me.

- In the meantime, I understood that someone from the NSC had contacted ambassador Krajeski in Dubai who, bless his soul, told them in no uncertain terms that he had left me in charge of the embassy and was completely supportive of any measures I chose to take towards its protection.

Needless to say, that got Washington off our backs. As it turned out, we were lucky. Yemeni security had the would-be perpetrator caught within a week, obviating the need for a CIA team to come and help catch him. Yes, it was taking longer than a week for help to arrive! I couldn't help but reflect on that experience a few years later, when our colleague Chris Stevens was killed in an attack on the U.S. consulate in Benghazi on September 11, 2012. To the best of our information, a CIA compound was 10 minutes away from the facility and could possibly have reacted to defend the consulate had they been requested to do so directly by embassy staff rather than wait for orders from Washington to arrive, or perhaps to wait for help from the navy offshore or from the U.S. mainland. Although in the end they proved unnecessary, the measures we took in Yemen were exactly the right ones. The first duty of an ambassador or CDA is the safety of their people—I'm still convinced today that in such emergencies, instructions from Washington bureaucracy come second, after any measures that can reasonably be implemented locally.

AQAP was launched in January 2009 from a merger of al-Qaeda's Yemeni and Saudi branches, as AQ central had weakened from the pressure exerted on them worldwide, branches or franchises had sprung up in Iraq, Yemen, and north-Africa, and AQAP was very quickly identified as the most capable of inflicting damage both inside and outside Yemen. Secretary Clinton classified AQAP as a terrorist organization in December 2009, by then it had made two attempts against the embassy, well after Tom and I had left Yemen.

Friends and Memorable Moments

Tom Krajeski was both my friend and ambassador in Yemen. His experience in the region and his knowledge of the Washington bureaucracy, not to mention his infinite patience with me, often saved the day and allowed us all at the embassy to sail through 3 years in Yemen unscathed. Upon his arrival in Sanaa, he invited me to brief him on the roughly two months during which I was in charge of the embassy in between Edmund Hull's departure and his arrival. As we sipped gin-tonics on the porch of the ambassador's residence, he told me to expect, as Deputy Chief of Mission, to be his full partner in running the embassy. "We will in fact be co-ambassadors, and short of Washington ordering me directly not to share something with you, you will know what I know," adding that he couldn't have been happier when he was informed that I had accepted the position of DCM.

True to his word, Tom and I began our days by receiving the daily intelligence brief together, we would then agree on a strategy for the day based on the intel brief and any instructions from Washington—and decide which meetings we would do together and which we could split up between us. Since we were both spouseless, at least during our first year in Sanaa, we also spent a fair amount of our free time playing Tennis or organizing dinners for friends and contacts. Tom quipped with a frown one day, as we got in the official car to drive to the presidential palace, "This is beginning to look like marriage you know!"

At one of our meetings with Saleh, the president brought out a dozen jars of Yemen's famous Dou'ani honey—a delicious thick honey from the Hadramawt region, drawn from palm-fed bees. He quipped to Tom as the latter was thanking him that it would strengthen his knees. Looking offended, Tom asked "What's wrong with my knees?" Saleh and I both laughed as I explained to Tom the Yemeni idiom, "He means it would enhance your sexual appetite." "Oh no, that won't do," Tom retorted, "my wife is not here you know!"

Saleh's cabinet was an interesting collection of ministers, deputy ministers, and bureaucrats—among them, the good, the bad, and the ugly. Saleh's foreign minister, **Dr. Abu-Bakr al-Qirbi**, stood out as a gentleman, a professional, and someone with whom we could always have a frank conversation. Extremely loyal to his president, Dr. Q—as I enjoyed calling him, would never openly voice disagreement with official policy but would indicate to us what comes directly from the top and whether or not there was any flexibility there. I recall him on one occasion confirming what I had strongly suspected, that Saleh would be totally dismissive of an instruction we received from Washington to suggest that he not meet with president Assad of Syria. Bashar al-Assad was coming to visit Saleh in 2006 and Washington, being weary of Assad for allowing foreign fighters to come through Syria on their way to fighting American soldiers in Iraq, wanted to put some screws to pressure the Syrian president. Ambassador Krajeski insisted we deliver the message as requested, even though it had come from a relatively low level at the State Department. I went along and we met with Saleh at the "Ma'asheeq" presidential residence in Aden. Saleh looked at us and chuckled in surprise when Tom presented the request. "It's really strange with you Americans," he said, "How can you expect me to refuse a visit from another Arab head of state when I have no problem with him?" Saleh did offer to relay any messages we might have to express our disappointment, etc, but he asserted he would definitely meet with his Syrian counterpart.

Qirbi's deputy, **Mustapha Noman**, was another story altogether. I still recall, after a first formal meeting where I handed him a demarche, sent through formal channels from Washington. The written message concerned the release of Yemeni Guantanamo detainees on whom the United States had no direct evidence necessitating their further incarceration. Among other conditions relating to the need to try them in Yemen and keep them under watch if released, was a curious stipulation that they be treated in accordance with international human rights standards. Mustapha scanned the paper quickly and on reaching that line looked at me with obvious irony and said impishly, "we promise to treat them no worse that you've been doing at Gitmo ..." We looked at each other briefly and both burst out laughing. We've been friends since that day.

Mustapha, despite his official position in government, always displayed a typical Yemeni irreverence toward authority. He reciprocated my skepticism toward some of our own policies by winking at me whenever he had to deliver an official line and followed with a frank assessment of what he thought was behind it. I learnt much from him on corruption and abuse of power in Yemen and I consulted with him when trying to suggest a policy to Washington on arms smuggling in particular.

Amat al-Alim al-soswa, Yemen's minister of human rights at the time, was so sincere in discussing prison conditions and the difficulties of championing human rights in her country that she established her credentials with us right away as someone who genuinely cared about positive change in Yemen. We immediately hit it off and Tom and I saw her often, both officially and at small dinners where we could talk and get to know one another. We briefly met her daughter, Sama'a, at her house one evening. Sama'a was a precautious high school student then, before leaving to study for a B.A. in the United States and become an excellent analyst of Yemeni events in her own right. Amat and Sama'a are in Washington these days and are both among my closest friends.

I recall Amat sitting between me and president Saleh one day at a meeting with a visiting U.S. Assistant Secretary of State for cultural affairs. After the Secretary's opening comments, Saleh jumped in with a loud and startling request, "I want you to give me twenty thousand visas for my people." An awkward pause understandably followed during which nobody knew exactly how to react to such a strange opening line from Saleh. Knowing him and his fondness for surprising and putting visitors on the defensive, I jumped into the breach in order to break the frostiness his remark had left. "Why Mr. president, do you intend to get rid of your opposition by sending them all to us?" Saleh looked at me startled for a brief moment then broke up laughing and said, "You are a Middle Easterner, you're dangerous!" Amat just smiled and nodded her agreement, saying, "he is, he is."

Mohamed al-Tayeb, another friendship gained while in Yemen, was with a member of parliament and a prominent member of the GPC, 2004–2011, and one of the main interlocutors with the western diplomatic community during my years in Yemen. Mohamed had Saleh's ear, on and off, or as often as Saleh would allow any member of his party to get close to him. Tom and I had many a dinner at Mohamed's house and he in turn was a frequent visitor to our homes. It was always easy to talk frankly with Mohamed who, while not expressing any opposition to his boss, was not averse to giving us some behind-the-scene information and advice, and always at his home to the background sound of several song-birds that he and his wife kept in their living room.

In particular, Mohamed let us in on the darker side of Saleh and why many around him, including his own family members, were intimidated and could not speak their minds in front of him. Although Saleh could not in any way be compared to dictators like Saddam Hussein of Iraq or Hafez and Bashar al-Assad of Syria, he nevertheless was capable of violently lashing out against those who opposed or connived against him. Consequently, Saleh lashed out verbally against those closest to him, and sometimes physically assaulted/slapped family members and ministers. During his rise to power in earlier years, people opposing him were known to have disappeared. During one meeting with Saleh I brought up the case of a journalist we knew who had reportedly been abducted by security forces. I told Saleh that acts of violence or intimidation against journalists would not go unnoticed and would earn him strong rebuke from western powers and international human rights organizations. "Oh no," said Saleh with a smile, "you don't have to worry, we don't overdo these things here, the guy might just be slapped around a bit and let go, just to teach him some manners!" Indeed, the journalist in question (a young man by the name of Khaiwani) was released two days after our intervention on his behalf.

In a similar vein, **Robin Madrid**, a dear friend and at the time director of the local office of the National Democratic Institute, was alarmed one day by an unflattering mention she received in a local rag. Indeed, I saw cause for alarm when I read the piece because yellow journalism served a political purpose in Yemen— that of sending coded messages and intimidating people. The rag in question was reputedly owned by pro-Saleh thugs and, in the case of the journalist Khaiwani, had written threateningly about him before he was picked up by the police. I called MOI Allimi right away and expressed alarm that someone might be intending to harm Robin. The next day, Saleh called me on the phone and said, "what's this I hear about someone threatening you?" He had got the message garbled, likely due to hearing it while at a Qat chew. When I explained that my concern was over Robin Madrid and not myself he invited me and the ambassador to drop by to discuss it. Tom suggested that I speak to Saleh directly in Arabic to make sure message and tone were conveyed clearly. I told Saleh that despite his disavowal of the paper in question (his first reaction had been to say that it was a Shi'i rag that often criticized him as well), people on the street assumed any messages there came directly from him and that some of his less couth supporters might take it upon themselves to harm Robin. "We want you to know," I said firmly and clearly, "that if any harm comes to Robin you will be held directly responsible by Washington."

Saleh said that he understood and that we were not to worry. A week later, Robin Madrid was invited by the palace for a meeting with Saleh and a photo appeared in the official press showing the two of them smiling at each other as she sat facing Saleh in the armchair usually used by official visitors. Message was thus delivered to any thugs that might have interpreted the negative article against her as license to harm.

CHAPTER 8

THE TROUBLE WITH WASHINGTON

Yemen has mostly occupied negative space in Washington's thinking. In 1990, during the occupation of Kuwait, Saleh took a stand in support of Saddam Hussein, hence breaking the international economic boycott against him. U.S. secretary of state, James Baker, promised that the pro-Saddam vote at the UN by Yemen would be "the most costly vote they ever cast." Indeed, aid to Yemen was cut, along with a downgrading of diplomatic relations. Saudi Arabia followed suit and evicted close to a million Yemeni workers who had been living and working in Saudi Arabia for years, causing a cut-off of their remittances to their families back home. Aid to Yemen was resumed as were full diplomatic relations in 1994 after Yemen's brief civil war. Saudi Arabia aided the secessionists in that war, but the United States took no action against Yemen's unity. Saleh cooperated fully in 2000 after the al-Qa'eda attack on the USS Cole leading to a large number of FBI agents and CIA analysts and security officials descending on Yemen.

Although security collaboration improved in leaps and bounds after that, U.S. economic aid to Yemen remained limited. Washington's attention was focused almost exclusively on the security aspects of the relationship. As a general rule, when a terrorist action takes place against an American target, Washington is all ears but when an embassy sends in a report suggesting we take the long view and deal with the underlying causes of terrorism, the yawn from stateside is almost audible. Ironically, it's the military officers who pay the most attention. When General John Abizaid, head of U.S. Army Central Command, 2003–2007, came to visit Yemen in November 2005, I took him to meet president Saleh. While we were waiting to be ushered in, Abizaid asked me, "What's going on in this conflict with the Houthis in the north, is this something we should be involved in?" I said, "this is not international terrorism and there's nothing there that can be seen as a direct threat against the U.S.," adding, "however, we should be helping Yemen economically and politically. Regional disgruntlement exists all over Yemen because of poverty and slow development. If the rebellion in the north succeeds other areas of Yemen, notably the south, will want to rebel and secede—if Yemen falls apart it would become worse than Afghanistan, and then you will have to intervene."

General Abizaid understood and brought back that message to Washington the next time he testified on the Hill. Getting Yemen to qualify for a Millennium Challenge Corporation (MCC) threshold grant, for example, was something that took hard work to accomplish. The MCC was established in 2004 by the Bush administration in order to both increase international aid while pegging it to progress in accomplishing reforms. The idea was to prepare a reform agenda and, once vetted by Washington, receive an initial grant to implement the reforms. Once implemented, the country would then qualify for a much larger grant to push a broader development agenda. In 2006, we worked for months with the ministry of international cooperation on developing a plan to fight corruption. The plan was approved in 2007 and $20 million were pegged to support it. Washington's knee-jerk reaction to the release of Jamal al-Badawi (one of the prison escapees who had given himself up in Aden) that same year was to cancel the MCC grant. It was a classic case of cutting off your nose to spite your face. The grant to fight corruption was as much in the U.S. interest as it was in Yemen's. The premature release of prisoners, and indeed sometimes their assisted escape, are often related to corruption or at least to a weak commitment to law and order. In helping Yemen overcome its corruption problem, we were in fact helping to lay the ground for the gradual strengthening of judicial institutions and the elimination of the smuggling of arms into and out of Yemen. The cancellation of the MCC grant was to say the least a short-sighted policy only narrowly and misguidedly focused on the problem of terrorism.

A perennial Washington problem is bureaucratic competitiveness—members of the NSC, for example, trying to conduct foreign policy on their own without consultation with State Department area experts. Yes, this problem did not start with Donald Trump, although he and his family have taken it to new lows. Both the Bush and Obama presidencies have also been guilty of this. One example on our watch in Sanaa involved then president Bush's assistant for counterterrorism and head of DHS from 2004 to 2007, Frances Townsend. The story concerns Abdulmajid al-Zindani, Islamist cleric, member of the Islah opposition party and head of al-Iman university, an ultra conservative school focused mostly on Islamic studies and to a lesser extent on the social sciences. Zindani was considered by the United States an al-Qaeda leader or affiliate, and in 2004, he was named a "Specially Designated Global Terrorist." He was reportedly once a spiritual advisor to Osama Bin Laden, though their relationship is not well documented. As the founder and leader of Al Imam University, he was in a position to influence the minds of the young in a salafi-jihadi direction. To our knowledge at the embassy, there was never an order for his arrest nor a request to the Yemeni government to arrest him. For us, he was simply one of many political actors, albeit not a savory one. Saleh called one day and asked us to meet him at the ministry of defense. Tom and I went to the meeting assuming another pitch for military assistance was on his mind.

Saleh wanted to discuss Zindani and to know why he was on the terrorist list and, more pointedly, why we wanted him arrested. "I have nothing against the man myself," began Saleh, "he heads a university, he is often in the public eye here and to our knowledge neither calls for nor practices violence." Saying that to our knowledge, there is no warrant for his arrest, despite his designation, Tom and I said that the embassy had not received any instructions on this. Saleh then took us to a different room, turned

157

on a tape recorder, and said, "listen to this": what followed was a phone conversation between him and Frances Townsend—a conversation we had not been notified about and received no advice on before or after it took place. We looked at each other, it was FT's voice alright and she clearly said, in answer to a rhetorical question from Saleh, that yes Washington expected Saleh to have Zindani arrested,

An awkward moment followed, broken by Saleh who took Tom and I by the hand saying, "Come, I want you to meet someone." Sitting in another part of the suite of offices was none other than Abdulmajid al-Zindani, looking regal in his flowing robes, red beard, turban, and a big smile on his face. Startled, Tom and I looked at each other wondering how to react. Finally, I whispered, "let's talk to the man, we're here, it's too late to back out!"

Zindani hardly projected the image or presence of a designated global terrorist. By reputation, he had espoused some cookie ideas like his claim to have discovered a cure for AIDS. He was also known to have made some ultra conservative pronouncements on women. Otherwise, his political statements were few and far in-between and tended to be in line with secular Arab nationalist rhetoric against Israel, colonialism, U.S. intervention in the affairs of Arab countries and such. He stood and came beaming toward us and shook hands. He was very soft spoken and came straight to the point. He was surprised by the State Department's designation of him as a terrorist, denied the charge and wanted to know if there was a way of removing his name from that list. "I have political disagreements with you for sure, in terms of your policies in the region, but I have never called for violence against you and always advocated that in war civilian lives must be spared. I don't even consider myself a political figure. I'm a teacher, no more than that."

After describing to Zindani that there was in fact a process for removal of listed names, an appeals process, we warned him that his reputation and rumors about the university he runs would make it difficult to disprove the charges against him. I asked him point blank: "If you're only a teacher and al-Iman university just a normal educational institution, why is it so closed and so difficult to get into? Why don't you, for example, invite me, an academic who has lectured in many universities in the region, to give a talk on your campus and meet and chat with your students?" Saleh immediately jumped in with, "Yes, why don't you invite Nabeel to visit?"

When we got back to the embassy, I drafted a cable about our meeting and mischievously titled it, "Can Zindani Come Out and Play?" I described our conversation with and our impressions of the man and asked if it was feasible to revisit the issue of his designation, if only as a response to Saleh's request. I referred to our conversation with Saleh briefly and said that he was under the impression that we wanted Zindani arrested and that we had not been aware of any such request from Washington. Diplomatically, the ambassador and I decided not to mention that there was a recording of FT making such a request of Saleh on the phone. We received only an informal reply denying that there was an official request for Zindani's arrest, that there was indeed an appeals channel but that Zindani would have to work with Yemen's ministry of foreign affairs to make such a request on his behalf. Next time Tom was in Washington he told me that Elliot Abrams, at the time special assistant to the president for near eastern and African affairs, asked him about this cable, saying, "Who is this Nabeel Khoury, and why does he refer so light heartedly to Zindani, an international terrorist?" Tom, came to my defense once more, "Oh, that's my deputy Nabeel, he just likes to inject some humor into his cables, there's no problem here."

Needless to say, no formal action was initiated by Yemen and therefore none taken by Washington to delist Zindani. Process there was, thoughtfulness in deciding such matters was another story.

159

While I would have enjoyed the challenge of speaking at al-Iman university and debating policy and religion with its conservative students, I could not do so without Washington's approval—which needless to say was not forthcoming, and I suspect Zindani was not fully at ease with my going there either, even though he did begrudgingly extend one.

Abdelaziz al-Maqaleh, on the other hand, Yemen's leftist scholar and poet, held occasional literary roundtables at Sanaa's public library and was known for his anti-American views. I paid him a visit, complimented him on his role as an intellectual agent provocateur, and suggested he invite me to give a talk. Since a political talk would have been deemed a little too provocative, I suggested a discussion of Lebanese-American poet, philosopher, and artist, Gibran Kahlil Gibran. I had in my possession numerous slides of Gibran's art, photographed for me from a unique collection at the Telfare museum in Savanah, Georgia. This proved too tempting for al-Maqaleh and a lecture at his center was agreed to. My talk and slide presentation was very well received by a small audience of invited guests and concluded with a discussion of Arab-Americans and their cultural and political influence in the United States. It was my cultural foot-in-the door technique to end up with a provocative political discussion with some of our critics after all.

The Preoccupation with Terrorism

Washington under both, the Obama and Trump administrations, kept its focus in Yemen on counterterrorism efforts to the detriment of development assistance and diplomatic attention to internal and regional problems. In December 2009, I gave a talk at Chatham House in London entitled, "Yemen, a Holistic Approach." I suggested not only increased economic aid but also diplomatic intervention in the ongoing war at the time, either directly or indirectly through regional partners. I argued again, as I

160

had done with General Abizaid and with my senior colleagues in Washington, that we needed to keep Yemen whole and thriving so it doesn't fall apart and generate chaos both within and outside its borders. I argued that terrorism's underlying causes were poverty and neglect and that a strong democratic Yemen would be less vulnerable to terrorist infiltrations. During the lecture at Chatham House, I suggested that Qatar would be a better regional partner than Saudi Arabia in terms of helping to end the conflict between the central government and the Houthis of Saadah. After the talk, a young political officer from the embassy of Qatar in London came over to talk to me and asked if I thought that Washington would welcome a Qatari role in Yemen. I answered in the affirmative, that to the best of my knowledge, the United States would welcome a regional initiative to end the fighting and help restore order and help with economic development in Yemen.

Qatar's foreign minister did in fact visit Washington early in January and proposed, while Saudi Arabia was militarily intervening in Yemen's war on the side of Saleh, a Qatari mediation in that war. Washington was receptive but Saudi Arabia nixed the idea and leaned on Saleh to say thank you, but no thank you to Qatar's offer, not only to mediate but also to pay for an ambitious plan to rebuild and develop northern Yemen so as to give the Houthis less incentive to rebel.

Tawakul Karman, one of the leaders of Yemen's Arab uprising in 2011, visited the State Department in October 2011 after receiving the Nobel prize for peace. Saleh had in June left the country for treatment in Saudi Arabia after being critically injured in an explosion inside the presidential palace in Sanaa. Tawakul was received by Secretary of State Hillary Clinton and had meetings with the Near East Affairs (NEA) bureau. I had met Tawakul during my stint in Sanaa as part of my meetings with civil society leaders and we had stayed in touch. After her meetings at the Department, and as I was escorting her and her husband out, we chatted about next steps in Yemen. Tawakul was concerned that the agreement which led Saleh to relinquish power was flawed in that it gave him and his family immunity and allowed him to return to Yemen if he so wished. I suggested that immunity from prosecution was probably necessary to avoid him contesting the transition of power but that president Hadi should move to consolidate the transition by removing Saleh's family members and former top security officers from their positions and replacing them with a new generation whose loyalty to the new government would not be in doubt. "But Nabeel," replied Tawakul, "your people here are telling me that Saleh's security team should stay on for at least a year for the sake of continuity in security and counterterrorism cooperation with the U.S." Tawakul reminded me in a recent phone call of my reply to her that day, "Is this your country or Assistant Secretary Jeffrey Feltman's?" I asked; "You are part of a new power elite now and you must guard against a counter-revolution from the old guard." It was not in fact Feltman who had made that suggestion to her but rather someone from the NSC staff she had met that day.

Tawakul remains today quite engaged in her country's debacle today, in addition to using her Nobel prize notoriety to lobby on behalf of democracy and human rights in the Arab world as a whole. I am convinced that, once the guns have fallen silent in Yemen, she will be part of her country's future in one capacity or another.

Both the Obama and Trump administrations have been guilty of looking at Yemen and seeing only Iran. Both also prioritized Saudi Arabia's needs and biases over Yemen's needs and over the very survival of Yemen's population—so much so, that the provision of arms and logistical support for the Saudi war on Yemen implicates the United States in war crimes being committed on a daily basis by the Saudi-led Arab coalition.

At a Camp David summit in 2015, President Barack Obama sought to reassure Arab Gulf states that the United States was committed to their security despite its trying to negotiate a nuclear deal with Iran. Saudi Arabia had just launched its war against the Houthis of Yemen, building a coalition of the willing to bomb, strike, and blockade Yemen ostensibly to prevent arms shipments from reaching the Huothis. Instead of counseling diplomacy first, President Obama reassured the Saudis that the United States was on their side and in fact for the next 2 years of this war, and the final 2 years of his administration, the United States provided targeting assistance to the Saudi air force, refueling their jets in flight and using U.S. warships to help enforce a blockade on Yemeni ports. During the last few months of the Obama administration, and after international human rights organizations raised the alarm over the impact of the war on Yemen's population—causing starvation, destruction of the infrastructure, and the spread of Cholera, John Kerry tried to mediate an end to the conflict, spending perhaps all of 48 hours on the issue via visits to Oman and Riyadh, to no practical effect. For that effort, Kerry and Obama received the wrath of Saudi Arabia—expressed in their media outlets—for having talked to a Houthi delegation in Oman and for "abandoning his friends" in the Gulf.

Enter Donald Trump. Displaying not even lip-service concern for the plight of Yemenis, the Trump administration went further in pleasing and appeasing Saudis, increasing arms sales to KSA, logistical support to their war effort in Yemen, and even promising and eventually pulling out of the Iran nuclear deal. Once again, U.S. action in Yemen focused on going after AQAP and assisting the Saudis in drawing a line in the sand against perceived Iranian encroachment. Yemen's social, political, and economic problems and the humanitarian disaster unfolding for the whole world to see somehow has remained invisible to American policymakers.

From a Beleaguered Northern Tribe to a Dominant Force

When the Houthi rebellion started in 2004, the Houthis were simply the largest Zaidi tribe in northern Yemen, leading a protest at the time against the Saudi supported attempt by the central government to spread Salafi/Sunni Islam in their region. Additionally, the northern region felt neglected and left out of development funds and projects given to Yemen by foreign donors. The former president Saleh attempted to subdue the Houthis by summoning Houthi elder, Badreddine al-Houthi, to Sanaa and by stationing troops in Saadah, the capital of the northern governorate. Defiance turned into resistance and led to 6 years of war between the Houthis and the central government in Sanaa—a struggle that only left the Houthis emboldened and toughened. After the 2011 uprising, and taking advantage of the political chaos and power vacuum in Sanaa, the Houthis fought off the Yemeni army and defeated and expelled the armed members of a major Salafi school, the Damaj institute, from their midst. Having faced Salafi militias from Sanaa (from the Muslim Brotherhood dominated Islah party) and occasional forays by AQAP, the Houthis, under the guise of fighting off these "invading" forces and supporting the uprising, continued their war into the governorates of Amran and Shabwa, reaching in the spring and summer of 2014 the outskirts of Sanaa.

Despite signing agreements with the National Dialogue Committee, brokered by UN envoy Jamal Benomar, and with the new president, Abd Rabbo Mansour Hadi, the Houthi's appetite had been whetted by successes on the battlefield and by growing assistance from Iran and Lebanese Hezbollah, into threatening Sanaa under the pretext of trying to force economic and political reforms. After establishing street presence via civilian demonstrations, the Houthis eventually sent troops into Sanaa and took the capital with only token resistance from the army. It was widely speculated that troops still loyal to the former president Saleh were ordered by the latter not to resist. Saleh, long angered by leading General Ali Mohsen, and the leading Islahi family, the al-Ahmars, struck an alliance with his former enemies the Houthis and gave orders to military leaders still loyal to him to stand down and allow the Houthis to advance unopposed. Saleh calculated that a Houthi takeover of Sanaa would soon allow him to return to the presidency of Yemen.

While the United States was busy (ineffectively) pounding AQAP members across southern Yemen, Iran's influence with the Houthis grew in leaps and bounds emboldening the Houthis to strive for full takeover of Yemen. I warned at the time that if the Houthis reached Bab el-Mandeb Iran would indirectly, and eventually directly be in a position to threaten the interests of the U.S. and international shipping through the Red Sea. In counseling tougher diplomacy with the Houthis, I argued that it would by then become too costly to try to reverse the facts established on the ground once the Houthis occupied the south.

In fact, after establishing dominance in Sanaa, Houthi forces continued south, taking Hodeida, the important commercial port city, and going East to the Hadramout region, taking Marib, the oil producing region, in the process. Instead of applying pressure and using diplomacy and/or deterrence to stop the Houthi takeover of Sanaa, the United States in fact had pulled a unit of about 300 special forces from a southern air base called al-Anad and closed its embassy in Sanaa, in effect signaling to the Houthis that they would not stand in their way. The Houthis were overly ambitious in trying to take over all of Yemen, but the ease with which their advance was accomplished certainly whetted their appetite for more gains. It must be added, that at least in the eyes of some of their leaders, the opportunity of reviving the Imamate presented itself.

Increased U.S. economic assistance to Yemen before and just after the Arab uprising of 2011 was too little too late. The highest investment of attention and money was given to pursuing AQAP elements with drone and airstrikes. The confluence of US airstrikes, and ground strikes by the Houthis against AQAP gave the impression to many in the region of connivance, especially during the Obama presidency. In fact, there was never any direct contact with the Houthis, except for that brief foray into Yemen diplomacy by John Kerry—something for which the Trump administration has shown even less enthusiasm.

U.S. Policy, How This Ends

Saudi Crown Prince Mohamed Bin Salman, in an interview [1] with Tom Friedman, reportedly said that pro-Saudi forces in Yemen controlled 85 percent of the country, but that anything less than 100 percent was unacceptable. A recent White House statement [2] called for opening the borders just long enough to allow humanitarian aid shipments and political negotiations to resume. The statement, however, said nothing about ending the U.S. role in the blockade imposed on Yemen and which itself forms a huge obstacle to humanitarian aid reaching those who need it the most. This is besides the fact that the idea of feeding Yemen while bombing it is an exercise in self-delusion.

Saudi Arabia, being the rich and powerful nation which took on this war in 2015, could easily choose to end it via a unilateral cessation of hostilities. After all, Houthi rockets, as provocative and destabilizing as they have been, have not been effective in changing the balance of power or inflicting much damage on KSA. Further, the Houthis did not start bombing Saudi territory until the Saudis put together the Arab coalition against them and started their air action. The Saudis would not be risking much by taking the first step toward peace. Washington should be the catalyst, prodding Saudi Arabia to put diplomacy first and becoming fully engaged itself in the peace effort. The prospects of that happening while Trump is in the White House and Mohamed Bin Salman (MBS) in Riyadh, however, are not good despite recent reports of a State Department proposal for peace in Yemen. Both men seem too preoccupied with their personal egos and their obsession with Iran to take the long view.

The Yemeni players in this tragedy could—and should—take matters into their own hands. After all, this is where it all began.

---

1   https://www.nytimes.com/2017/11/23/opinion/saudi-prince-mbs-arab-spring.html

2   https://www.whitehouse.gov/the-press-office/2017/11/24/statement-press-secretary-humanitarian-crisis-yemen

Yemeni youth, hoping to end a corrupt and authoritarian regime, joined their brothers and sisters in the protests that erupted during the Arab uprisings of 2011. Their sheer will and popularity with Yemenis from all walks of life led to the abdication of Ali Abdullah Saleh but also, unfortunately, to the now defunct National Dialogue Conference (NDC) of 2013. The conference, coupled with Gulf Cooperation Council mediation, led to the installation of Abd Rabbo Mansour Hadi at the head of a transitional reconciliation government. The failure of this reconciliation—and the Houthi takeover of Sana'a—precipitated the military debacle that followed.

The NDC process was flawed from the start. For all its participants (over 500 members), it failed to build the necessary consensus among the principal players in Yemen on a power-sharing framework that could have led the country to a more stable and prosperous future. A difficult task in 2013 has become even more so today with the rising number of players, militias, and foreign armies. Nevertheless, a reconciliation effort can still stave off the literal decimation of the Yemeni people. The selfishness and corruption of all sides to the conflict in Yemen have prevented that from happening thus far.

Personal Attempts and Frustrations

I have always believed that peace and prosperity in Yemen were in the long-term interest of the United States, if nothing else in order to deny strategic space to terrorism and extremism. I wanted the USG to, directly or indirectly, push for a full recognition of all the power brokers in Yemen and involve them in a serious push for peace. I also wanted the United States to recognize the value of Yemeni civil society and to facilitate a role for the country's youth to play in shaping a secular democratic future in Yemen.

It was very frustrating for me, having developed a personal attachment to the country and its people and developed friendships with Yemenis from all walks of life, to watch Yemen disintegrate and not be able to get Washington to do the right thing by it. White House and top State Department officials during my time there were simply not motivated to invest financial, political, and diplomatic capital to help keep the country together. Part of this disinterest was the complexity of tribal and political life in Yemen and a certain disdain of getting too deeply involved in it. Yemeni friends from government and opposition to the conflict have often asked me for advice—this was the case while I was at my job in Yemen, and has remained the case since my return to Washington and during my retirement. Southern opposition leaders, for example, often called me to confer on internal and regional issues. They invited me to join them at some of their meetings in Cairo while I was still at the Department. I thought at the time that closer contact with southern leaders would help me assess their potential to be effective at the national level and would give the United States a more direct role in peacemaking. NEA leadership at the time would not give me permission to do so on the grounds that it would get out in the papers that Washington was taking sides in Yemen's internal conflict. Never mind that the United States was already seen as intervening regardless to whom its diplomats were talking.

Another personal intervention I offered to make was to convince former president Saleh to remain in Riyadh, where he had gone for medical treatment in after the attempted assassination against him in 2012. He had arrived in New York for further treatment and sent me a message that he would very much like to talk to see me if I could visit him at the hospital where he was staying. I asked NEA for permission and was again denied the opportunity to be helpful. Our ambassador to Yemen at the time and NEA apparently decided that the best way to deal with Saleh was to shun him and to apply pressure by giving him a hard time before finally granting him a visa to come to the United States for treatment. Keeping Saleh out of Yemen was the right thing to do in order to give the political transition there a chance to take place without his intervention. He was not in my opinion however a man to be pressured simply by being shunned. Unless you had some real means of intimidating him into staying away, you had to cajole, bribe, or otherwise convince him it was the right thing to do. I argued that I had a special relationship with Saleh that allowed me to speak quite frankly to him and that I could convince him to stay out voluntarily. Again my offer of help was rejected on the grounds that it would get out in the press that "the Department" was meeting and plotting with Saleh against the rest of Yemen.

I did manage to get a message to Saleh via his ambassador and brother in-law, Abdelwahab al-Hajry, to the effect that he would do better to seriously retire and enjoy a few years of quality time with his family away from all the chaos and violence. When he returned to Sanaa, much to the surprise of our ambassador who thought that Saleh was bluffing when he promised to return to his country—he gave a speech in which he said, "a friend from a major power suggested I should travel and enjoy myself instead of coming back to Yemen, but I responded by saying that I wasn't a tourist and only cared about being back among my people in Yemen."

The Powerbrokers

The main Yemeni players in this tragedy appear today to remain equally matched. The Houthis, even without the former president Saleh's assistance, dominate the north militarily and are unified under one leadership. They wield more than 100,000 fighters and have an imposing arsenal of stored weapons, artillery, and rockets—add to that a fighting spirit and a strong sense of purpose and you have a formidable force. There can be no peace without their full cooperation. By now, the Houthis recognize their overreach in trying to take over the whole country in 2014. To boot, the break with Saleh and his murder may have deprived the Houthis of much of the military units that have now shifted their loyalties to his family and supporters within the former ruling party. At best, and after several more years of conflict, and that's assuming that the Arab coalition forces tire first and leave the county, the Houthis might hope to be the last force still standing in Yemen and could presumably rule over the rubble and a devastated population in the north: not a happy prospect, given that none of their fellow Arabs would recognize or accept them as a legitimate state within the Arab fold.

Ansar Allah, the Houthis political party, lacks sophistication, organization, and a sufficient cadre of leaders. Their political naivete is compounded by religious fervor and slogans, in part derived from Iran. This makes them a difficult partner for peace. They do, however, form an integral part of Yemen and have as much interest in a fair deal as anyone else. If this war has shown them anything, it is that they will have to give up on any dreams of conquest that some of their hardliners may still entertain. A fair deal would grant them autonomy within their region, fair representation in any future government, and a fair share of the economic benefits of a peaceful union.

Islah and the Joint Meeting Parties with which it is affiliated have long served as a loyal opposition to Saleh. Militarily, they played a role in resisting the Houthi takeover of southern Yemen and have mostly thrown in with Saudi Arabia. Their old leadership, however, has atrophied and can no longer contribute much to a new path forward for the country. They can however designate youthful representatives and should not seek to place their old guard in any future government.

The secessionist movement known as Hirak, founded in 2007, boasts at least nominally the loyalty of several million southerners yearning for independence and willing to fight for it. All told, however, fewer than 100,000 men now fight under different banners of the Southern Transitional Council (STC), the Security Belt and Elite forces—both supported and directed by the UAE. The total number of anti-Houthi fighters includes several small mercenary armies with hard-to-identify loyalties. Split in this fashion, Hirak cannot hope to build a separate state without significant Arab Gulf support, which would deprive them of the independence they desire. The STC led by the former Aden governor Aidarous al-Zubaidi has yet to merge the various Hirak factions. Uncertain support from the United Arab Emirates (UAE) and Saudi ambivalence to an independent south has further frustrated his efforts. The UAE-armed Security Belt force (*al-Hizam*) makes for an uncertain ally as it pursues its own self-interest and has been implicated in intimidation, assassination, and other human rights violations[3]. Add to that odd mix the fighters from al-Qa'eda in the Arabian Peninsula and ISIS and you have a combustible situation in the south.

Politically, Hirak leaders agree on an independent southern state, but differ on tactics. Some call for unilateral secession, others a referendum, and others still a negotiated secession with Hadi and the northern government. Regional intervention has not helped either, in that their loyalties are split between those indebted to Saudi Arabia and those under the influence of the UAE. Ultimately, President Hadi or his successor will need to convince these leaders that a better future for them lies in reconciliation with the north. That kind of leadership has yet to be demonstrated by Hadi or anyone in his circle.

Alternate Leaders

At this writing, the current leadership across all the factions in Yemen seems bankrupt and incapable of making peace. President Hadi has been hopelessly stuck in Saudi Arabia with only brief visits to Aden and elsewhere in the south. To say the least,

---

3   https://www.hrw.org/news/2017/06/22/yemen-uae-backs-abusive-local-forces

he has been an ineffective leader of his own people and has not been able to negotiate independently inside or outside Yemen. He comes across as a mouthpiece for Saudi Arabia and looks very bad to at least half his population when he supports the continued bombing of his country by the Arab coalition. Looking beyond his presidency, his vice president, currently Ali Mohsen al-Ahmar, has been a military man all his life, working in the shadow of Ali Abdallah Saleh, and has not appealed very widely even after Saleh's demise. As president, he can be expected to perhaps prosecute the war with a little more efficiency than has been the case so far for the current government, but as a politician, he would likely leave much to be desired.

On the Houthi side, Abdel Malek al-Houthi has inherited the mantle of leadership from his father and older brother but has not shown much creativity in striking alliances and responding intelligently to international peace overtures. He is still a young man however and is unlikely to be challenged by anyone from his own party and tribe in the foreseeable future.

Whether from the old guard or newly emerging civil society leaders, Yemen needs skilled individuals with a vision who have not yet played a major role in trying to bring the warring parties together to forge a new way forward for the county. From the older generation, several wise men and women, while not totally untainted by the past, could take the initiative in this regard, but their voices have thus far been muffled. I suggest here just a few names by way of example, some from the old guard, some from the new generation, and with no pretense that they're the only ones in that category by any means.

Rashad al-Allimi, a longtime member of the inner circle of the late president Saleh, MOI for 10 years prior to Saleh's departure from Yemen in 2011, and a member of a strategic advisory role during the transition. Allimi has a Ph.D. in sociology and is one of the most experienced government officials in security matters in the country, having been in charge of the CSFs and the Counter Terrorism Unit during the Saleh years.

Rashad was the deputy prime minister for Saleh and is currently a deputy prime minister for president Hadi. He has represented the Hadi government in peace talks with the Houthis and has considerable political skills. Allimi, however, is mostly viewed as an efficient bureaucrat and not someone with a broad political base to back him up for a leadership position. Further, Allimi, despite Saudi support, has domestic and regional enemies and has been tainted by the corruption of those he has worked for, including both Saleh and Hadi—all of which would complicate his playing a significant role in the future of Yemen.

Abu-Bakr al-Qirbi, another outstanding bureaucrat and policy advisor, a foreign minister who put the best face on Yemen's foreign policy for both western and Arab interlocutors and was extremely loyal to Saleh while he lived. Qirbi currently lives in Jordan where he continues to be an active member of the GPC based in Sanaa and opposed to Hadi. Any new leader might well rely on his sound advice and guidance, especially in dealing with the international community. His role inside the country would necessarily be a circumscribed one.

Mohamed al-Tayeb, a member of parliament and once the favorite interlocutor with the western diplomatic community in Sanaa, is also a man with wasted potential, given his inability to play a role in the transition to a post-Saleh government. A man of no ideological inclination or unquestioned loyalty to any leader, al-Tayeb does not have a large popular base to be the needed leader himself but could easily be an advisor on political and economic matters and an excellent foreign minister when the right kind of cabinet comes along.

Amat al-Alim al-Soswa, minister of human rights 2003–2006, when she left Yemen to become Assistant Secretary General at the United Nations for the Arab region within the UNDP program. Amat is one of Yemen's strongest and most prominent women leaders and is a match for anybody from the old guard, man, or woman. Completely at ease in Yemeni, Arab, or western circles, she is a principled nationalist who would like to see a developed, democratic Yemen that respects the rights of all its citizens, men, women, and children. She has a good political vision, does not abide fools and easily speaks truth to power. Her UN and World Bank experience speak volumes as to her expertise. Under the right circumstances, Amat could be a national leader in her country.

Mohamed Abu Lahoum, a youngish son of the former leader of the Bakil tribe, former member of the GPC, left to start his own third way party after 2011, the "building and justice"—as an alternative to the two main adversaries in Yemen's internal conflict, the GPC and the opposition Islah party—at least when the struggle for power started in 2011—and a potential mediator between the two main adversaries in the ongoing war, the Houthis and the Arab coalition. Now that the conflict has both a regional and an international dimension, Abu-Lahoum's challenge is more complex, but he still is someone who can talk to all sides and should be at least a partner in promoting peace, reconciliation, and reconstruction in Yemen.

Civil Society

At this writing, Yemen is at a crossroads. The war has been going on for almost 5 years with no sign of abatement. The regional powers, and principally Saudi Arabia, have been fighting from air, land, and sea, directly and through proxy forces, to repel the Houthi rebels from the capital Sanaa and from lands they occupied south of the capital. In principle, they want the Houthis to pull their forces back to the northern Saadah region, and preferably give up all their heavy weapons to a restored central government under the presidency of Abd Rabbo Mansour Hadi. Despite all their technological superiority, this Arab coalition is not any closer to accomplishing their goals now than when they started their intervention. The UAE displays regional goals of its own, primarily the control of ports and waterways in Yemen, to include the island of Socotra—objectives that would enhance the Emirates' economic power in the region. The north and south of Yemen each started this war with their own goals that harken back to previous conflicts with the central government, conditions that no longer pertain given the fading authority of that government.

When I left Yemen in 2007, having served as Deputy Chief of Mission at the U.S. Embassy from 2004 to 2007, I gave an interview to "al-Ayam" which was the premier southern publication at the time and my favorite during my stint in Yemen. In that interview, I expressed concern about both north and south Yemen, saying that the central government needed to pay attention to their legitimate grievances to prevent constant warfare in the north and a potential secession of the south. The late president Saleh did not allow foreign diplomats to visit the Saadah region in the north, claiming that security conditions made any trip there a dangerous proposition. The south however was open space and my colleagues and I went there frequently.

There was not one trip south where I didn't get an earful about southern grievances. They all centered around feeling disrespected by the central government: Not enough southerners in government positions or the military and security establishments, and much was taken from southern resources with hardly anything given back. For many, the south had its own identity: more secular and worldly than the north and more capable of joining the rest of the modern world and, to that end, south Yemen ought in their opinion to be called southern Arabia and not south Yemen. Hardly anyone, however, said they were not Yemeni at heart or that the people of the north were somehow totally unrelated to them. The same is true for northerners who identified as thoroughly Yemeni but felt imposed upon by a central government which in their view conspired against them with Saudi Arabia and Wahabi Salafis. They felt they were totally ignored when borders with their northern neighbor were being negotiated and they felt neglected when the benefits of governance were being distributed. Despite sectarian differences, however, and some dreams of going back to a lost Imamate they once led, Houthis and others in the northern region of the country still largely felt they were Yemenis first and foremost.

The 2011 uprising in Sanaa was a reflection of its sister uprisings in Tunisia and Egypt. Ruled by a corrupt government and a single ruling party, the GPC, which was a mechanism for exchanging loyalty for goods, services, and money, good governance in Yemen was an afterthought. The same problem that plagues every authoritarian regime in the region plagued Yemen. That Arab regimes have been bankrupt for years has become a cliché. The wooden language of the rulers, justifying their authoritarianism on the grounds of being part of "the resistance against Israel," or that the west would somehow exploit any signs of weakness on their domestic front and that terrorist organizations would take power and make life for citizens a living hell. All these arguments have proven false over the years. With no war and no peace with Israel, these regimes have had very little to contribute in this regard. Domestically, with their failure to promote the living standards of their citizens and their cynical use of extremists to scare skeptical friends and allies, their scare tactics ring hollow. Arab youth, on the other hand, have proven that they are now a new force to be reckoned with. From Morocco to Lebanon, civil society leaders have risen to champion the rights of citizens to a decent standard of living and to freedom of organization and expression. Their own divisiveness and the forces arrayed against them have thus far stood in the way of their success. Despite their varied political views and affiliations, however, they have more in common than they have differences and I strongly believe the future is theirs.

Throughout my posts in the Middle East, I always sought out civil society leaders and tried to support them with USG grants and to lobby Washington on their behalf. In Yemen hundreds if not thousands of young leaders who are worthy of note, whether as gadfly critics and lobbyists or as alternate national leaders from a new, well educated and open to the world generation. Again I mention here a few by way of example not exclusivity.

Tawakul Karman, a Nobel prize awardee, Tawakul comes to mind as someone with potential because of her early involvement with 2011 uprising and despite her affiliation with the opposition Islah party. My first encounter with her was in 2005 while on routine visits, I asked our Public Affairs Officer to organize for me with civil society organizations. Tawakul was at the time a journalist and a human rights activist. I was a strong believer in encouraging democracy movements in the Arab world and in the assistance, the United States could give to encourage civil society leaders. Tawakul sought advice and assistance from us and other western countries in promoting a women's media group. She called me once for advice on a name for her new group and wanted to know how "Unchained Women Journalists" sounded to a western ear. Knowing that English at that time was not her strong suit, I suggested the title would have to be amended a bit so it didn't have unintended nuances to English speakers. She faxed over the announcement she was working on and I suggested the title that was eventually adopted, "Women Journalists Without Chains."

Tawakul was, and still is, a very energetic and strong willed person. These qualities helped make her one of the leaders of the protest movement against Saleh when the youth uprising began. She, however, also was and still is a very controversial figure. A member of the conservative Islah party and a devout Muslim, she wears the head scarf and conservative, if often colorful robes, and is almost always accompanied in her travels by her husband. This in itself would only put the most liberal of her colleagues and compatriots on guard. Add to that she at first sounded like her party's spokesperson rather than an independent youthful voice, that she at first seemed to support the Saudi-led war against the Houthis, then turned against them and adopted Qatar as a sponsor and patron. She has, since the Nobel prize, distanced herself from the old guard of the Islah party and struck out on her own, armed with her own Tawakul Karman Foundation and a host of international colleagues and supporters. Her involvement in international causes beyond the borders of Yemen are an advantage should she choose to help unite and lead the nation once the war stops.

Rahma Hujeira led another women's media group. I was told, in 2004, that she had turned down a Fulbright grant because of her strong hostility to U.S. foreign policy, particularly in Afghanistan. I took that as a challenge and went to visit. At a roundtable with her and her colleagues, I challenged her to explain her rejection of an excellent learning experience like Fulbright and she mentioned Afghanistan. I asked what she and her group had to do with Afghanistan, or Iraq or any issue with U.S. policy in the Middle East. "Is this a priority for your group, or an area of particular expertise?" I asked. I proceeded to explain that on civil society and media matters, we were in full agreement and that a Fulbright grant aimed at enhancing her experience and knowledge of those areas where she and her group could make a difference. I clearly had her group's support as I made my arguments so I finished with, "Why don't you to go and reap the most benefit from this trip and while there, by all means, criticize U.S. foreign policy to your heart's content, no one will mind." Eyes widened at that and she asked for a week to consider. She came back to us later with an acceptance of the grant. I saw her in Washington when she was still on her grant and she was a transformed person. She did mention that she had not changed her mind about U.S. policy but that she totally valued the experience gained, all while blasting U.S. policy at every roundtable and forum.

Rahma is back in Yemen and though an early participant in the 2011 uprising inexplicably switched alliances and sided with the former president Saleh—something that baffled her friends who wondered why she would turn back to the old corrupt regime. It is one of the sad facts of the ongoing Yemen war that divided communities and broke up old friendships. Everyone in Yemen has been politicized by this war and only some of those who left the country have had the luxury of retaining some neutrality and objectivity in their writing and analysis of events.

Afrah Nasser, a young journalist, 2011 activist and bloggist, Afrah gained her experience in journalism before leaving to Sweden to study for a Master's degree in the field. Like many journalists in Yemen, Afrah decided it was not safe to come back to practice in her native country. She was accepted as a political refugee in Sweden where she has dedicated herself to writing about the plight of Yemeni victims of war, famine, and disease with a particular focus on the disrupted lives of journalists of all political persuasions writing under pressure from the various authorities and militias in the country, or writing from exile and feeling the burden and stigma of exile.

Afrah was awarded the International Press Freedom award for 2017, which brought her to New York and Washington, DC, giving me the chance to meet her. While in DC, she met with several members of Congress who were alarmed by their government's support for the Saudi war and lobbied them to work for a more peaceful role for the United States in the region. Afrah, like many of her compatriots abroad, is very active in social media and her online magazine, the Sanaa Review, is a publication dedicated to providing information to Yemenis and to carry Yemen stories to the rest of the world. Hence, one can find articles about young Yemeni entrepreneurs, Yemeni singers, artists, and just young Yemenis who managed to live and thrive inside Yemen despite the harsh and dangerous conditions there. Afrah is currently the main Yemen researcher at Human Rights Watch.

And, speaking of Yemeni stories, no one tells them more graphically and more effectively than **Khadija Assalami**, an internationally recognized film director, documentary maker, and author. Her movie *Amina* (2006) tells the story of a child bride who was sentenced to death for the murder of her husband, with virtually no evidence; the movie offers a rare glimpse of life in women's prisons in Yemen. Her movie *I Am Nojoom, 10 and Divorced* (2015) is inspired by the true story of Njoud, a 10-year-old who walked to a courthouse in Yemen and asked for a divorce from a much older man she was forced to marry. Al-Salami portrays some very jarring aspects of Yemeni culture, with the goal of awakening, educating, and hopefully motivating young people to push for change in her country.

Hafez Albukari, an early advocate of citizenship education—starting with young people and teaching them what good citizenship means as building democracy from the grass roots. I recall us helping him with this program which awarded young students with a good-citizen passport at the end of the course. Currently, Hafez heads Yemen Polling Center which, in collaboration with international public opinion experts, helps provide a sense of Yemeni public opinion.

These are a few of the hundreds of young Yemeni men and women working mostly outside Yemen and showing great promise because of the expertise they are developing and the dedication they have for their country. While the conditions in Yemen are currently miserable, they give me hope of a better future ahead.

The Peace Effort

Authoritarian regimes, whether ethnically or religiously or tribally based, use and abuse their minorities to the point where these groups rebel or try to secede whenever an opportunity presents itself. Such behavior, understandable though it may be, rarely ends well in the Middle East. Whether it's the Kurds of Syria, the Kurds of Iraq, the Houthis of Yemen, or the south Yemenis, they all fall into the same traps. In the case of the Houthis, it's the dreams of grandeur, spurred by a vacuum of power at the center and an encouraging hand from a regional power. For the southerners, the same opportunity and regional inducements spur them on.

It is precisely, however, those enticing conditions that complicate matters. Chaos at the center is also a manifestation of chaos at the periphery, and the same regional encouragement for secession is itself a complication when the regional powers are themselves victims of their own selfish desires and their own limitations. The Saudis—who were and still are obviously incapable of achieving their stated objectives in Yemen without the importation of foreign fighters—are themselves in need of advice on how to manage their role in the region, and indeed even their own economy which faces some serious challenges. The Emiratis dreams of an empire is way too ambitious for their small size and inexperience in playing the regional leader.

The youth who started the uprising of 2011 and exposed the weakness and total corruption of the central government have been left with no leg to stand on inside their country because of the total war and chaos which consume it. They have taken their activism abroad and are showing the world what Yemenis can do in civil society, journalism, and organization building. Their time has not yet arrived, but who knows what dreams may come and what directions the country might take once the guns have fallen silent and good governance is again in search of champions to lead the way.

When a handshake between the various warlords, domestic and foreign alike, ends this bloody conflict, the details of a federal democratic system of some sort will have to be worked out. It is at that point that the talents of Yemen's youth will be called upon to draw a political path forward.

We Will Always Have Socotra ... or Will We?

Socotra.

Socotra catch.

Socotra.

I had the rare privilege and opportunity to visit Socotra while I was in Yemen. Not many, whether foreigners or Yemenis get to do that—the island being a bit off the beaten track and with almost nonexistent infrastructure. British Council friend and visiting friends from Prague, Pavel, and Nadia, accompanied me, along with two colleagues from USAID. The island was recognized by UNESCO as a world natural heritage site in 2008 because of its unique flora and sea-life.

The Blood dragon tree is probably the most famous feature of the island, but actually rock formations, bird, and sea-life are also uniquely preserved from antiquity and the small population and simple life-style have not caused any damage to the island's unique features.

We spent a long weekend, sleeping in tents and barbequing fish for meals. A school of dolphins came close to the boat we were in at one point and I could not resist the urge to jump and swim with them. They of course swam off in a hurry when I did that. Goats which have a run of the island are very bold and came in close one evening to get a closer look at the foreign interlopers. One enterprising goat came up close and, not finding any scraps of food around us, carefully approached a tissue box and snatched a tissue. Not seeing any reaction from us, the goat returned on another run. The third time, it grabbed the whole box in its mouth and ran off with it.

Socotra has largely been spared the chaos and destruction of the Yemen war, but it has come under the gluttonous eyes of the Emiratis who have sent a small naval force to the island. Not currently accessible to tourism, archeological research and preservation experts from international organizations, the UAE and Saudi Arabia are using it as a military and naval outpost. The UAE likely has economic and commercial exploitation of the island in mind for the future. During my stay in Yemen, Yahya Saleh, the former president's nephew, wanted to build five-star hotels on Socotra and bring plane-loads of tourists to it. Those of us in the diplomatic corps who truly appreciated the island's uniqueness were horrified and lobbied against the idea. Now, with the island under UAE control, one is not sure if their idea is to take over and turn it into another Dubai, or to simply use it as a naval listening post and prevent any Yemenis or international companies from developing the island to in any capacity so as not to compete with their own ports and islands.

Yemen in 3D.

184

Amidst ancient ruins—Yemeni girl eating a banana.

CHAPTER 9

A DIPLOMAT IN THE MILITARY AND INTELLIGENCE MIX

The security establishment of the United States, reviled by many in the Middle East as an instrument of oppression and at home by the ultra-left, many of whom call it the constant war state—and more recently, attacked by Donald Trump both during the campaign and after his victory at the polls because of the investigations they launched into Russian interference in the elections, and presumably because secrets they may have uncovered that could jeopardize his presidency. A bit of a mystery to me, even after two decades in the foreign service, I got to know both military and the intelligence community a little more intimately during my last 5 years in the service. My 4 years with the Bureau of Intelligence and Research (INR) at the Department of State were sandwiched between 1 year of teaching at the Marine War College (MCWAR) in 2008, and teaching another year at the war college at the National Defense University (NDU) in Washington, DC. Add to that a year as a member of the State Department's Senior Seminar—a year-long training course in 1998, primarily for senior DOS officers but open to representative from each of the military services and the intelligence agencies.

As a result of these 5 years, I have nothing but respect and admiration for members of the military and for the analysts of the intelligence agencies (primarily NSA and CIA). I speak nothing here of the top leadership of these organizations, always political appointees and often subject to the will and caprices of the elected leaders in the White House. I speak, rather, of the rank and file military and intelligence officers and FBI agents who are almost to a man or woman dedicated, professional and self-sacrificing to the utmost. They perform critical tasks that should not be politicized, stereotyped, or underestimated.

187

Senior Seminar: State-led

Our Senior Seminar visit to New Orleans took place in January 1999, just in time for Super Bowl XXXII. I must admit here to a very un-American thing: I have never had any affection for or familiarity with American Football and have only rarely watched the Super Bowl. My friend and companion during most of our senior seminar travels, Charlie Vasilakis and I, were walking down Bourbon Street when he spotted a hotel and insisted we go in and watch the game on their big screen in the lobby. I agreed, with the proviso that he help me understand the complex rules of the game. "Soccer is very straight forward," I said, "You keep kicking the ball until you can drive it into the net, but this measuring of yards and stopping each time the ball hits the turf is beyond me." Once inside and Charlie heard all the silly questions I had (such as how come they change teams each time someone loses the ball?), he hushed me up and suggested I save my questions till after the game, saying, "you're embarrassing me with these naïve questions, they might throw us out!"

The New Orleans visit—seeing the special mix of ethnic groups, classes, and cuisine, gives one a special appreciation of the city— all the more in light of what happened after Hurricane Katrina, the damage that resulted and the neglect that followed. The visit left me with a very sympathetic view of the city, its streets and the music that follows you everywhere you go, not to mention the crawfish, hot sauces, and beignets. The endearing, Let the good times roll spirit, made it all the more heartbreaking when Hurricane Katrina struck in 2005, to watch the slow response of the federal government and the long time it has taken for the people there recover from it.

From watching the economy of crabbing on the Chesapeake Bay and eating our haul on Tangier Island, to sampling the special crawfish followed by sugar-covered beignets in New Orleans, our group of 30-some senior government officials adopted the motto "Eating our way across America!" We were the 40th class of a great State Department program called Senior Seminar, a training program that has now unfortunately been cancelled. It was a great opportunity for senior or about to become senior foreign service officers, chosen from across the various departments of government, to develop a deeper knowledge of the various branches of the foreign service and what the various issues were in domestic politics and economies across the United States. The largest contingent came from the State Department officers, roughly 12 out of the 30 members, with the rest coming from the intelligence community, one from each of the military services and one from each of the Commerce Department and USAID.

Aside from listening to speakers from various government agencies in Washington, we spent the majority of our time traveling, often in military planes, to various military bases and facilities, we received briefings at intelligence agencies and met with private sector businesses including Wall Street stock market and several financial companies on Madison Avenue. The year was both intensely interesting, useful, and fun. My guess is that the fun part is what caught the eyes of budget cutters who decided it had to go—after all, if any government work is fun, there must be something wrong with it!

It would be hard to pick the best and most memorable visits during that year. Alaska, New Orleans, and San Diego would probably be at the top of my list of visits however. Of all the military sites we visited, San Diego stood out as the most hands-on military experience. We visited the Marine recruiting center, stood in the spots marked for new recruits just arriving and were yelled at by a staff sergeant doing his best to give us a taste of the humiliation and brow-beating that fresh recruits receive. Part of the briefing later explained the need to break down egotism and any expectations of any special treatment that some might be carrying with them from the civilian world.

The second stop in San Diego was the Navy Seals training area—where we watched the trainees swim underwater with first hands, then hands and feet tied together. The exercise looked quite dangerous, but trainers were closely watching and ready at both ends of the pool to jump in and assist in the case of need. The Seals were very welcoming and their show and tell included a display of the various weapons they use. The fun part included a ride in their new (at the time) $20 million boat—an armored speed boat which seats 18 with room below the deck for sundry gear, equipment and weapons. As I recall, the boat reached 40 miles per hour within seconds and stopped on a dime, better than any car I've ever tried to bring to a sudden stop. It then spun around 180 degrees and took off at the same speed as before in the opposite direction. The Seals of course would not expect to fight anyone at sea unless they absolutely had to, but they would use the boat to get to their destination, use diving gear to get to shore or to any target at sea, complete their mission, and get back to the boat. It was our first James Bond experience during the program.

Our second experience was even more fun—and educational, of course! We "trapped" onto a moving aircraft carrier in mid-maneuvers. The word trapped refers to a small plane, seating roughly 16 as I recall, which takes off a very short runway for a quick steep ascent and lands on an equally short one on board the carrier, again on a remarkably abrupt descent. We were warned that this was not for the faint of heart—actually it was the stomach that was more at risk and barf bags were to be kept handy for that purpose!

The landing on a moving carrier in mid-maneuvers was impressive enough, but watching those 18–20 year-olds orchestrating and executing the maneuvers was amazing. Young men and women were conducting traffic on deck for take-offs and landings of F-16 jets and making sure the landing aircrafts hooked to a cable on deck to ensure they stopped before the end of the runway. We went up to the observation deck where the overall control of operations took place and the precision with which everything was done was impressive to say the least, all the more to see the weight of the responsibilities given to such young officers—a contrast to several other countries whose military—observed during overseas visits with the Marine War College—where the leadership at least was left to older more experienced officers.

Tradition versus Modernity

The bus driver into Sitka related to us what was probably his stock joke for tourists, a cautioning note about wandering off into wooded areas and possibly running into a bear. So, the common wisdom he imparted was: If you are in a clearing and see a brown bear, run to the first tree and climb and you'll be safe; if the bear is black, you should still run to the first tree you see and you'll probably make it, but the bear will then shake the tree so fiercely that you'll fall off and he'll eat you. If the bear is a white one, forget about running, you're not going to make it to the tree ...

The purpose of visiting Alaska was twofold: to understand subsistence economy and visit the coast guard to see their unique responsibilities there. When representing the U.S. abroad, it makes an impact upon one's hosts when you know your country well and can speak to the social diversity and the variety of life styles and the needs around the country. The subject of the rights of the different ethnic groups in the United States is often a topic of conversation overseas where the impression tends to be a negative one in this regard. The semi-autonomous status, for example, of Indian and native American tribes is not well known. The Alaska Federation of Natives, as one example of such ethnic associations, was organized in 1971 and includes 151 federally recognized tribes, 134 village corporations, and12 regional corporations. Knowing the history of the Federation and meeting some of the people involved in it was one of the goals of this trip.

Federal law protects the cultural and economic uniqueness of the various indigenous populations of Alaska, practicing what has come to be known as subsistence economy, i.e. the dependence on wild foods for nutrition and other customary and traditional uses—for medicine, furs, transportation, and ceremonies. Whaling, for example, is permitted in certain communities in contravention to the otherwise legally restricted fishing certain sea-life species and certain times of the year. There's also the question of storing and distribution of big catch like a whale—interesting to see how traditional methods used work well for small communities but difficult to see replicated in larger ones. In the end, the small villages we saw where the Yupik Indians lived, we were told that the villages were perfectly content to keep their communities small so they could continue living as their ancestors once lived and, of course, when in need of certain products, whether food, medication, or other supplies, they had no trouble spending some time acquiring those in nearby cities.

Learning about life in Alaska was fun. Things one always heard but never had the chance to see or learn about in detail were there in living color. Salmon making their last trip up river, for example, to go back to where they were spawned—quite a sight to see the bottleneck as the salmon gathered in large numbers at the point where ocean meets river and wait for their turn to swim upstream. I recall thinking of a Star Trek episode where aliens—considered casualties in a digitally fought war (fought by computers instead of real weapons in order not to destroy their cities)—dutifully gathered at designated chambers in order to have their lives terminated per agreement with the enemy).

We also flew to Admiral island—sealed off from any mechanized transport in order to protest wildlife—to watch bears in their natural habitat. The flight in a small propeller plane that landed on water was the worst part of this particular experience. My friend Charlie and I were seated in the back and smoke from the plane's diesel fuel wafted right to us as the plane had no doors or windbreaker flaps. We looked at each other smiling gingerly and wondering which one of us was going to get sick first. Luckily, we both barfed at the same time and neither one could claim to be tougher than the other—the guys sitting in the front of course made fun of us for the rest of the Alaska trip.

The highlight however was walking along a designated path, singing or whistling per instructions to ward off any hungry bears in the vicinity. We then climbed up a treehouse overlooking a stream and saw a large bear sitting in the shallow water looking like an oversized child taking a bath in a small bathtub. The bear was actually fishing, and if you haven't seen that sight anywhere it's a definite a remedy for shaking off the blues. It was hilarious!

Being briefed about the receding ice and the role of the coast guard in rescue missions was the more serious part of the trip.

Rescue missions, assisting mariners, monitoring for drug trafficking, assisting law officers in maintaining stability, law, and order—assisting the military in ensuring that any "regional instability and unilateral action by state and non-state actors do not pose a threat against the Homeland, our allies, and partners;" are some of the main functions and services performed by the coast guard, the strategic portions subsumed under the rubric of counterterrorism—protecting the homeland and allied countries. The role of the coast guard during hurricanes and coastal floods— something that definitely doesn't get the publicity it deserves— became much clearer to us after the visit.

Back in the Washington area, a visit to the Chesapeake Bay area took us on a boat ride to Tangier Island, a small island in the middle of the Bay that I had never heard of before our Senior Seminar trip. Another slice of Americana, and another aspect of the variety of communities, one finds in different parts of the country. A small very religious community of inhabitants lived there, made a living from crabbing and running restaurants for visitors—southern cuisine and southern accents were almost startling to find in the DC–Maryland area.

MCWAR: Marine-led

The pleasant experience of walking down the streets of Phnom Penh and being greeting by friendly Cambodians and seeing young and old couples walking hand in hand belies two grim reminders of it violent past, the Tuol Sleng Genocide museum from the capital and the ongoing search for the remains of U.S. soldiers still listed as MIAs. The fact that I was traveling with U.S. marines from the Marine War College (MCWAR) made this visit to this site all the more poignant.

The site of the museum is a former high school which was used as a prison and torture facility known as **Security Prison 21 (S-21)** by the Khmer Rouge regime in 1975–1979. With no warning signs on the outside, you enter what looks like a normal school yard and walk up to a very ordinary looking school building. The photo displays you see from room to room however are a veritable horror show. It was tempting to suggest that such a museum should be built up and better presented to the world as evidence of man's cruelty to man and part of a Never Again campaign, were it not for the continued practice of such horrors with impunity in today's Syria and Yemen. If one were to represent all the horrors of the past and the present where would they all fit?

In Cambodia, we actually participated in a token digging for remains, joining the group actually doing the digging on a full-time basis at the Cambodian–Vietnamese border.

Vietnam and Cambodia horrors have been relegated to history books and are rarely mentioned in conversation or media articles—so much so that a new generation of Americans is almost oblivious to what transpired there and to the anti-war movement in the late sixties and early seventies. Data released by the Clinton Administration showed that between 1965 and 1973, 2,756,941 tons of bombs were dropped on Cambodia mostly as a result of B52 carpet bombing. The U.S. also secretly deployed troops to lead South Vietnamese into Cambodia to confront North Vietnamese troops assisting and resupplying the Viet Kong on the Ho Chi Minh trail inside Vietnam. 100,000 Cambodians are estimated to have died in that effort.

The same trip to Cambodia also took us to India. We spent three days in Delhi visiting with the U.S. embassy, to be briefed on U.S.–India relations but also with the Indian military to understand their perspective on the same subject. Our hosts were very gracious and not only treated us to a fantastic lunch but also invited us to watch their special forces training. They repelled from helicopters and a rooftop into the middle floor of a three-story building in a mock exercise to root out terrorists who had taken hostages. The point of the exercise was to show us what worthy partners they were in the war on terror, while making the point over lunch that the United States just didn't understand their feelings about Pakistan, and acknowledging that they in turn didn't quite understand our feelings toward Pakistan and why we afforded them such a special place in U.S. interactions in south Asia.

I was in India for the first time in my life. I was astonished at first to see New Delhi with its vast avenues and almost no pedestrians on the streets. The embassy was apparently in this posh part of town and the bus driver taking us on a tour was clearly focusing on the old imperial highlights. I finally told the driver that I wanted to see the real India, "where are all the people, this can't be typical!" Sure enough, the driver then detoured and took us into the more popular neighborhoods with teeming streets, rickshaws, and three-wheeled cars, the Indians cleverly designed for cheap but reliable transportation on crowded city roads. In the midst of a very crowded area sprang the Jamaa mosque, a beautiful edifice constructed in the seventeenth century with a vast square outside the mosque where worshippers and tourists mingled. Another rich and poor story is the Taj Mahal, and its sudden appearance after a long drive on a narrow and crowded road with tin shack shops of street vendors. The edifice, standing clean, tall and proud looking, appears so picture-perfect, and out of place in the midst of obvious poverty and squalor.

As an FSO with an academic background, I was twice honored with appointments to teaching positions at the nation's top military colleges - the Marine War College (MCWAR) for the 2007-2008 academic year, and to the National Defense University for 2012-2013. Both these institutions are open to all U.S. members of the military, with a smattering of representatives from civilian agencies of government - in both cases, students studied strategy, history of war and international relations. The degrees obtained enhanced the students' chances for promotion to senior military and foreign service ranks.

Mission statements at both MCWAR and NDU stress that the education they provide is to prepare students for "assuming senior leadership positions in a complex and dynamic security environment—grounded in enduring principles and values while continuously adapting to ensure relevance." Hence, many of the Lt. Colonels who came to study strategy and international relations were picked for promotion to Colonels, and many who came in as Colonels were eventually picked to join the senior ranks as Generals.

What I found refreshing was the encouragement of critical thinking and objective analysis. This was as true in Senior Seminar as it was at the war colleges. In fact, I found the military men and women were even more prepared to be critical of their government's foreign policy than the civilians. These were men and women in their late 30s and early 40s who had just come back from assignments in Iraq and Afghanistan. They had seen war up close, talked to civilians about the impact of war on their lives, and were therefore more prepared than civilians who had never left Washington to discuss questions like, "what got us there in the first place?" and, "what's the alternative to our policy there?"

Team teaching was a challenge, particularly at MCWAR where it felt a bit like being on an assembly line where you did your bit and hoped it fit in nicely with the efforts of other faculty members. The students, as with all military officers, generally displayed remarkable respectful and hard working attitudes and even though a bit shy to discuss their experiences, nevertheless, had much to contribute from having worked and fought in Afghanistan and Iraq.

NDU is part of a broader national system of education and the curriculum was more thorough and the courses better integrated than at MCWAR. Almost daily, general lectures by invited guests were followed by individually run classes where the teacher had full control of the material—though coordinated with other professors on a weekly basis to enhance integration and synchronization of the general lectures. Students came from various parts of government, though the majority were from the three military services. International students generally came from countries with friendly relations with the United States and included some defense attaches from embassies in Washington. These officers often go back to senior positions in their governments and/or military establishments. General Abdelfattah al-Sisi, for example, is one recent case who went back home after 1 year at Carlisle's Army War College to gradually assume command of Egypt's military and then run for office officially after running off the country's elected president Morsi.

I particularly enjoyed being part of a team-taught Strategy exercise at NDU—which happened to be on the subject of China and the south-China sea. This topic was chosen partly because of President Obama's vaunted "Pivot to Asia" policy goal. The majority of officers felt that the initiative was not well thought out on the part of the president and that, while it made sense to follow with interest China's quest for supremacy in that region, it was not practical for the United States to pull military resources from other parts of the world—notably the Middle East where vital interests remained—and move them to the Pacific.

It was particularly opportune, in 2012, that I was able to introduce a course on the Arab uprising in two parts at NDU. While I found official Washington unresponsive to the situation and tied up in knots over it, the military officers were fascinated by developments in the region and anxious to explore the implications of a democratic wave possibly sweeping through the Middle East.

Best memories: On the same trip with MCWAR to India and Cambodia, we also stopped at Stuttgart. The purpose of the trip to Stuttgart was to visit African Command, set up in 2007 along the lines of eight other unified combatant commands like CENTCOM for the Middle East/South Asia and Pacific Command. We visited it in 2008 when it was still brand new and controversial because it was set up in Germany and not in an African country. The facilities were already impressive with a center for cyber space monitoring and warfare, an intelligence outpost, and a command center to coordinate the staffing and operations of the various services that might participate in any conflict on the African continent and would not necessarily be deploying from bases in Germany. The real issue during the early years was how useful this base would be and how it could serve all of Africa with so many different issues and conflicts. For the political side of things, four senior foreign service officers served as advisors and experts on various subregions of the continent.

The real joy on that trip was a side visit to Nuremberg—a real jewel of a city right on the the river Pegnitz and on the Rhine–Main–Danube Canal. I couldn't get enough of walking around this city, and I couldn't stop thinking how incongruous its beauty was with the serious and grim trials conducted there after WWII to bring to justice some of the most prominent Nazi war criminals. Now, post Arab Uprising and the wars that came in the wake of it, I reflect on how many young Arabs very much hope that some of the Arab world dictators—at least the ones who have actually massacred their own people—would one day be brought to justice—and of course if and when that happened, it would likely not take place in such a beautiful setting as Nuremberg, though the Hague, which hosts the International Criminal Court, wouldn't be such a bad site itself.

The Marines were generally very kind to me, appreciated my lectures and discussion sessions but were most impressed with my ability to keep up with them while walking in Nuremberg, Agra, and especially our off-road jaunt in Cambodia. My certificate of appreciation upon ending my stint at MCWAR read: Nabeel, Staff-Time Tough, essentially saying, "Not bad for an old guy, and a civilian at that."

The Question of Israel

My only involvement in the Middle East Peace Process (MEPP) consisted of attending the Oslo agreement signing at the White House's rose garden on September 13, 1993. I was invited to attend in order to mix and mingle with the international media in attendance, but like everybody else there I stood in awe of that famous handshake between Yitzhak Rabin and Yasser Arafat, with the arms of a beaming Bill Clinton around the both of them. I recall the optimism of the moment and the sense that we were all witnessing a historical turning point in front of our very eyes.

The Clinton administration came close, but in the end failed to move Israelis and Palestinians forward toward a two-state solution and a full peace. The second Palestinian Intifada followed in 2000 and, despite Israeli withdrawal from Gaza in 2005, that moment of optimism in 1993 was never to return. Israel continued to surround Gaza by land, sea, and air and the occupation and building of settlements in the West Bank continued apace. Palestinian frustration and suffering continued to grow.

Despite 25 years in the foreign service, always with a focus on Middle East issues, I had never desired an assignment to Israel and in fact never even wanted to visit Israel. This was mainly because I was never sure I could separate my personal feelings from my professional duties while witnessing first hand the occupation of Palestine. As the director of the Near East South Asia office of the Bureau of Intelligence and Research (INR), however, I hosted several meetings in Washington with Israeli analysts who regularly came over to compare notes with us and discuss regional issues. I got along very well with on particular Israeli diplomat of Egyptian origin who often represented his embassy in Washington at those meetings. The Israeli embassy officers eventually said it was their turn to host us in Israel and proffered an official invitation. My boss, Philip Goldberg, the Assistant Secretary for INR, asked me to put together a team to be headed by him to travel to Israel. It was an invitation I couldn't refuse.

Where Israel is concerned, the dilemma of being Arab-American manifests itself in a big way, at least it did for me and several of the Arab-Americans I know. The American diplomat in me wanted very much to be professional with all foreign diplomats, to understand their thinking and perhaps contribute to a better understanding on their part and ours of the issues of mutual concern. By and large, I was always easily able to put my personal feelings aside in order to accomplish this goal. Israel, however, presented a difficult challenge for me. Despite being an important part of the Middle East puzzle, Israel's history with the Palestinian people has always been impossible for me to put aside. Where Israel was concerned, the Arab in me was always at loggerheads with the diplomat in me trying to stick to the matters at hand and offer objective analysis to the best of my abilities.

As we set out on this trip, I recalled sitting down for the Baccalaureate exam in Lebanon in 1967 as our proctor was listening to the radio and following news of the six-day Arab–Israeli war. Regardless of what our various religious sects and political orientations were, students and faculty felt the let-down by Arab regimes that first falsely claimed victory and then had to admit the ignominious defeat they suffered. The sense of humiliation was universal and deeply felt. My own political awareness on this issue had not come from family (my father was a moderate and a pragmatist on all issues and did not often express strong political views). It did not come from political parties either, having been turned off by them all at an early stage life. The songs of Fairuz, however, had had a great impact on me—and relevant to the question of Palestine, her songs about Jerusalem had a profound effect on me. That the holy city was under a hateful occupation, that Israel had made refugees of hundreds of thousands of Palestinians who were taken in by Lebanon and other countries and that Israel was deeply at fault in the harm that had come to Palestinians over the years.

I had warned my Assistant Secretary and my Levant analyst—both of whom were Jewish—that my emotions could get the better of me and that they should take care to reassure me and hold me back if I got too carried away in any arguments while there. As it turned out, our hosts went out of their way to make sure we were all well received, from our arrival at the Ben Gourion airport to our departure four days later. Our meetings at the foreign ministry were at once professional and friendly. In fact, their counterpart of our Assistant Secretary for INR—noting that I was impressed with the instant Turkish coffee they served, singled me out for a gift of a large package of that at our final session. Our exchanges at the Israeli ministry of foreign affairs were always calm, rational, and professional in the extreme.

Ironically, the only time my emotions got the better of me was when we visited the old city—the streets of which are in at least two of Fairuz's songs. West Jerusalem is ultra-modern and frankly does not inspire. East Jerusalem however is another story altogether and evoked strong feelings—in particular, when touring the old city, we stopped to see the Church of the Holy Sepulcher, or the Church of Resurrection within the Christian Quarter. As someone who has philosophically roamed between agnosticism and atheism, and certainly a fallen Catholic by my family's standards, I was quite surprised when my tears flowed—to the alarm of my companions—with A/S (Phil) asking, "You're not going to turn religious on me, are you?" The only way I could explain my reaction was that I had heard about this place all my life, and whether from the political standpoint or simply the history of Christianity and its many stories I heard since childhood about Christ, it was just overwhelming to be right there on the spot where Christ's body had been laid after taking it down from the cross. I finally joked that just as Helen of Troy possessed the face that launched a thousand ships, Christ launched millions upon millions of believers—even though I wasn't one of them—and one had to feel a sense of awe standing in the place where he had walked and died.

Other moments of reflection included walking along the corniche in Tel Aviv, a promenade by the sea which was not only very similar to the one in Beirut further north, but also less than 200 miles south of it—yet one couldn't just walk or drive directly from one to the other. It was surreal, like being on the flip side of a coin. One could not even communicate freely with anyone in Lebanon lest the call be monitored on both sides, putting the person at the other end in Lebanon under suspicion and, in fact, putting yourself under a spotlight by whoever was monitoring communications inside Israel. Standing at the point in Israel furthest north where Israel, south Lebanon and the Golan Heights meet—an area that had witnessed several wars and where Israel's IDF and Hezbollah keep a watchful eye on one another was another strange moment.

Our side trip to the West Bank was also noteworthy. The exit we took off the Jerusalem highway into Ramallah was clear, almost deserted looking, with only one Israeli checkpoint waving us through in our U.S. embassy cars. Within easy sight was the other entry point used by Palestinians—chuck-full of cars and pedestrians wading their way through long lines and numerous checkpoints—a daily ordeal for many which we, as privileged visitors did not have to endure. We did not, while in Ramallah, meet any Palestinian officials but we did have very useful and meaningful conversations with Dr. Khalil Shikaki, Palestinian pollster, and an NGO that works on people to people peace with Jewish volunteers.

There were certainly a few humorous moments as well during this visit. At one point, walking back to our hotel along the Corniche in Tel Aviv, my colleague Ruth Citrin was some distance ahead, having crossed the road before the light had changed when I was approached by a Hassidic couple who started talking to me in Hebrew. I had no idea what they were going on about so I called out to Ruth who came back and explained that they were asking me about where the bus stop was and how often the bus stopped on that street. I chuckled to Ruth after they walked off, "You realize this means I've now passed as a local in Tel Aviv!"

Osama Ben Laden was killed on May 2, 2011—a momentous day worldwide, but especially in the Middle East and Israel. We were checking out of our hotel in Tel Aviv that day and waiting for what seemed an eternity in long lines at the reception. When we finally got to the desk the receptionist, seeing our U.S. diplomatic passports, asked "So is Ben Laden really dead?" I quickly quipped, "Oh yes, he checked out a long time before we did!"

INR

The Bureau of Intelligence and Research (INR) is the State Department's link to The intelligence community and one of the least known to the general public and even less known to many of the foreign diplomats in Washington. With offices that cover the globe, the mostly civil service analysts have the highest security clearances in government and routinely access the highest classifications in material that the intelligence agencies bring in. The job of the analyst is read and interpret the material relevant to their area of expertise, decide what is of most significance to the policy community and write short assessments (usually 850 words) for the Secretary of State and the Assistant Secretaries for the geographic areas in question. INR analysts also sit in on meetings with members of the intelligence agencies, particularly those from the CIA, NSA, and DIA—to compare notes and discuss the meaning of the raw information coming from overseas. INR contributes to the President's Daily Brief (PDB) and to the National Intelligence Estimates (NIE) that are required by Congress on a yearly basis.

Though small in number and limited in resources compared to the much larger intel agencies, I found State analysts worth their weight in gold. Most of them were civil service employees who had done this work for years and were real experts in their field. Whereas the bigger agencies like CIA could field 30 or 40 analysts on one country like Iraq and even more for a subregion like the Gulf, we had two analysts for each of these two as an example. I found however that numbers do not easily translate into better/ sounder analysis. Thirty-some analysts looking at one country led to dividing the country into many subspecialties with one analyst or a team of two looking at each. This often seemed to me like an assembly line analysis. I found that asking any particular analyst about an area outside their immediate areas of focus, even if only just, produced a shoulder shrug. Our analysts by contrast had to look at an entire country, organization, or issue and had thereby an incredible overview and could link individuals and overall issues.

The competence and independence of INR's take (already mentioned in an earlier chapter) on the intelligence presented by the

CIA in 2002 which was used to justify the Bush administration's decision to invade Iraq. Congress (the Senate select committee on intelligence) eventually[1] concluded that the Bush administration had "overstated" its dire warnings about the Iraqi threat, and that the administration's claims about Iraq's WMD program were "not supported by the underlying intelligence reporting." This in fact was INR's view from the start and the Bureau's dissent was highlighted in the first footnote in the NIE's executive summary page and acknowledged in unclassified documents early on.

The *Financial Times,* on July 30, 2003, reported INR's warning to Secretary Powell in January of that year as follows : "The Bureau of Intelligence and Research (INR), the State Department's in-house analysis unit, and nuclear experts at the Department of Energy are understood to have explicitly warned Secretary of State Colin Powell during the preparation of his speech that the evidence was questionable. The Bureau reiterated to Mr. Powell during the preparation of his February speech that its analysts were not persuaded that the aluminum tubes the Administration was citing could be used in centrifuges to enrich uranium."

My role as the director of NESA was much like that of the chief editor of a major newspaper—the individual analysts did most of the legwork of researching the intelligence in their particular areas of expertise and wrote the assessments which I edited and made sure were logical and presented an important policy issue to our policymakers. I also discussed the important events of the week at weekly staff meetings and suggested topics to the analysts that I thought were both important and timely. It was without doubt the most interesting and often fun job I could've landed in Washington. I had access to all the highest intelligence reports on the region I most cared about and, combined with open sources material, I was able to closely follow all the latest developments in the region and have discussions with some of the best analysts in

---

1   http://www.intelligence.senate.gov/phaseiiaccuracy.pdf

and out of government—as we often sponsored and/or attended academic conferences in order to see what the scholars in our field of interest thought about current issues.

Briefing Hillary

Because of the high level of classification of the material we handled at INR, our material was not available to others in the building who did not have the Secure Compartmented Information Facility (SCIF) that we had. We had to physically carry selected pieces of raw intelligence to the NEA bureau and others who had SCI clearance on request to brief them. I regularly briefed the NEA Assistant Secretary (for most of my time at INR it was Jeffrey Feltman) and some of the top NEA officers. It was also my privilege to have briefed Secretary Clinton on several occasions, usually with invited analysts from CIA and DIA and normally at her request. I had met Hillary Clinton before when she was First Lady and had accompanied her husband, the president, on a trip to Morocco. At the time I organized a roundtable for her with men and women civil society leaders to discuss democracy, women's rights, and human rights in Morocco and the broader Middle East. I have mentioned the briefing on political Islam in an earlier chapter, where Hillary displayed not only her respect for the briefers and her excellent questions but also how personable she can be—by recalling the roundtable I had organized for her and by listening to a story I told her about the first time I met Morocco's Islamist prime minister at the time, Abdililah Benkiran. On another occasion, I and two colleagues briefed her on the Syrian opposition in the presence of the NEA Assistant Secretary and the U.S. ambassador to Syria upon his return from Damascus due to the rising level of violence there.

Robert Ford who had just returned from Syria after shutting down the embassy there was debriefed by me and my Syria desk colleagues. He also attended some of the Syria briefings we offered to NEA. He and some of my NEA colleagues were rather disparaging of the Syrian opposition—disappointed with their lack of unity of their weak connections to what was happening on the ground in Syria. Indeed, our own report to the Secretary about the various opposition groups stressed their divisiveness and ineptitude. I was however personally still very much in favor of giving them all the assistance they needed to help them become stronger and more unified. My reasoning was that the opposition Syrians earnestly wanted to work with us and could, with our assistance, become better equipped and financed, thereby attracting more fighters to their ranks. I could see from the Secretary's body language and comments that she felt that way too. The president, however, was not of that mind and that frustrated those of us who identified very much with the Syrian uprising and wanted it to succeed. Radical Jihadists eventually secured funding as foreign fighters poured into the country in the latter part of 2012 and, together with the more secular opposition pushed the Assad regime to the limit, each faction of course fighting for their own agendas. In turn, the regime's supporters—read Iran, Hezbollah, and eventually Russia came to support the regime in full force. The United States, with its meagre and reluctant support for the opposition, was essentially missing in action.

Briefing the NEA team gave me the chance to chat with them about the intelligence coming in from the region and what it might mean to the overall picture. Feltman was always in a hurry and so did not have much time for a general discussion, unless he had some specific questions to ask. Since we were on friendly terms, I was able to put some questions before him as he was reading the material, which normally generated short answers on his part. I recall discussing Libya before the U.S. intervention as he was looking at intelligence on the threats made by Qadhafi and the progress his troops were making toward Benghazi. We discussed the likelihood of the success of his campaign, the ability of the resistance to withstand it, and the destruction and loss of life that might ensue. Since he was attending higher level talks at the White House than I was, he would on occasion discuss his impressions of the way the wind was blowing on policy. The Principal Deputy Assistant Secretary, Ron Schlicher, was both a colleague and a friend from my very first posting in Alexandria. He was always more relaxed even when very busy and always enjoyed a good chat on the issues and an exchange of views. Ron understood my passion for making a difference, particularly in Yemen. He understood why I wanted to direct the US government's attention to the internal problems there and why it could make the difference between Yemen thriving and Yemen falling apart and causing everyone grief, especially its own population. But Ron was also realistic enough to know that it was almost impossible to turn the ship of state on a dime and make it go the other way when it was going full steam ahead in the counterterrorism direction and could not be bothered with the complex problems of a little nation in the south of the Arabian Peninsula.

Ambassadorship Opportunities

I was nominated by the NEA Bureau for ambassadorships in 2011—The D committee (Deputy Assistant Secretary level) considered me for Yemen, Beirut, and Qatar—though my understanding was that the Bureau formally supported me only for Yemen. Ron Schlicher's support was crucial for this opportunity to be offered, as was that of Undersecretary Patrick Kennedy who was one of my bosses in Baghdad. When the D committee met to fill ambassadorial posts worldwide, the Director of the Foreign Service, called to let me know that while the positions I wanted were being given to others, the committee was offering me instead an ambassadorship to Mauritania.—It was the sort of bargaining that took place among committee members, Undersecretaries and Assistant Secretaries—to give some positions in one region of the world to someone who had primarily worked in a different part of the world, almost as a favor from one bureau to another. It took me only a few seconds of reflection while on the phone to reply with, "I'm honored of course, but I regret that I have to decline this offer." The Director, surprised, asked me to sleep on it and talk to her the next day. I went straight to Ron's office to let him know about the offer and my reply. He was surprised at my refusal as well and genuinely urged me to change my mind and take it—for the benefits the title would bring when looking for work after retirement, and of course for the prestige while still in the service.

I went to see the Director the next day and said that even after sleeping on it I still preferred to keep my job at INR for two more years before mandatory retirement rather than go to Mauritania. I explained that becoming an ambassador was never my goal when I joined the foreign service. "I want to make a difference; I want to believe in what I'm doing, which means going where the action is—given the Arab Uprising in my region, that would not be in Mauritania. I don't mind danger or hardship, but I know what I can do for you in Yemen, which is on the brink and needs our attention—I can even make a difference in a complex environment like Lebanon, but I honestly don't know what I can do for you in Mauritania—I feel I would just be out of the area where my concerns and my skills would make me the most effective and the most fulfilled." Though an Arab country, Mauritania was placed in the Africa Bureau at the State Department. It was also not a country where the Arab uprising had taken off as a democracy-seeking movement.

That same year, I also turned down an offer to be Consul General in Afghanistan, at a site planned to be established in Mazar el-Sharif, northern Afghanistan. The DCM at the time, David Pearce, was a friend who called to make the offer. I turned him down right away during that phone call—I did not have to think about it and call him back. The reason I gave was simple enough:

I did not believe in what we were doing in that country. We had gone into Afghanistan in the wake of September 11, 2001, attack on the World Trade Center in New York with the purpose of driving out al-Qa'eda. Once that mission was accomplished, we stayed to fight the Taliban to make sure al-Qa'eda did not return to the country. At the time I was offered the job, we had 100,000 troops deployed there. At the same time as Afghan citizens and U.S. troops were dying in the process (roughly 4,000 troops back then), we were secretly talking to the Taliban about ending the war and having them join in a coalition government—an arrangement we could certainly predict would end with the Taliban taking over from corrupt war lords and government officials. Further, building a large U.S. consulate in northern Afghanistan was both overly optimistic and cynical. The situation in the country was nowhere near as stable as it ought to be when considering the expansion of U.S. diplomatic presence. Further, U.S. presence there could only be viable via an agreement with warlords and drug merchants. I saw this as both futile and hypocritical and did not wish to be a part of it.

What I didn't tell my friend was that, in addition to matters of principle, and although it would have been a pleasure to work with him again, I did not wish to serve under ambassador Ryan Crocker, then a decorated career ambassador who had been recalled from retirement by President Obama to serve as ambassador to Afghanistan—his fifth ambassadorship at the time. I had first met Ryan at my first posting in Alexandria, Egypt, when he was the political counselor at embassy Cairo. I liked him and thought he was one of the most intelligent people in the service, and certainly one of the best Arabists in the Department. By the time I saw him again in Iraq, 2003, however, it seemed to me that the years in service had taken their toll on him. I found him to be irritable and difficult to work with. I had no regrets turning the offer down. He ended up serving there for only one year and then returned to retirement and academic life where he now shares with his students the valuable experiences he gained from over 35 years in diplomacy.

My premonitions regarding a new U.S. consulate in the north of Afghanistan proved right sooner than I thought. The Washington post wrote on May 5, 2012, "After signing a 10-year lease and spending more than $80 million on a site envisioned as the United States' diplomatic hub in northern Afghanistan, American officials say they have abandoned their plans, deeming the location for the proposed compound too dangerous." This made me even more glad I had turned down the offer to head such a post

The Arab Uprising

The Arab uprising caught scholars, diplomats, and analysts alike by surprise. The prevailing theory had for years been that Arab populations had become adept at absorbing and submitting to dictatorship and authoritarian rule, that the rulers of the 21 Arab states had become so entrenched and all-powerful that a rebellion in any one state, let alone a general wave against Arab regimes as a whole was highly unlikely.

The U.S. government had to make some tough calls that year, on Egypt, Tunisia, Yemen, Libya, and Syria—the countries where the 2011 uprising hit hardest. The Obama administration, despite the president's eloquent rhetoric in support of democratic change in the Middle East and the need for the United States to be on the right side of history, managed to wrap itself up in soul searching and asking "the tough questions" that hindered rather than informed any definitive action. In Egypt, did the events of January 25, 2011, constitute a revolution? Was the election of the Muslim Brotherhood's Mohamed Morsi to the presidency the beginning of a revolution of a different kind—one which would prove a setback to democratic development and perhaps detrimental to U.S. interests? Was General Abdel Fattah al-Sisi's non-coup (considering that millions supported it in street demonstrations) a step to be condemned and shunned or encouraged and rewarded with U.S. recognition?

These definitional questions were not merely interesting academic ones. I saw firsthand that the administration was preoccupied with such questions at the highest levels of government. President Obama himself seemed a Hamlet-like figure, entertaining deeply troubling questions and posing them to those of his advisors who advocated pro-democracy action. Their inability to answer the president's questions had, for the most part, a crippling effect on U.S. policy from Egypt to Syria to Iran. Even in the case of Tunisia, which early on showed signs of a potentially smooth transition—the dictator having fled the country voluntarily and the popular movement in the streets appearing unified, with the army not acting against them. In every case, actions not taken were merely deferred, only to be taken at a later time at the least propitious moment, when a Shakespearean denouement was all but inevitable.

The truth is that government analysts themselves (to include INR) were caught flat-footed by the events in Tunisia and Egypt as they first unfolded. The magnitude and import of Tunisia's uprising eluded even the most astute among us. By the third day of events in Egypt, however, we were sure Hosni Mubarak was going to fall. Seeing, on live TV, the total lack of fear among protesters as they chased after and burnt police vans was sufficient to underline that something fundamental had changed. Those who discounted Tahrir Square as a genuine revolution argued for staying the course, out of loyalty to Mubarak and for safeguarding U.S. security interests from the unknown to follow should he be toppled. Values and accurate, if delayed forecasting fortunately won the day, and Mubarak's denying the will of his people was decried.

We then inclined toward fair and free elections as in the best interests of Egypt, the region, and the United States. We got some big things right. We projected a Muslim Brotherhood (MB) victory at the polls—not because we thought they represented a majority, but because they were the largest plurality and the most organized one at that point. We projected further that the military, given that it had abstained from using force to keep Mubarak in office, would not deny the MB its victory at the polls, not just because international observers were there but in order to avoid a certain bloodbath. In analytic and political circles, the prevailing educated opinion was that the MB would respect certain redlines, particularly in foreign policy and regional security matters. Those redlines would be the United States', Israel's, Saudi Arabia's, and, consequently, those of the Egyptian armed forces as well. In return, the military would allow the MB its turn at the wheel. The 20 percent portion of the parliamentary polls for the Salafis was certainly a surprise, but not so much so that it distracted from the potential of a moderate MB having to steer a careful middle course between its critics on both sides of the isle.

Enter Morsi—the man who would be president. At first, we were impressed. The new president made some pragmatic moves on the foreign policy side of things, such as his acceptance of Egypt's security arrangements with Israel (to do otherwise would have opened him up to a dangerous confrontation for which he certainly was not ready) and his visit to Iran while maintaining, in public at least, respect for Saudi Arabia. Less admirably, Morsi waded knee-high into an ugly dance with Egypt's judiciary and governmental bureaucracy, hiring and firing civil servants seemingly at will and following, it seemed, only the advice of the MB's Shura Council in making those decisions. Again, those among us who did not think of January 25 as a revolution decried the desecration of particularly the Egyptian judiciary, with its long (though checkered) history of professionalism.

Knowing the bad history between Egypt's military and the MB, and realizing that high-level bureaucrats were all Mubarak appointees, it was logical enough that Morsi would try to remove pillars of the old regime. Students of revolution will certainly recall that Salvador Allende committed a fatal flaw in trying to reason with the old regime and openly invited them to share in governing the new Chile, only to be outmaneuvered by civil servants, labor unionists, and the military—not to mention the helping hand of Uncle Sam to the north. Morsi could not, logically, be faulted for trying to build the new regime with new people, more loyal to "the revolution" than to Mubarak. Where he can, and should be faulted, lies in his misconception that his 52 percent victory at the polls allowed him to build the MB's long-awaited dream state in total disregard of the wishes of the other half of the Egyptian population. Morsi assumed that, as president, he had full legitimacy on his side. He did not realize how badly he needed some allies outside his own party in order to proceed safely and, more importantly, that the new Egypt could not be, totally at least, in the image of the MB, and that he had, of necessity, the obligation to include the other dreamers who were instrumental in driving Mubarak from office.

Egypt's military played the game well. Biding its time and, perhaps doing more behind the scenes than was evident to its American and European friends, it waited for the right moment to pounce on the unsuspecting Morsi. Egyptian comic, Bassem Youssef, nailed it in portraying the man as a buffoon: He had no clue and, in the end, no business running the Egyptian state. But the question of where Egypt's military might take the Egyptian state, once it has taken away the keys from the MB, still troubled the administration. Surely it couldn't be thinking of bringing Mubarak back (practically from the dead)! To be sure, even that seemingly ridiculous proposition had its advocates within and outside the administration. Some were still thinking we owed it to Mubarak to support his return out of loyalty to the man if nothing else.

In a rational world, the MB, the military, old Mubarak figureheads, and, yes, even the idealists of April 6 and the other secular or liberal oppositionists would have all sat down to truly and honestly assess their options of working together and building a truly democratic state, much as the U.S. founding fathers had done over 300 years ago. To some extent, the national assembly that drafted a new constitution and prepared for elections in 2012 could have also set the stage for a genuine national reconciliation, but that was clearly at best an incomplete achievement.

The late Saudi philosopher Abdallah al-Qussaimi wrote (from exile of course) a book about exactly such a supposition and offered the answer in the book's title: *The World Is Not Rational* (al-Alam Laisa Aqlan). In the real world of 2011, and even now, there is no rational rewriting of social contracts. A brutal struggle for power ensued in Egypt, one which the military was best equipped to win, as indeed has happened elsewhere in the region where a void at the center resulted from the Arab uprising.

In Syria, Obama's and the State Department's policy planning office asked the following questions: Is the Syrian opposition worth supporting? And, since the answer from the intelligence community was equivocal (Yes, but), then why take the risk? From Policy Planning (PP), is it your assessment that Assad will fall? In this case, and since the answer was largely "Yes, sooner or later," the retort was, "well then, if he is going to fall anyway, why should we do anything about it?"

The militarization of the Syrian conflict came roughly 1 year after the initial demonstrations against the regime, which started in Der'aa in eastern Syria in March of 2011. BY 2013, Islamist fighters began to gain ground, followed by the increasing role of Lebanese Hezbollah, which was able to liberate the town of Qusair close to the Lebanese border from rebel forces which had occupied it. The full militarization of the conflict was well underway and the Obama administration, having done little to shore up the secular opposition forces, ended up with a significantly diminished role in Syria, 2 years before the Russians set foot there.

Libya, the only uprising where the U.S. military played a role, albeit reluctantly, was a case of leading from behind after the French took the lead in confronting Qadhafi—the talk in the Near East Bureau of the State Department focused on the need to stop Qadhafi's government forces from launching a full-scale attack on Benghazi where tens of thousands might be killed. Stopping Qadhafi's forces proved a much easier affair certainly than intervening in Syria—given that no other foreign forces had intervened. Russia was not interested in helping Qadhafi and the armed opposition had not splintered early as it did in Syria. Military intervention over, the United States, the EU, and the United Nations were at a loss how to help in the political transition to a unified democratic government. Qahdafi had left the country bereft of any state institutions, calling it a populist Islamic republic—read, the man wanted no institutions between him and his people so he could rule unimpeded. Given tribal and regional schisms, political transition was a challenge indeed, and the Obama administration was neither prepared nor even interested to play a major role in that regard. The United States did not start the Libyan uprising, but NATO had a definite hand in the downfall of Qadhafi—ergo, going on the principle of if you break something you need to fix it, the U.S. and NATO countries should have invested more diplomacy in reconciling and help Libyans rebuild.

Yemen's uprising fizzled out fast, with the National Dialogue Conference (NDC) sponsored by the UN in 2011, ending with a seemingly good agreement. The GCC countries mediated an agreement that allowed the election of Abdrabbo Mansour Hadi as president. As it turned out, it was not the end of the saga. The NDC recommendations, arrived at by over 500 conference participants, were not genuinely agreed to by all parties, especially the ones that controlled guns and fighters. Hadi was not an effective president, which left a power vacuum at the center. The Houthi rebels marched south to fill that vacuum and perhaps take over the reins of power completely. In 2015, Saudi Arabia intervened to prevent a Houthi-controlled country at its southern borders and all hell broke loose. The United States stepped in to help Saudi Arabia win the war against the Houthis, while pretending it was not a party to the war. Once again, the United States did not start the Yemen uprising, but, given its interest in counterterrorism and stability in the region, it should have played a more direct role in finding a diplomatic solution to the Yemen conflict—a conflagration that has claimed the lives of thousands, displaced millions, and placed three quarters of the Yemeni population in food insecurity and subject to the spread of famine and disease. The lack of American sensitivity, let alone leadership, has been nothing less than astounding.

Of the four Arab countries that experienced the jolt of the Arab Uprising season in 2011 and had their longtime leaders toppled, only Tunisia can thus far be considered a success story. A fifth country, Syria, split into a civil war which still rages, but the ending looming ahead is definitely in favor of the dictatorial regime reasserting itself. In Tunisia, President Ben Ali left in January 2011 with relatively minor violence, given that the army did not support him and suggested he depart to spare his people the bloodshed that surely would have followed had he stayed. Tunisians proceeded to elect a constitutional assembly, two successive national assemblies, an interim, and now a fully elected new president without any major clashes either between army and populace or between the competing Islamist and secular parties. The real test lies ahead in the ability of the winning party to lead the people, integrate the factions, uproot corruption, and balance Tunisia's need for security and economic progress with the original purpose of the uprising—democracy. President, Parliament, and civil society have been struggling with corruption, a sluggish economy and still, 6 years after the uprising, with the concept of justice. The success in Tunisia was due to several factors, the army's refusal to support the dictator, the Islamist party (An-Nahda) acting pragmatically and not stubbornly clinging to power after the first election, and not least for regional and international powers staying out of the fray and not trying to exploit the situation. Ironically, however, a little more foreign intervention, albeit of a benign nature, may well be called for to assist in the needed economic development.

Where does that leave the United States and its allies? The Arab Uprising was not predictable, at least in its timing and depth. Once it was underway, however, we should have been better, and faster, at predicting consequences, gaming options, and deciding on strategies to adopt. The military's intervention in Egypt, given Morsi's blundering, should've been anticipated. Taking three weeks to decide on which definition of a coup to apply is not acceptable for a super power. One of the reasons for our flat-footedness when it comes to Egypt is a result of our having accepted for years the limitations on our access and ability to offer advice, imposed on us by the Mubarak regime. The fault lies not with the fast pace of events but in ourselves. The United States and the world cannot just watch as bloody events unfold in the most populous Arab country, both on the edge of the Nile and bordering as it does both Gaza and Israel. Cutting off U.S. aid to gain leverage won't work at this late stage in the game. Egypt needs above all else political reconciliation and a bold multi-year economic plan. The United States, given the low regard most Egyptians have for it at the moment, cannot wade into this quagmire alone. We can and should be helping put together a concert of donors to include the European Union, Japan, and even Russia and China if they'll come along, to press for a credible national dialogue under the auspices of the United Nations, with the serious carrot of an international Marshall plan for lifting Egypt out of the economic disaster in which it now finds itself. The United States needs to shed the doubts that have plagued it and face up courageously to the challenge that lies ahead. Saudi Arabia did step in with billions of dollars, once the military was firmly in power. This assistance however does not come free of strings and Saudi conditions do not generally favor democratic development.

Testifying before the senate intel committee on one occasion and the Department of Defense's policy committee on another were fun occasions. Senator Diane Feinstein, whom I have always admired, chaired on the first occasion and was such a lady and a scholar. She took time out at the start of our briefing to thank me and my colleagues from CIA and DIA for our service and for testifying before her and her colleagues. She then singled me out as representing INR and the State Department, saying how much she appreciated the work we do and the insights we bring to the analytical table. Her questions were always direct and to the point without speechifying. Briefing DOD's policy committee was like walking into the defense establishment's hall of fame, featuring former defense secretaries and national security advisors from previous administrations—all the more so when Henry Kissinger walked in the room some 15 minutes late. Looking robust for his age, he proceeded to chat a bit and poke those next to him as presentations were being made. After I finished my presentation on the Arab Uprising and possible impact on the balance of power in the region, Henry the K's hoarse accented voice came across with a question, "What about China, how does it figure into this situation in the Middle East?"

It was an unexpected question from left field, but I couldn't resist venturing a reply just to engage a walking legend (good or bad). I described how, up to that point, China had only shown interest in commercial projects and had not tried to interfere in any way in the politics of the region. The projects China took on in the region were all turn-key operations. They tended to bring in all the labor and equipment needed, their people tended to stay on isolated compounds, not mixing with local populations, and they all left, lock, stock, and barrel when it was all over. I suggested however that they were gaining a positive reputation for getting things done without meddling, and that the credit they were accruing could well be cashed in for political influence at some point in the future when they felt ready to play a larger role in the Middle East.

CHAPTER 10

FINAL THOUGHTS

The Arab world now stands in the middle of a maelstrom—the season of uprisings in 2011 having mostly given way to chaos, counter-revolution, and further repression. A historic transition has nevertheless started and western interests are implicated in the outcome. Finally, after nearly a century of authoritarian and often abusive rule, the region's youth have risen, not primarily for sectarian or narrow ethnic or personal rights but for democracy and for freedom from corruption. The United States can, while maintaining its national security interests, lead a reasoned well-balanced international effort to advise and assist in the ongoing political transition—hence demonstrating that the principles of democracy, human rights, and rule of law are sincerely held and apply outside the United States and not just for domestic audiences. The image of the United States as a benevolent and caring big brother is not an easy one to maintain if the policies do not match the rhetoric. I recall at a State Department meeting in the nineties discussing with the Under Secretary for political affairs why public affairs officers weren't being able to better explain Iraq sanctions under Bill Clinton—we were told that we were losing the battle for hearts and minds. My retort was, "if the product is bad, no number of public affairs campaigns can help." Asked what I meant, I added, "if most of your friends and enemies are telling you that your (sanctions) policy is bad, perhaps they are right and what is called for is a policy change not better salesmanship."

This image of the United States as a benevolent and caring leader of the free world is not the one most people in the Middle East see. If they haven't even lived in the United States, they are also likely unaware of the distinction between the American people as open and fair minded and U.S. Foreign policy which can often seem alien, self-interested in the narrowest sense and completely detached from the suffering of others. This wasn't always the case. After WWII, the United States was perceived as having saved the world from Nazi Germany and as a donor country that distributes wheat to food insecure countries and extends a helping hand to the needy. The Kennedy years, brief though they were, also projected idealism and optimism to the rest of the world. The cold war, however, saw the U.S. side with dictators and authoritarian regimes for the sake of blocking the spread of socialism and communism. For the Arab world, U.S. support for Israel, especially after the 1967 war, was seen as unconditional, an extension of western colonialism and always at the expense of the Palestinians.

The end of the cold war in 1990, and the Arab uprising of 2011, offered the U.S. chances to live up to its values of democracy, respect for human rights and sensitivity to foreign cultures. Unfortunately, U.S. policymakers found it hard to pivot from the cynicism of relying on foreign dictators as allies against the Soviet Union in the cold war to alliance with the people of those countries and consistency in practicing what they preached, in terms of respect for everybody's right to democracy and not act as if these values only applied at home. American reactions to terrorism in the late nineties and in the aftermath of 9/11 also brought back arrogance and paranoia in a big way. The invasions of Afghanistan and Iraq in 2001 and 2003, respectively, re-emphasized the image of a super power throwing its weight around in alliance with authoritarian regimes and in total disregard of the impact of its security policies on the lives of the people on the ground who became victims of war and mere collateral damage. The image of American troops entering and occupying an Arab capital in 2003 was very jarring on the Arab psyche, and the consequence of the Iraq war, whether intended or not—and unfortunately it was perceived as intended by many in the region—was the unleashing of extremist religious forces whose terrorism has yet to fully subside.

Even the advent of a deep thinker, a sensitive African-American man to the White House in 2008 failed to alter the negative image, largely due I think to his failure to respond strategically to a fast-changing world during the 8 years of his presidency. Barack Obama began his Middle East policy with his famous Cairo speech in 2009, hosted by al-Azhar and Cairo University—the heart of the Arab/Islamic world, where he pitched a new beginning in the U.S.–Arab relationship. The Arab uprising however caught him flat-footed, unprepared for placing the United States on the right side of history, as he had often preached during his campaign for the presidency. He sought to withdraw U.S. troops from the region without divesting from authoritarian Arab regimes or investing in youthful democracy movements and civil society organizations. His democracy rhetoric was not matched with real policy changes on the ground—hence his famous "Assad must step aside" dictum was unmatched with any real support for Syrian opposition, leaving the country wide open for Russia, Iran, and Lebanese Hezbollah to step in and fill the void, shoring up the Assad regime and their own special interests in the process. While his administration worked hard on the Iran nuclear deal, a singular achievement in the region, he failed at building a more comprehensive understanding with Iran on regional issues and policies.

Perhaps his worst legacy in the region is his appeasement of Saudi Arabia in order to win its grudging support for the nuclear deal with Iran. Before and during the Arab uprising, he touted Yemen as a success story for U.S. counterterrorism strategy. This consisted mainly of drone strikes against al-Qa'eda and ignored the historic opportunity to support the youthful revolution and the stumbling start of a democratic transition. In 2015, when the Saudi-led Arab coalition started a vicious and unrelenting campaign against the Houthis, who had taken the Yemeni capital Sanaa by force, Obama supported their effort even when it became obvious they would have to destroy Yemen entirely in order to liberate it. By ceding Yemen to Saudi Arabia, he implicated the United States in a reckless policy that has left Yemen devastated, committing war crimes, and creating the worst humanitarian disaster since WWII—the desires of Yemeni youth for democracy and a decent life be damned.

With the Donald Trump presidency, the international public opinion needle on U.S. foreign policy has moved back considerably into the cynicism mode. In the Arab world today, there is a split between authoritarian rulers who see an opportunity to use U.S. power to their own advantage, and young civil society leaders who now perceive the United States as completely useless to them, if not an outright hostile enemy. Trump's erratic nature does not completely take the blame for this. A hawkish and totally selfish ultra-right-wing is perceived to have moved into Washington with him and to have taken over the reins of U.S. policies, foreign and domestic.

Regrets, I've Had a Few

I had originally chosen to begin this book with the title "No Regrets," to say that on balance my chosen career as a diplomat was interesting enough and enriching enough to offset the negatives. Writing the book has however reminded me of the personal cost, both to me and to my family - a cost I chose not to dwell on in this volume. Suffice it to say that the pressures my foreign service career imposed on my personal life with my family, on my sense of identity and the complex issues with which I chose to grapple the better part of my life were often overwhelming. Being a member of the foreign service certainly put me awkward situations, especially when I had to stomach and explain U.S. policies that were not in line with my own values, let alone with those of the journalists and academics with whom I interacted over the years. I was certainly not shy about expressing my disagreement in internal meetings at the Department and the NSC. I can safely say I was never able to change policy, nor did I ever witness anyone at the Department convince the White House to change course on any matter of substance. I had to contend myself with little victories such as expressing myself in my own words in foreign media, informally expressing my understanding of the strong objections expressed by Arab critics of U.S. foreign policy and the ability at times to positively influence our critics to see a value in retaining their friendship with the United States despite their strong objections to policy.

The foreign service life, as I have often told students who came to me for career advice, is not for everyone. You have to really love your work, appreciate other cultures, and be able to accept and deal with perspectives totally opposed to your own—both inside and outside the foreign service. In other words, no one out there owes you a comfort zone, you have to create your own. Secondly, you have to like travel and be able to put up with the life of a Bedouin, picking up your tent and moving from country to country and from job to job. This life-style is tough on family life. Despite having a very understanding spouse who was willing and able to organize every move and look after our two children when the demands of my job did not allow me to share in those responsibilities, my constant absences, demanding work schedule, and a busy social life, all put a strain on my marriage that in the end was hard to ameliorate. To put it simply, I was too distracted to focus on the impact of the life I chose on members of my family. I could have and should have done better.

There was a psychological toll as well. I was literally disoriented sometimes on waking up in different cities, hotels, and beds. I had to rub my eyes on some mornings and remind myself, "OK, I arrived late last night at Dubai airport so I'm in a hotel in Dubai this morning.... Right?" Or waking up in Baghdad and wondering for a moment about which universe I was really in, and why the gunfire. Throughout my career, but in Yemen especially, I had to take security decisions that potentially affected the lives of those who served with me. I never thought that I suffered from actual PTSD but I have had to deal with the repercussions of moving in and out of war zones and being exposed to live fire. I recall that on arriving in Yemen after Baghdad, and while sitting on my porch on a quiet Saturday morning, I literally jumped from my armchair at a sudden loud noise nearby, which turned out to be a neighbor dropping a large tin roof he was fixing on top of a chicken coop on his roof.

I also recall my first 4th of July event back in Washington, DC, after returning from a trip to Beirut during which I was caught while visiting my family there in an all-night street battle. I was so rattled by the fireworks that day that I couldn't handle it had to turn back from the event. This aversion became endemic after my Baghdad experience. I literally cannot to this day stand being around fireworks—it just sounds too real and brings back disturbing images and memories. I have also become rather claustrophobic and really hate to be hemmed in.

The question of identity is a more complex one. It is a common complaint among immigrants in general on going back to their native country to say, "I no longer feel at home here, but I'm not sure I'm quite at home there either." I love Lebanon, there is no doubt in my mind about that and, if for a period of time this love wanes or goes into an exasperation mode as it has done over the years of war and conflict there, all it takes is listening to a song or two by the immortal Fairuz to bring back the love in full force. It is also true, however, that Lebanon is no longer the country I remember from my childhood days. Beirut, and in fact all coastal cities in Lebanon, have become overcrowded, noisy, and dirty. The feeling one gets also is of a population that has turned totally cynical. While hardly anyone mentions the 15-year civil war anymore, it is clear that it has had a severe psychological impact, along with the several mini-wars and armed clashes since the major war ended in 1990. The Lebanese now often strike me as selfish in general and intentionally nasty when behind the wheel—always in a mad rush and always with zero patience for anyone who gets in their way. In the heat and dust of summer and given the garbage crisis of the past few years, summers in Beirut have become intolerable for me. When I go back to Lebanon these days, I go directly to my hometown, Hammana, a small village in the Matn mountains which has remained largely unaffected by war and undisciplined urban growth. There, the beauty of nature and the peace and quiet of my extended family's neighborhood put me at ease and I feel at peace with myself and my surroundings.

There is a poster photo of Mount Sannin covered with snow and another black and white photo of the mountain right next to the family's ancestral home in Hammana. I have carried these photos with me everywhere I've been in the foreign service and have always displayed them over my desk at every office I've had, and now at home in DC. It's almost like a turtle that carries its shell, which is also its home everywhere it goes. These photos remind me of where I came from and give me inner peace. But there is also a sense of peace I feel upon returning to the United States after a long trip abroad or upon returning from war zones and official meetings in the Middle East. It's the practicalities of life and the ease with which people communicate across social, economic, and racial stratifications that appeal to me. I recall coming back from a particularly tense trip overseas one time, exiting from JFK airport and onto a waiting bus. The driver, an overweight African-American woman, was chatting amiably with a gray-haired man in a suit and tie. The two were so relaxed bantering with one another that I just breathed and relaxed. This is the America I chose, one with friendly people who easily cross class and racial lines and where wealth and position mean very little, whether on the street, in an office building or on a city bus.

In the end, the Arab-American identity suits me perfectly. Arab-American identity and politics are issues I have grappled with since I came to the United States in 1971. I was always proud to be Lebanese but I have also always deeply identified Lebanon as an Arab country. Americans in the seventies had positive impressions of Lebanon but negative ones of the Arab world—associating the first with the many Lebanese immigrants among them dating back to the late nineteenth century. The word Arab on the other hand has over the years evoked the Arab–Israeli conflict which and more recently the specter of terrorism, along with the negative imagery of the Arab often propagated by Hollywood and the media—not to exonerate here the behavior of Arab leaders themselves and extremists of all varieties.

I have often had to correct people who on meeting me would follow up with the question, "so you speak Lebanese?" I would patiently say, "no I speak Arabic, which is a beautiful language." I had trouble with the melting pot theory from the start, feeling that it was a fantasy and one that counted on minorities ignoring or hiding their ethnic origins and cultures. At the same time, and despite my having assisted the efforts of others in Arab-American organizations, I never felt quite at ease in making a career out of fighting for the Arab-American cause. In the early days in Albany, I wanted to be accepted as an academic who happened to be Arab-American not an Arab-American who happened to be an academic. When writing about the Middle East, I sought to write objectively and in pursuit of truth, and when teaching I sought to educate not to be the proponent of a cause and preoccupied with a single issue. As a diplomat, I wanted to be accepted as an American foreign service officer who happened to be an ethnic Arab—not as an Arab who somehow ended up working for the U.S. State Department. I often had to remind Americans of the diversity of their society, hence controlling my anger at civilians who, on being told I was a diplomat, would say, "Oh, for which country?"

I am a blend of at least two cultures and I have nothing but respect for the efforts of those who struggled for Arabs to be treated fairly and decently in the United States. The Arab-American lobby organizations have worked hard over the past three decades to enhance the acceptance of the latest wave of immigrants to hit U.S. shores. James Aburizk, James Zogby, and Khalil Jahshan are three names that come easily to mind, having built the Arab-American Anti-Discrimination Committee, the Arab American Institute, and the National Association of Arab-Americans during a difficult time in the history of the community when it faced political discrimination, ridicule in the media, and personal attacks by pro-Israel lobby groups that vilified them. Hala Maqsoud and Helen Samhan also played leading roles in the Arab-American community and toward making sure that the ethic of political correctness and fairness covered Arab-Americans along with other ethnic groups in the country. If the Arab lobby and the Arab-American community enjoy more respect and acceptance by the general public today, it is largely due to the efforts of the men and women who have worked in these organizations and Arabs who succeeded and excelled in the arts, sciences, and the entertainment industry. At this point in my life, I have spent more years in the United States than in my native Lebanon. The fact that I represented the United States as a diplomat overseas gave me a pride in American values and an attachment to the institutions of law and order. I have taken particular pride in the work of American NGOs whose work overseas I observed as a diplomat and a scholar studying the Middle East region in particular. The selfless work they have dedicated themselves to in promoting democracy and human rights around the world fills me with pride and appreciation, and a belief that the world is one after all is said and done.

Retirement Goals and Perspectives

I retired from the State Department in 2013 and was immediately recruited by the Chicago Council on Global Affairs. While there

I also offered courses at Northwestern University. Essentially, I wanted to get back to my academic roots and to teach and write about my experiences in the foreign service. I loved Chicago. The educational, cultural, and artistic scenes were superb and in particular, I couldn't get enough of the Jazz and Blues clubs, outdoor concerts and even street musicians in the summer. By the end of my 2-year contract, however, I decided not to play the think tank game anymore—it was way more competitive and fickle than working for the Department of State. I also felt that I no longer wanted or needed a paymaster. Instead, I wanted to focus on finishing this book to make a statement on what my years in the foreign service meant, and to write in social media, freely expressing my opinions and sharing with friends and colleagues some of my experiences and impressions.

For the past 2 years, I've been doing exactly that: writing opinion pieces for the Atlantic Council and the *Cairo Review* as a nonresident scholar, giving TV interviews on current U.S. foreign policy issues and writing this book. I feel fulfilled, reflecting back on my career and the concerns that led me to it. I now understand the foreign policy process and international interactions much better than I did when I started out as a professor in Albany. I have lost my innocence though in hoping that I could actually make a meaningful impact on U.S. policy, let alone on conflict resolution in the world—for this, the bureaucratic process and the political agendas of elected officials were too much of an obstacle. I nevertheless continue to be engaged through my writings, interviews, and contacts—always willing to lend a hand to students, researchers, as well as activists and peacemakers who seek my advice.

Seeking closure might be too much to ask. I still travel frequently and spend summers in my hometown in Lebanon and winters in Washington. The diplomat in me still wants to deliver messages and weigh in on the conflicts and issues of the day, though the messages necessarily become vague and garbled with the passage of time, and as the world becomes more complex. A short poem by Palestinian poet, Murid Barghouti, called *the postman,* describing life in the diaspora, has stayed with me throughout my travels. My translation of its closing lines follow:

I have become a postman

The letters are still in my bag

But the addresses have faded

And I no longer know to whom they should be delivered

Also, no one today anticipates my footsteps or the knocking in my heart

But, satchel on my shoulder

I continue to roam

BIBLIOGRAPHY

Brandt, Marieke. *Tribes and Politics in Yemen: A History of the Houthi Conflict.* Oxford: Oxford University Press, 2017.

Burns, William J. *The Back Channel: A Memoir of American Diplomacy and the Case for Its Renewal.* New York, Random House, 2019.

Caton, Steven. *"Peaks of Yemen I Summon": Poetry as Cultural Practice in a North Yemeni Tribe.* Berkeley: University of California Press, 1990.

Cavafy, C.P. Rae Delvin, translator. *The Complete Poems of Cavafy.* Durham: A Harvest Book, 1976.

Gerges, Fawaz, Ed. *The New Middle East: Protest and Revolution in the Arab World.* Cambridge: Cambridge University Press, 2014.

Hull, Edmund. *High Value Target.* Lincoln, NE: Potomac Books, 2011.

Jamestown Foundation, The. *The Battle for Yemen.* Washington, DC, 2010.

Johnsen, Greggory, D. *The Last Refuge: Yemen, al-Qa'eda and America's War in Arabia.* New York: Norton & Company, 2013.

Khalilzad, Zalmay. *The Envoy: From Kabul to the White House.* New York: St. Martin's Press, 2016.

Mackintosh-Smith, Tim. *Yemen: Travels in Dictionary Land.* London: Picador, 1999.

Mahfouz, Naguib. *The Sons of Gebalawi.* London: Heinemann Educational Books, 1981.

233

Merouazi, Khadija. *Sirat al Ramad* (The Story of Ashes). By Afriqia al-Sharq, Morocco and Beirut, 2000.

Miles, Hugh. *Al-Jazeera: The Inside Story of the Arab News Channel That's Challenging the West.* New York: Grove Press, 2005.

Mourid al-Barghouti. *Al-A'mal al-Kamilah (Complete Works)*, By al-Mou'assasah al-Arabiya Lilnashr, Beirut, 1997.

Rugh, William A. *Arab Mass Media.* Westport, CT: Greenwood Publishing Group, 2004.

———. *Front Line Public Diplomacy: How US Embassies Communicate with Foreign Publics.* New York: Palgrave, 2014.

Shaheen, Jack, G. *The TV Arab.* Bowling Green: Bowling Green State University Press, 1984.

Soufan, Ali, *Anatomy of Terror.* New York: Norton and Co., 2017.

———. *The Black Banners.* New York: Norton and Co., 2011.

Wolf, M. L., A. R. Ferris, and A. D. Sherfan. *The Treasured Writings of Kahlil Gibran.* New York: Castle Books, 2011.

Zogby, James. *Arab Voices: What They Are Saying to Us, and Why It Matters.* New York: Palgrave Macmillan, 2010.

ABOUT THE AUTHOR

After twenty five years in the Foreign Service, Dr. Nabeel A. Khoury retired from the U.S. Department of State in 2013 with the rank of Minister Counselor. He taught Middle East and US strategy courses at the National Defense University and Northwestern University. In his last overseas posting, Khoury served as deputy chief of mission at the U.S. embassy in Yemen (2004-2007). In 2003, during the Iraq war, he served as Department spokesperson at US Central Command in Doha and in Baghdad.

Follow Nabeel on Twitter @khoury_nabeel.